D0122016

SHERMAN J. MAISEL

Managing the Dollar

W · W · NORTON & COMPANY · INC · New York

Library of Congress Cataloging in Publication Data

Maisel, Sherman J
  Managing the dollar.

  Includes bibliographical references.
  1. United States. Board of Governors of
the Federal Reserve System. 2. Monetary policy—
United States. I. Title.
HG538.M28 1973   332.4'973   73–7956
ISBN 0–393–05494–2
ISBN 0–393–09337–9 (pbk.)

Contents

Contents

Preface

MONETARY POLICY is among the most discussed but least understood of all major influences on the economy. The Federal Reserve System is often blamed for everything that goes wrong with the economy—for inflation or deflation, for causing stock prices to sink or to soar, for high or low interest rates, for unemployment, for overprotecting the dollar or for causing its devaluation. The actions of the Fed are the subject of a wealth of articles, books, courses of study, and debate in both financial and academic circles. Yet misunderstandings abound as to what it is trying to do, and why. Although, in comparison with other central banks in the world, the Fed is very open and outspoken, a certain aura of mystery and awe surrounds its operations.

Before my appointment to the Board of Governors of the Federal Reserve System in 1965, I had spent nearly twenty years studying and teaching monetary economics. I thought I understood what the Fed did and how it affected the economy. I soon discovered how little I knew. I also found that the Fed itself, while it had a definite philosophy, had no clear concept of how monetary policy worked. I searched for an official statement of doctrine or an outline of operating procedures. None existed, except at the most general level. I felt from the beginning of my service on the Board that the policy decisions themselves, their

effects on the financial world, and the public's comprehension of
the Fed would all be improved if its techniques and operations
were more widely understood and were explained in more concrete terms.

While it is true that the more that is known about the workings
of an organization, the more criticism it attracts, it is also true that,
the better its powers and limitations are understood, the more realistic will be expectations for its performance. My purpose in this
book is to promote a realistic conception of the use of monetary
policy and how the formulation of it has developed in the past ten
years. Those years have been among the most active and interesting in Federal Reserve history, for in this period the full arsenal
of the Fed's policies was called upon to meet the crises that con-
fronted the economy and the U.S. central bank. I attempt to show
how policy results from an interplay of history, personalities, and
doctrine, all reacting to events in the economy and the Washington world. The book is meant for the intelligent layman with an interest in economic affairs, for the college student of economics or
business, for the professional analyst. It aims to give a feeling for
how the dollar is managed so that they may improve their own
judgment of what is happening in financial and money markets.

My background as an economist equipped me to analyze the
pressures, procedures, and techniques used to make monetary
policies. My membership on the Board of Governors gave me a
unique opportunity to do so. The result is an inside view of how
policy is actually made. It goes without saying that the impressions
and judgments of events and policy making described herein are
my own. I am sure that in many cases other members of the Board
would interpret identical events very differently. In some situations, a majority might not concur in my analysis and viewpoints
—a state of affairs that frequently arose in the course of policy
making. These pages present a personal, not an official, view.
They describe how I saw monetary policy developing and decisions being made. Clearly, my analysis of what needs to be done
and my recommendations for the future are entirely my personal
judgments.

The contrast I have drawn between the periods before and
after 1966 is much sharper than most within the Federal Reserve

would accept. Many who were involved in decision making in that earlier period would say that the Fed did an excellent job of gauging the need for monetary policy, given the lack of knowledge that existed. A large body of outside critics disagrees. Since I was not at the Fed at that time, I have little special insight to support either side in that debate. I think, however, that a knowledge of the underlying theory of that era—one which stressed greater or lesser accommodation to the demand for credit—is necessary to an understanding of the controversies surrounding the development of policy in recent years.

My debt is great to many for aid in completing this work. Most of the writing was accomplished while I was a Fellow at the Center for Advanced Study in the Behavioral Sciences. Only those fortunate enough to have had this unique experience can appreciate how much it facilitates the completion of major analytical endeavors. Among the many who have read various drafts of this book, I want to thank for their helpful comments George L. Bach, Frederick A. Breier, Howard Craven, James Duesenberry, Lyle Gramley, Harry Kahn, Thomas Mayer, George Mitchell, Frank O'Brien, Charles Partee, and Merritt Sherman. None of them, of course, is responsible for the errors that may remain. My task was greatly eased by the willing and efficient cooperation of Joan Warmbrunn, who was my secretary, and of my wife, Lucy, who did a great deal of editing and polishing. The same is true for my editors, Donald Lamm and Mary Shuford.

The entire book would not have been possible if the Federal Reserve were not the dynamic, forward-looking institution that it is. It has recognized the need for constant development and has tried to keep an open mind to promote progress.

Managing
the Dollar

CHAPTER ONE

What Went Right?
What Went Wrong?

ON JUNE 1, 1965, William McChesney Martin, Jr., Chairman of the Federal Reserve Board, spoke before the Commencement Day luncheon of the Columbia University alumni. His speech, "Does Monetary History Repeat Itself?" shook the stock market and the financial community to a degree not experienced in many years. The text was released to the press at noon on that Tuesday; by the time the stock exchange closed, the Dow Jones industrial average had dropped 9.51 points. The next day's front-page article in the New York *Times* was headlined, "Talk by Martin Batters Market." The Dow Jones average fell 19 points the first three days and about 60 points during the three weeks following the speech.

While many other crosscurrents were also at work, the financial press and analysts attributed the severe change in national sentiment to the Martin speech. The national reaction reflected a tremendous respect for Chairman Martin as an acute observer. His fear that some of the excesses of 1929 might be repeating themselves in the current booming market struck a sensitive nerve. It also reflected respect for his position as Chairman of the Federal Reserve Board.

Even though a careful reading of the speech showed that it was primarily a warning against excesses in the private credit and stock markets and a strong plea for international cooperation and

1

maintenance of the fixed price for gold at $35 an ounce, observers assumed that the speech was an attack on the Johnson Administration's economic policies. They feared that it signaled a shift in monetary policy from accommodative to restrictive, with a consequent pressure on stock prices. On June 25, the Chairman gave another commencement speech at Rutgers. This speech was optimistic and stated clearly that the Federal Reserve would continue to furnish the funds needed by American business for expansion. Whether by coincidence or not, within a day or so the decline ended; the market shot back up.

June 1, 1965, also marked the end of my first month as a member of the Board of Governors of the Federal Reserve System. I had barely learned the way through the marble halls to my office when I suddenly found myself in the middle of an economic donnybrook. President Lyndon Johnson and Secretary of the Treasury Henry Fowler both felt obliged to respond to Martin, to let the country know that no change in economic policy was contemplated. The Federal Reserve entered a period of tense relations with the Administration.

While no one knew it then, June 1965 was also the last month of the relatively steady economic expansion that had begun in early 1961. The concerns raised by Martin's Columbia speech were shortly overshadowed by other forces. For at least the next eight years (past the end of my term at the Fed) economic events were dominated, or at least strongly influenced, by the surge of spending on the Vietnam War and the private and governmental economic policy reactions which it engendered.

As a result, Martin's question, "Does Monetary History Repeat Itself?" was superseded by an entirely different set of problems. People soon wanted to know why interest rates reached their highest level in over 150 years and remained high, why prices rose at near-record rates even though unemployment was high, why the U.S. dollar was devalued, why wage and price controls were necessary. As it was succinctly put to me by Kenneth Arrow, Nobel laureate and then president of the American Economic Association, "You were in Washington for seven years—what went wrong?" More importantly, however, What did the events of the sixties and early seventies foreshadow for the future? Such questions permit no simple answers. Yet to plan intelligently for the future and to lessen the chances of still greater inflations, recessions, or depressions, we need to analyze the past.

The Federal Reserve and Monetary Policy

Among those who play a key role in the making of economic policy, we find The Federal Reserve System, the central bank of the United States. To be able to explain and forecast what will happen to the dollar, interest rates, credit, and related economic forces, we must understand how the Federal Reserve works. It both influences and is influenced by movements in the overall economy. It alters monetary policy in reaction to many forces, including instability, financial changes, gold, psychological shifts, uncertainty, and doctrinal debates.

When we speak of monetary policy, we mean the government's influence on the economy through changes in bank reserves, money, and credit. In formulating monetary policy, decision makers at the Federal Reserve select targets for growth in money, for credit, and for the behavior of interest rates, with the objective of helping the nation reach its economic goals. They manipulate bank reserves, discount rates, interest ceilings, and a variety of other monetary instruments in an attempt to hold the economy on a desirable path. When the targets are properly selected and the instruments correctly used, monetary policy helps achieve prosperity. When the targets are wrong or operations ineffective, monetary policy aggravates inflation or unemployment.

For more than fifty years, Federal Reserve decisions have aroused controversy. But, because there is still so little understanding of just what the Fed is trying to do and how it does it, most of such debate has failed to improve decisions. During the seven years I served on the Board many things went wrong; but many other things went right as well. I shall relate some of the important developments and show how new concepts of monetary policy and operations emerged from the trauma of attempts to battle large-scale inflationary pressures.

What Went Right? A Panic Averted

It is perhaps appropriate to start with a major event that went right: that our financial system withstood two tremendous shocks in a two-month period in 1970, the Cambodian invasion and the failure of the Penn Central Railroad, episodes of a kind which previously had led to financial panics and crises.

How Depressions Occur

Economists always fear that a shock to the financial structure will become cumulative and lead to drastic contractions in output and jobs. Some of the worst depressions in United States history have followed liquidity squeezes. In 1873, 1893, 1907, and 1933 the inability of banks to obtain reserves led to major financial panics. There is almost unanimous agreement that a primary reason for central banks to exist is their ability and duty to intervene in such situations to forestall a cumulative monetary contraction.

No matter how a recession or depression starts, it can be greatly exacerbated by monetary events. Spending and output depend on a smooth flow of money and credit. If this flow becomes erratic, income and jobs disappear. Such chains of events can easily be recognized in the past. An occurrence such as the failure of a bank or a large debtor raises questions as to the safety of existing credit arrangements. Creditors and debtors reexamine their positions. They decide that it would be safer to be more liquid, that is, to have more cash on hand in case they have to make unexpected payments or fail to receive expected inflows of money. But the attempt of everyone to become more liquid is self-defeating, as can be illustrated by one of the most typical depressions caused almost entirely by monetary events: the "Wall Street rich man's panic" of 1907.

In that year, when the Knickerbocker Trust Company failed, even though the economy was basically strong, depositors immediately began to withdraw funds from other banks. These banks had to call loans to obtain the necessary funds. Interest rates on call money loans leaped to over 70 percent and reached 125 percent in some cases. Banks everywhere scrambled for cash. Within a week, banks in New York could no longer supply currency to their depositors. Instead they began issuing clearing house certificates (scrip issued by the banks against their joint frozen assets through their clearing house). Within two weeks banks throughout the country had suspended cash payments and were also issuing scrip. Loans were called. Interest rates rose. As is typical in such situations, when loans were needed, banks either could not or would not lend. As a result, the damage was not limited to banks. As interest rates rose and loans were called, business confidence evaporated; industrial stock prices fell by 50 percent; business failures rose by 30 percent; national output in 1908 was 10 percent less than in 1907; unemployment jumped from under 2 percent to over 8 percent; the amount of saving and investment fell by over 40 percent. This depression was one of the shortest, but also one of the sharpest and deepest, in history.

The 1970 Crisis

It is because they are aware of how dangerous financial squeezes can be that monetary historians, recognizing the contrast to prior panics, will cite May and June 1970 as most significant, although far from typical, months in the financial world. The decisions of the Federal Reserve Board and the Open Market Committee in these two months illustrate monetary policy at its best. The Fed performed the oldest and most traditional central banking function: acting as a lender of last resort. It forestalled a liquidity squeeze by guaranteeing banks the necessary cash and reserves to meet the demands of their customers. In 1970, the economy experienced a mild controlled recession, but not a disastrous depression such as had followed major shortages of reserves in the past.

Toward the end of 1969 the longest economic expansion in U.S. history had ended. The fact that the growth rate of money and credit had deliberately been held well below that of spending was one of the causes of the downturn. Scarce credit led to one of the highest interest-rate periods in history. Early in 1970, however, the

Fed relaxed monetary policy. Reserves and money were expanding at a moderate pace. Short-term interest rates were declining. Long-term rates were stable, but at very high levels.

Then, in fairly rapid succession, came events that altered the entire financial picture. The credit markets were thrown into a panic when, on April 30, news broke that United States forces in Vietnam had extended the war into Cambodia. This was followed by the shootings at Kent State University and a major eruption of protest and strife on campuses and in cities throughout the country. And, on June 21, the Penn Central Railroad filed in federal court for a reorganization under the Federal Bankruptcy Act. Together these events threatened a major liquidity crisis. Each situation struck at a somewhat different part of the financial structure, however. Cambodia and Kent State together menaced security markets and institutions dependent on security values. Plummeting stock prices deepened gloom and uncertainty. The Penn Central collapse then threatened a major source of funds for the nation's large corporations.

In the sixteen months following its peak in December 1968, the stock market had fallen by 25 percent. It fell another 10 to 15 percent in May 1970. Long-term interest rates had reached record highs at the turn of the year; the Cambodia invasion saw them shoot up again. Financial problems were exacerbated by the fact that the news of the expansion of the war hit in the midst of a delicate Treasury financing. The markets would have been completely demoralized if the Federal Reserve and the Treasury had not come to their support with several billions of dollars.

Falling security prices meant higher interest rates. Hardest hit by declining values was the investment community; some of the country's largest investment bankers and brokerage firms became insolvent. Large contractions in net worth threatened the stability of other financial institutions as well, including savings and loan associations, mutual funds, and a billion-dollar bank (the Bank of the Commonwealth in Detroit, a city which had been a center of major troubles in the Great Depression).

The history of previous financial panics indicated that, if repeated, banks, individuals, and corporations would all attempt to become more liquid, they would want to hold as much money as possible to insure themselves adequate cash and guaranteed solvency; they would dump securities in favor of money; interest rates would rise and security prices fall; loans would be called; net assets would be wiped out. Such a rush to hold money and other liquid assets appeared to be in progress in May, with the demand for liquidity surging. If the Federal Reserve failed to meet the demand by increasing the supply of money available, a true monetary crisis could develop. Even if a crisis did not occur, a failure to meet the demand would have unfortunate effects on output and employment, since available money would not be spent, but would be hoarded or used for improving liquidity instead. Demand for goods and services would fall.

The Federal Reserve Response

Alerted by previous experience, the Fed did not stand by to watch a financial panic develop. Although wracked by a strong internal debate, in May the System furnished the reserves necessary to stabilize financial markets (see pages 37–41). While the probability of a true liquidity crisis might not have been great, as a central bank the Fed had a primary duty to assure that a crisis did not actually occur. Business and consumer confidence was deteriorating; the Fed could help support the economy by attending to its liquidity needs.

The money and credit added calmed the markets upset by Cambodia and Kent State temporarily. Then the second crisis threatened on Sunday, June 21, when the officers of the Penn Central Railroad filed for a reorganization. The Federal Reserve was greatly concerned because this failure jeopardized a major credit market—that for commercial paper. Commercial paper is securities sold by borrowers to lenders with very short terms, from 1 to 270 days. Borrowers generally hold commitments from their bank for funds to pay off loans coming due if the lender decides not to renew, or roll over, the loan through commercial paper. The firms issuing commercial paper (the borrowers) have prime financial ratings, and much of the paper is sold through reputable underwriters. Although most of the nation has never heard of the commercial paper market, from 1965 to May 1970 the amount being borrowed in this market at any given time rose from $9 billion to $40 billion.

Thousands of firms, individuals, trusts, foundations, and other lenders had purchased commercial paper on the assumption that it was a completely secure repository, with a rate of return from 1 to 1.5 percent above the yield on ultrasafe Treasury bills. However, the rapid growth of the market and its high rates had attracted inexperienced lenders, and even some experienced lenders had become careless of the criteria they used.

The Penn Central failure threatened the entire structure because it cast doubt on the basic assumption that the commercial paper of large, well-known companies was good security. Penn Central had $80 million in commercial paper outstanding when it went into receivership. Lenders on Penn Central's commercial paper suffered major losses. People who had lent money on the commercial paper of other companies suddenly, with the specter of the supposedly secure Penn Central before them, realized that they had agreed to unforeseen and unwanted risks. Lenders asked themselves whether they should not withdraw their money and put it into safer securities as soon as possible.

The problem which faced the Fed was to make certain that there would be sufficient money available to permit all those who held maturing commercial paper to be paid off if they did not wish to renew. Banks had made such commitments to borrowers on commercial paper; but would they and could they meet them? Although banks were fully loaned up, they might now have to lend several billion dollars a week to those corporations which would need it to pay off their commercial paper. Before making such loans, banks would have to decide whether their previous commitments were still valid, given their own liquidity position, the altered condition of the economy, and doubts about the solvency of borrowers. Banks could back out of these commitments by invoking responsibility to their depositors not to take undue risks; but this would cause failure for the rejected borrower.

The shock waves from the Penn Central failure could spread rapidly if reinforced by failures of additional firms. As working capital disappeared and customers were lost, corporations unable to borrow would shut down. Massive unemployment could ensue.

At this point the Federal Reserve informed the major banks of the country that its discount window—where it makes short-term loans to member banks—was wide open. If they needed funds to make loans to their customers who were having difficulty in rolling over their commercial paper in the market, they were invited to borrow from the Fed. Further, to enable the banks to attract more money, the Board raised interest rates permitted to be paid on certificates of deposit (CDs), which are funds that banks receive from large customers. Of course, if they preferred, they could find other sources than the Fed's discount window for their increased needs for funds.

The commercial paper market remained precarious for several weeks. Banks had to make numerous loans to many companies having trouble rolling over their paper. Almost all banks met their commitments, using Federal Reserve discounts and new deposits attracted with the higher CD rates the Fed permitted. All told, they borrowed an additional $1 billion from the Fed over the following month. In the next three months, their certificates of deposit virtually doubled, a rise of nearly $11 billion. During the same period, the volume of commercial paper outstanding fell by $6 billion. In that quarter reserves furnished by the Fed grew at a 25 percent annual rate. The money supply increased at slightly over a 5 percent rate. All interest rates retreated from their record highs.

The Differences between 1930 and 1970

In the summer and fall of 1930 the economy was poised between stabilization and a drastic fall. Stock prices, which had reached their peak in September 1929, had fallen sharply but appeared to be stabilizing. The same was true for real output and expenditures. Interest rates on Baa (medium-grade) corporate bonds had gone from 6 to 6.25 percent. Then, on December 11, 1930, the Bank of the United States (despite its name, simply a large commercial bank) failed, an event that played a large role in setting off the secondary deflation which plunged the country into such a deep and long depression.

In the spring of 1970, the country was similarly poised between stabilization and decline. Stock prices had been falling since December 1968. Real output and expenditures had been dropping since 1969. Interest rates on Baa corporate bonds were at near-record highs—9.25 percent on older bonds and almost 12 percent on new issues. Then came the failure of the Penn Central, the seventh largest corporation in the United States.

But there was a major difference between the events which followed these bankruptcies. In April 1933, nine quarters after the failure of the Bank of the United States, the unemployment rate was more than 25 percent. Spending and industrial production had decreased by almost a half since 1929. Stock prices were down by over 75 percent. The interest rates on corporate Baa bonds had risen to a peak above 11.5 percent, almost twice their starting point. More than seventy-five hundred banks had suspended payments, causing inconvenience and major losses to their depositors and customers. Prices had declined by about a quarter.

In October 1972, nine quarters after the failure of Penn Central, unemployment was only about 2 percent above its prerecession level. Spending and industrial production were at record highs. Stock prices also had surpassed their previous peaks. Interest rates on Baa corporate bonds had declined to within 1 percent of rates reached in 1968. The number of bank suspensions in the nine quarters totaled only six. Prices had not dropped, but had risen 9 percent. After the downturn of 1969, there was no cumulative contraction and no monetary deflation and collapse of the banking system.

A major difference between the two periods was the introduction of a conscious economic policy aimed at maintaining jobs and production. After the 1969 downturn the economy was not left free to contract at its own pace as it had been in the thirties. Instead, governmental policies were used to lessen and then to counteract the natural deflationary forces in the economy. One of the most significantly altered policies was the Federal Reserve's management of the dollar.

What Went Wrong? Inflation Unchecked

Although the policies of the 1960s and 1970s avoided the disastrous experiences of the 1930s, these decades too witnessed problems.

The question, What went wrong? can be answered either by enu-
merating the undesirable conditions—inflationary price pressures,
relatively high interest rates, the need for peacetime controls over
wages and prices—or by citing the inability of government policy
to cope with them.

Inflation is simply a condition of generally rising prices. Like
sin, everybody is against it. People hate inflation because it is unfair. It takes real income and wealth from some and gives it to others in an extremely arbitrary and accidental manner. There is little
or no relationship between what a person does or what he is worth
to society and how he is affected by inflation. Social and political
tensions increase because of the injustice of this form of redistribution. Furthermore, those who profit from inflation tend to credit
their own individual skills and wisdom, while the losses are far
more obvious and blamable on others. For these reasons, everyone
—including those who profit—wants more stable prices.

If an inflation becomes rapid, it may cause a decrease in productivity and efficiency. Economic decisions at all levels can be
warped by the fear of rising prices, straining the whole structure of
the financial system. Because they do not want to put savings in
deposits or monetary assets whose real value will fall, people over-
invest in goods which they hope will retain their purchasing
power.

The distress over rising prices has been particularly great at the
Federal Reserve. For many years preservation of the value of the
dollar has been considered a cornerstone of policy. Yet the value of
the dollar has still been falling. People want to know why this was
tolerated by the Fed. Is not the failure of the Federal Reserve to
halt inflation one of the key things which went wrong? The answer, I believe, is that the Fed did not tolerate inflation. In 1966,
1969–70, and 1973, it fought inflation hard. It is true, however,
that it failed. Other weapons besides monetary policy which were
needed were not brought into the battle.

Interest rates fluctuated over a wide range to highs which would
have seemed unbelievable only a few years previously. Long-term
rates remained high. While those who held deposits had less purchasing power because of the inflation, those who held other assets
found their values decreased as interest rates rose. In addition,
there were periods when many borrowers who were good risks

found it either impossible to raise money or found money available only at rates they believed they could not afford. Finally, in an effort to halt the inflation, government wage and price controls were imposed. The need to introduce controls in a period not marked by an all-out war was a blow to our traditional concepts of free enterprise. That the high potential costs of compulsory controls ought to be avoided at almost any cost has been a basic tenet held even by those who believed that some governmental programs were needed to handle excessive wage-price increases.

The cause of the inflation was a major increase in excess demand and an inability or unwillingness to combat it through the use of fiscal (governmental spending and taxes) and monetary power. The demands that broke the back of stability arose from government deficits; from speculative investment in plant, equipment, and labor by business corporations; from use of economic power to raise wages and profits; and, some believe, from mistaken monetary policy. But most significant were the government deficits.

The Vietnam War was the most potent cause of governmental excesses. Because of the way in which it was fought, its widespread lack of public acceptance, and its shifting fortunes, it was not supported by the fiscal actions essential to maintain economic stability. The necessary cutbacks in other demands were not imposed until mid-1968, and they were later relaxed. Of course, this same reluctance to finance wars on a current basis has always been characteristic of governments; but it was to be hoped that we had learned from past errors.

Overinvestment and overspeculation—excess business investment in plant and equipment, labor hoarding, and speculation in the stock market—had many causes. Apparently business and investors, after such an extended period of prosperity, had accepted the idea that the government would permanently maintain close to full employment. The risks of losses would be diminished; increased profitability would be assured by rising prices. The thrust of economic policy making, both fiscal and monetary, was overbalanced toward expansion. Once a decision had been made to widen the U.S. involvement in Vietnam, policy which had previously been sound became highly inflationary.

The rapid run-up of Vietnam deficits is an example of how many of even the most vital decisions concerning economic policy are made for other than economic reasons. A case in point involves my appointment to the Federal Reserve Board. On the morning of April 1, 1965 I met with President Johnson, who asked if I would be willing to serve as a member of the Federal Reserve Board.

One of the periodic crises in the British pound was threatening. The Administration feared that the Fed might overreact to such a crisis, as it had in the past, and so endanger the domestic expansion. While neither this nor any other future policy of the Fed was mentioned in my discussions with the President and his staff, it was clear that they had reviewed my speeches and publications and believed that on the Federal Reserve Board my approach to problems, my analysis and decisions would probably fit the economic patterns and programs the Administration was trying to foster.

The White House recognized, of course, that, once appointed, a member of the Fed is completely independent, beholden to no one. As is true with the Supreme Court, a President's impact on future decisions derives mainly from picking appointees with compatible values and the necessary skills to make them effective.

I accepted President Johnson's offer willingly. Within the hour, he announced my nomination at the swearing-in ceremony for the new secretary of the Treasury, Henry Fowler. The next day's papers commented on the changes in the economic team and on the economic problems looming on the horizon due to the balance of payments and the length of the existing expansion.

It was not until seven years later, looking through the "Pentagon Papers," however, that I learned of other decisions made that day which were to have a far greater impact on the economy than a new secretary of the Treasury and a new member of the Federal Reserve Board. Immediately after the swearing-in, President Johnson had lunched with his major national security advisers. At that lunch the decision was made to escalate the war in Vietnam. This decision dominated most of the economic developments for the next eight years; yet escalation of the U.S. role in Vietnam clearly was never thought of as a basic economic decision. In fact, for the next year, economic policy was made with no clear picture of the developing war and its economic consequences.

The Limits of Monetary Policy

The price indexes show that monetary policy did not halt the inflation. The critical factors involved in this failure can be easily summarized. They are the same forces which must constantly be re-examined as we make monetary decisions in the future.

—There is a trade-off between idle men and a more stable value for the dollar. A conscious decision must be made as to how much unemployment and loss of output is acceptable in order to get smaller price rises. A major depression, however, with its severe losses of output and jobs and other untold hardships, is unacceptable as a primary anti-inflation weapon. Monetary policy has to ease its pressure when a crisis threatens.

—Some price increases originate on the cost side or in particular industries. These cannot be halted by monetary policy, which acts principally on the overall or aggregate demand for goods and services.

—Because significant costs arise specific to the use of monetary policy in contrast to other anti-inflationary tools, the nation's welfare may be better served by substituting other weapons in the battle. Some sectors of the economy are hit disproportionately. Certain forms of wealth decrease and income is redistributed in an arbitrary way.

—If monetary policy pushes too hard, it can cause a liquidity crisis. The consequent problems of the financial world can then lead to a major depression.

—Policies often do not work out as well as hoped because we do not know enough and because we make mistakes. More is expected of economic policy than it can yet deliver. The best mix of fiscal, monetary, and incomes policies is not clear. Although we have learned to avoid the major errors and disasters of the past, we still know too little to halt economic fluctuations completely. We cannot yet fine tune the economy; while the band of fluctuations beyond control continues to narrow, it remains wider than we like.

—Furthermore, errors are more likely on the inflationary than on the recessionary side. It is particularly hard to make a prompt political decision since each one aids some at the expense of others. Thus policy decisions are delayed and action to curtail rapid growth often comes too late.

—Even as we learn how to solve old problems, new ones develop. We live in a dynamic world. Human ingenuity can create new economic patterns of fluctuations almost, but fortunately not quite, as fast as we recognize and stabilize old ones.

—In my judgment, the techniques used over the past twenty years have tended to overemphasize monetary policy and underutilize fiscal and incomes policy. The benefits and promises of monetary policy have been so widely sung by politicians and other policy makers that newspapers, financial writers, and so-called experts have often given the impression that it is a panacea for economic ills. As with wonder drugs, the bad side-effects are either soft-pedaled or not recognized at all. The costs of and limitations to its effectiveness are never explained; one of the most unfortunate effects of this tardiness in recognizing the limits of monetary policy is that it has delayed the use of other governmental action tools that might have been more effective. Meanwhile, inflation has become a more pervasive and difficult problem. The Federal Reserve itself has sometimes been guilty of promising more than it can deliver through monetary policy, while minimizing the costs involved.

Monetary policy simply could not accomplish alone the tasks assigned to it after 1965. The scope of its role was too great for existing instruments and knowledge. Although I believe that, on the whole, the Federal Reserve did an excellent job, its batting average was well below 1.000. If monetary policy is forced to bat too often, the resulting fluctuations in interest rates, money, and credit cause unacceptable hardships. How far it can go is limited by the distortions in jobs and income it causes and by the ever-present possibility of a financial crunch.

The Impact of Monetary Policy

The Federal Reserve had never accepted the idea that minor sin should be winked at, that a little inflation could be a good thing. It believed that the spread of such a doctrine was the chief danger to price stability. In speech after speech and in numerous publications, Fed spokesmen attacked the concept of the trade-off, that is, the idea that because of the difficulty of maintaining both price stability and full employment at the same time, it is necessary to choose more of one at the cost of less of the other.

The Fed rejected as false the idea that prices had to rise to get higher output and more jobs. This made no sense; it only tended to promote inflation. Either inflationary excesses or the cost of fighting inflation would eventually cause output to fall below the true equilibrium level. The losses in jobs and output from recessions would be as large or larger than the gains in the boom. Since, in addition, there would be losses from the inflationary redistributions, everyone would be worse off. There was no need to choose among goals. A proper monetary policy geared to maintaining an orderly market, safe banks, sound credit, and resisting price increases would benefit everyone.

Unfortunately, the actual policy choice faced was not that of small price rises versus a few additional jobs. The question was what policy should be when prices were rising rapidly, unemployment was high and growing, and plants were only partially employed. This was the situation in 1970 and 1971 when the country experienced a large-scale inflation accompanied by a high unemployment rate.

It turned out that a problem of trade-off really did exist. (In Chapter 11 [pages 282–85] we see why the trade-off exists.) Inflation does not arise merely from the demand side—"too much money chasing too few goods." Prices can also be pushed upward by wage-price pressures, accompanied by rising income, greater demand, and a potential wage-price spiral—the cost-push. In such a situation, stable prices per se cannot be the sole objective of monetary policy if the level of unemployment required for complete price stability is too high. If forces other than monetary demand raise prices, as, for example, corporate and union price-wage policies, then a monetary policy capable of reducing demand to a point where prices remain constant can lead to so great a fall in output and jobs that it will be unacceptable. Large or prolonged increases in unemployment set a limit on the extent to which a policy can be pursued.

Even before such a limit is reached in terms of the nation's welfare, a continued squeeze on demand may be politically impossible. It was the recognition of this fact that in 1971 and 1973 brought a widespread demand for wage and price controls.

In addition to the difficulties raised by the price-job trade-off, monetary policy pushed beyond a given point, which may still be short of that required to halt inflation, runs into opposition and limits set by the high costs it engenders in particular spheres of the economy.

When monetary policy attempts to lower the demand for goods and services, sharp fluctuations in interest rates and the availability of money cause high costs to the economy. The goals of monetary policy cannot neglect the size of movements in money, credit, and interest rates. The burdens of monetary policy are not shared equally; the impacts upon different sectors are grossly uneven. The sectors hardest hit by tight money, such as small businesses, housing, and local governments, are often those with a high social priority. For example, in 1966, housing starts dropped by nearly 50 percent, while plant and equipment expenditures of businesses were virtually unaffected. In 1969, the differences were not as large, but housing decreased by 20 percent, while businesses raised their expenditures nearly 10 percent.

But it is not only a case of soak the weak; rapid changes in interest rates have large-scale impacts on monetary wealth and well-being as well. In 1969, the market value of both bonds and common stocks was far lower than in 1968. Investors had lost large sums and few owners of financial assets were happy when they saw what tightening monetary policy did to their net worth. There was also a redistribution of income. When interest rates move up, those with wealth to lend get more income, while those who must borrow incur a greater drain on current resources, even though both may have lost net worth. Furthermore, just as with inflation, monetary policy brings about an arbitrary redistribution of wealth. Families gain and families lose income in a way unrelated to their contribution to economic productivity.

Whatever their indirect impact, the direct effects of interest rate rises are inflationary. Interest plays a major role in the consumer price index, especially through the housing and consumer credit component. It is a large factor in utility costs. Regulatory agencies allow interest increases to affect rates and prices almost immediately. Movements of interest rates increase the uncertainties and therefore the risks and costs of doing business. Tightening monetary policy has an effect on productivity and efficiency. Investment for the next several years will be less and its costs more because of past interest rate gyrations.

The Penn Central episode underscores the problem of a financial crunch. It may be that this was primarily a case of a declining industry and not the best management; but still, large-scale shifts in interest rates and in the availability of money can shake even the strongest corporations and financial institutions and can topple those that happen to be caught with their liquidity down. In 1970 most corporations, even though hurt, were saved from bankruptcy. But the danger lies in the possibility that, if monetary policy is pushed beyond a certain point, many essentially sound businesses may be unable to withstand the vagaries of financial pressures.

An economy in which spending and prices respond promptly and smoothly to policy changes would make life simple for economic policy makers. Problems of income redistribution, large losses in production and jobs, corporate bankruptcy, or inflation would be less likely to arise. Unfortunately recent experience in using monetary policy has raised serious questions as to what costs were being engendered and what burdens the nation is willing to bear. The high costs experienced mean either that other and better ways may be needed to fight inflation, or, at a minimum, that other policies must be used in conjunction with money in order to spread the burden over broader segments of the economy.

The Gap between Monetary Policy and Events

In addition to reaching the limits of monetary policy, the Federal Reserve made errors. I acknowledge my full share. But it was not merely a case of avoidable mistakes. The art of economic policy making is still imperfectly developed. Although it has moved forward rapidly, so have the problems which must be solved.

The Vietnam War was only one of the factors which caused trouble for economic policy makers. Another factor, less tangible but nonetheless real, was the speeding up and proliferation of economic events. Faster communication, better knowledge in the business and investment world, more public interest in what goes on, have all made managing the economy far more difficult. It is true that these same factors have increased our ability to manage the dollar; but the growth in monetary knowledge has not been adequate to cope with the complexities created by an increasingly dynamic economy.

My answer to such questions as 'Has the economy changed? Are economic problems different? Is it true that the old rules are not working?' is that the rules never did work very well. They are working as well as or better than they ever did, but recognition of their inadequacies has become widespread. A famous story which the governor of the Bank of England and chancellors of the Exchequer frequently tell, illustrates the old saying, "Ignorance is bliss." For over one hundred years England had no official balance of payments statistics and it experienced no balance of payments crises. Since the balance of payments has been calculated, one crisis has followed another in rapid succession. The story is more than apocryphal. Knowledge of what is happening in the balance of payments sphere has compounded the difficulties of the Bank of England and the Exchequer in handling their reserves. When no one knew whether England was an international bankrupt, it was much simpler to obtain credit and trust. When the extent of her losses in reserves became known, everyone with money fled to other currencies.

The change in communications and in knowledge was more than just a matter of degree; it put an entirely different face on policy problems. For example, the tremendous growth of multinational corporations and multinational banks has caused vast sums to flow through the international exchanges. These institutions are aware of the risks and profits in exchange movements. The Bretton Woods Agreements and the International Monetary Fund were simply not equipped to handle the problems resulting from this increased knowledge and activity. Nowadays a great deal more is known about how to handle exchange problems, and numerous policy tools have been developed; yet, in the face of crisis, the policy tools have been overwhelmed by the ability of the private market to transfer funds. In June–July 1972, for example, the United Kingdom lost more than a third of its large reserves in only a few days. In 1973 most exchanges were buffeted by tremendous flows of money across borders.

Throughout the financial world, we see evidence of a new look. It is to be found in the stock market and in investment policies. Bank trust officers used to be solid, staid pillars of the community. Almost overnight institutional investments became the forte of youth, constantly promoting new ideas. This was a factor in the unprecedented increase in volume in the stock market and the failure of some brokerage firms that found themselves unprepared to cope with the sudden rise in volume and subsequent contraction. It was another clear sign that reaction time has become much faster.

The banking system of today is far different from what it was even in 1960. When new ideas or techniques appear that are useful and profitable, the word spreads rapidly. Success stories become known almost instantaneously throughout the financial community, and there is a rush to get on board. The one-bank holding company is a good example.

Another illustration is to be found in the money markets, which have seen rapid expansion in the use of formerly little-used instruments, most of which have turned out to be extremely volatile. The certificate of deposit came into being in its modern form in 1961. Over $24 billion were outstanding in 1968. In the following year the number outstanding had dropped to less than half the previous peak. In the next year it shot up by an additional 150 percent. Fluctuations of similar or even greater magnitudes can be found in the borrowing of Euro-dollars by banks in the United States. We have seen the same type of movement in the commercial paper market.

Along with the spread of economic knowledge, expectations grew as to what economic policy could accomplish. This was due in part, no doubt, to the successful attempt, beginning in 1961, to return the economy to its path of rapid growth and full employment. The drive for economic growth under Presidents Kennedy and Johnson brought about the longest sustained growth of the economy in history. Output expanded for 105 months; and the expansion was accompanied by a constant discussion of economic policy. From the President down everyone tried to educate the public as to what economic policy was and what it could achieve. The situation had changed drastically since the 1950s, when members of the Council of Economic Advisers boasted of their success in moving out of a recession despite the fact that they could not admit to using modern fiscal policy. Any hint that increasing public expenditures could raise income would have been anathema to the fiscal conservatives who dominated the Eisenhower cabinet.

Through speeches, interviews, and in the media, the potential of these new economic tools and the success with which the Administration was using them were enthusiastically described. As a result, expectations of what economic policy could accomplish zoomed. It seemed to have worked. But there was one major negative result of this success: It was accepted perhaps too well by business and common stock investors. Looking at the world through new rose-colored glasses, they saw increased possibilities of profits. Whether they actually overestimated these opportunities or not is still uncertain. The results from the nation's point of view were, however, clearly unfortunate. The spurt in demand, coming when the economy was fully employed, could only be met by bidding resources away from other uses at higher prices. While real investment lowers costs over the long run, it can be extremely inflationary in periods when it causes a sharp spurt and an excess of total demand.

As the decade progressed, it began to become apparent that economic policy was not the panacea that many had been led to believe. To fine tune the economy and maintain it at full employment with reasonable price stability was a vastly different problem from that of bringing it up from recession levels. Policy makers now realize that in the range close to full employment they need much more knowledge about the impact of policy changes before they can regulate the economy as closely as the public seems to expect.

The Federal Reserve's Record in Perspective

Problems of rising expectations and others even more difficult plagued the Federal Reserve as well as the Administration. Our knowledge and ability to conduct monetary policy improved rapidly, but the problems the Fed had to handle arose at a still faster rate.

Our initial conception of what could be accomplished through monetary policy may have been wrong. Choices looked clearer than they turned out to be in practice; problems were oversimplified, and many elements were neglected. In some cases the choices made may have been the popular and easier ones; in retrospect, some people are sorry that greater sacrifices were not demanded. We knew less than we thought we did, both as to what had to be accomplished and how to do it.

A recognition of the difficulty of the problems, the lack of knowledge, and the limits of policies may account for the fact that many economists have treated the Federal Reserve more kindly than has the popular and financial press. Economists recognize that monetary policy must be made in the context of other forces in the economy; it cannot overwhelm them. Recent price, wage, and interest rate movements resulted from the interactions of economic policy with war and with the decisions of businesses and households with respect to investments, prices, wages, and employment. In rating economic managers, the main question to ask is not what were the final results, but how skillfully did they use the available tools in this interactive process.

Looking back at history, many economists feel that the Federal Reserve policy from 1930 to 1933 was disastrous. It failed to avert a financial crisis at that time. In the late 1940s the problem was complicated by the aftermath of World War II, but the Fed still failed to bring the economy back to normalcy. In fact, most people believe it aggravated inflation by maintaining its support of the Treasury for too long. Perhaps in reaction to its stance in the late 1940s, the Fed maintained a tight rein on money during the 1950s. While the Fed dissents from the view, most critics believe that monetary policy was too restrictive in 1957 and 1959, which was one of the principal reasons for the slow growth rate of output in the ten-year period from 1951 to 1961. During this time unemployment more than doubled, from 3.3 to 6.7 percent.

In the opinion of many qualified observers, the Fed's performance in the 1960s improved markedly. Paul Samuelson, the first American Nobel Prize laureate in economics, has said,

Let me begin by stating flatly an unpopular view. I believe that Federal Reserve policy in the decade of the 1960's has been very good. It has not been perfect. But when I consider the situation within which the decision makers have had to operate, I suspect that we are not likely in a future decade to do as well. And certainly Federal Reserve policy in the 1960's has been superior to that of the 1950's, both in terms of technical proficiency and the social welfare goals that the central bank has pursued.[*]

I am not certain how widely the Samuelson view of the Fed's record in the 1960s is shared. Certainly a group of very vocal critics dissents from it. As we examine the problems which plagued the Federal Reserve in the sixties, we can see why. These problems and the Fed's reactions to them are the foundation upon which current and future monetary policy must be made. When monetary policy is used as the cutting edge in battling inflation, the difficulties of managing the dollar become immense. This is a key lesson of recent history. The Fed saw a clear goal, but it lacked the necessary policy tools to reach it. Its vision outreached its grasp. Partly the inability stems from inadequate techniques; more, however, it originates in the fact that monetary policy by itself does not have the strength necessary successfully to combat significant swings in spending patterns without major costs. Learning this basic lesson has not been easy. Many analysts do not accept it yet. I believe, however, it is much more useful to start from the premise that the scope of monetary policy is limited and build upon this knowledge than to start with the idea that monetary policy can solve all our economic problems if it is only operated properly.

[*] *Journal of Money, Credit, and Banking* 2 (February 1970): 33.

CHAPTER TWO

What Does the
Federal Reserve Do?

"MONEY MUST BE MANAGED" is the unblazoned motto of the Federal Reserve System. History shows that unmanaged or poorly managed money results in increasing instability and economic disaster. Like fire, money is useful under control; but running wild, it can do great harm. The Federal Reserve exists to keep money (currency and certain types of bank deposits) under control. Its policies affect everyone and everything. Good monetary decisions make possible more jobs, more goods, and greater wealth. Poor decisions can lead to unemployment, falling stock and bond prices, inflation, and bankruptcy for thousands of firms.

The Need To Manage Money

Congress delegated its constitutional power to coin money and control its value to the Federal Reserve through the Federal Reserve Act of 1913, thus giving the Fed considerable freedom to manage the dollar. Actually, this independence is both ill-defined and circumscribed; Congress furnished no specific instructions. And, although the Fed has an almost unlimited ability to create and cancel money and thereby to raise or lower the dollar's value, forces other than law effectively limit its actions. Monetary policy is only part of a general economic scene in which the strongest thrusts come from other sources.

Fundamentally, money is a commodity. Like the value of wheat or meat or anything bought or sold, the value of the dollar rises or falls depending on the amount supplied relative to demand. How

24

many dollars are created is limited by the desire to maintain the value of each one.

In making monetary policy, all of the members of the Federal Reserve Board face a constant dilemma. Outside events shape the economic context in which money must be managed. With the information available it is not possible to determine with any degree of accuracy what impact a change in monetary conditions will have on the economy. Yet the Fed cannot avoid making the decision as to how much money should be created.

Whether the Fed existed or not, the amount of money would fluctuate because of the way in which our financial system works. Millions of independent decisions made daily at all levels of our banking and credit structure operate to create and cancel money. If they are not properly orchestrated, the result is chaos. History shows that money is not automatically generated in desirable amounts. The record of money not managed is a history of intolerable instability. Sad to say, the record of money managed often has not been too much better.

How the dollar is managed has been a constantly evolving process. While there is no authorized version of the framework for decisions and operations employed by the Federal Reserve, we now can get a clearer picture of how monetary policy is made than we could in the past.

Members of the Federal Reserve System are badly split over the fundamentals of both the theoretical framework and techniques of operation. Although I have made every effort to do justice to all points of view in the discussions which follow, the reader will doubtless become aware that I am far from being an impartial observer, as a recent incident illustrates. I was delivering a speech and participating in a discussion with the senior staffs of the Ministry of Finance and the central bank of a neighboring country. After an hour or so of give and take, I prefaced an answer by remarking, "Remember that this is my interpretation, and hold in mind that I was one of the more liberal members of the Federal Reserve Board." The minister of finance at once replied, "Governor Maisel, you didn't have to say that. We've been listening."

The way in which the Federal Reserve makes and operates monetary policy probably developed as rapidly in the past decade as in any previous period in its history. Monetary policy and doctrine

were forged in a crucible of criticism from both within and without. A series of shocks and crises in the economy evoked drastic
shifts in policy. The authority to create and cancel dollars was employed to an unprecedented degree. The chapters which follow describe the old doctrine and the events and ideas that shaped the
new. They explain how money is now managed; how one can interpret and predict what monetary policy is doing and will do, and
how to analyze the dynamic process through which monetary doctrine continues to evolve.

The Critics of the Federal Reserve

The Federal Reserve was slow to react to the accelerating expectations and explosion of new ideas that marked government in the
1960s. New concepts and procedures were needed to bring monetary policy into phase with new developments. A great deal of
pressure came from events; but part came from new ideas in economics as well. The rapid growth of computer techniques made it
possible to quantify economic measures and to handle complex
data to a degree never before feasible. The Fed has always resisted
being too specific about its methods and its goals, clothing its operations in a kind of mystique that left it more freedom for maneuver. It took the position that the complexities and psychological
factors inherent in the financial system were best dealt with by use
of intuitive judgment. Experience and discretion were needed
rather than reliance on formal theories and stated targets for performance. The Fed's able staff economists gathered and published
a great deal of valuable data, but they were not asked to analyze
the information in the coordinated form necessary for the development of more precise policies.

This failure of the Fed to spell out its objectives and methods
brought it under mounting criticism from at least four important
and articulate groups in the economy. With each succeeding year,
with continuing improvement in data and knowledge, their attacks
grew stronger and gained more public credence. The Fed found itself on the defensive. Specific accusations of bad judgment could
no longer be countered by generalities. The System had to develop
a more comprehensive theory of monetary policy and clarify its
own views.

The Proponents of Low Interest Rates

One group of critics constantly pressed for lower interest rates and greater availability of credit. Their roots are populist; from the era of Andrew Jackson many political forces throughout the nineteenth century pushed the government to make money more abundant. More recently, President Lyndon Johnson and Congressman Wright Patman of Texas have been prominent spokesmen in this low-interest tradition. In their view, the country would be better off with lower rates and more money available for farmers, small businesses, and housing. They accused the Federal Reserve of being in league with the banks and failing to force them to lower the price of money sufficiently.

The home-building and labor lobbies are among the important political forces in this camp. Both are politically active and spend a great deal of money on congressional elections. At times they have been joined by the strong savings and loan lobby, an industry which was shaken drastically by higher money market rates and increased bank competition.

The Financial Community

In almost complete opposition to the complaints of populists were periodic bursts of criticism from the financial community, the traditional major supporters of the Federal Reserve. Commercial bankers, executives of large insurance companies, investment bankers, and others who hold large amounts of savings have had faith in the Fed as an independent organization whose main function was to impose financial responsibility on the President and Congress. It was the last citadel protecting the dollar and the country from disaster.

This group has now become critical of the Federal Reserve for failing to maintain stable prices. They are concerned that the Fed may have given too much weight to boosting output and employment when it has furnished the money necessary to keep the economy going ahead in the face of the higher wages and prices forced by union contracts and of the high costs of war in Vietnam. While they recognize the political problems, many feel the Federal Reserve ratified the inflationary impacts of government spending and the cost-push. Its task was to hold back on money and credit to insure that the wage-price cycle would not gain momentum, even if this meant high interest rates and rising unemployment. In their view, it failed to do its job.

The Post-Keynesian Economists

A third group of critics was based in the school of academic, governmental, and business economists who have dominated much of economic thought since World War II. These post-Keynesian or "new economists" included the chief economic advisers of the Kennedy and Johnson Administrations. Men like the successive chairmen of the Council of Economic Advisers, Walter Heller, Gardner Ackley, and Arthur Okun, and directors of the Bureau of the Budget, Kermit Gordon, Charles Schultze, and Charles Zwick, all recognized the problems of the Federal Reserve. They were on the whole understanding, but felt it could do better. They came into office pledged to speed up growth and improve stability. They were extremely critical of the Federal Reserve's performance in the 1950s, feeling that tight money had retarded growth and raised unemployment. They wanted to insure a better record for the 1960s.

Their criticism centered on two spheres: The Federal Reserve was not operating as efficiently as it could because of its faulty theories and antiquated operating procedures. But, more importantly, they considered the Fed to be biased in its goals. Because of the individual values of Board members and the System's traditional relationship to the financial community, too little emphasis was placed on the advantages of full employment and increased output.

The Monetarists

The final group of critics were economists of the monetarist school, whose number and influence expanded rapidly during the sixties. They too believed that the Federal Reserve made poor policy because it used improper guides and operating techniques. The monetarists hold that control of the money supply is the key to economic stability. The majority specified that the Federal Reserve ought to hold money growth steady in the neighborhood of 4 percent a year. This school of economists has developed a theory of how changes in the money supply affect spending and prices (see Chapter 11). In the popular and academic press, they have trumpeted their belief that failure to follow the prescriptions developed from their theory has caused many of the economy's recent problems. Supporters in academic, business, and political circles have flocked to their banner.

For both philosophical and political reasons, President Nixon embraced this viewpoint. It predominated among his advisers, Paul McCracken and Herbert Stein at the Council of Economic Advisers, and George Shultz, who was successively secretary of Labor, director of the Office of Management and Budget (OMB), and secretary of the Treasury. Even more importantly, it was accepted completely and uncritically by the noneconomists who dominated the White House staff.

Initially the group within the Nixon Administration was extremely critical of the Federal Reserve for creating too much money in the late 1960s. In 1971, however, when the economy failed to respond to their initial prescriptions, they reversed their criticism and became proponents of a much faster growth rate for money.

The Framework for Monetary Policy

The process of making monetary decisions is a useful starting point for understanding what determines the dollar's value. A description of procedures also serves as an introduction to the language, the meaning of commonly used terms, involved in monetary management. It forms a background that enables us to see in proper perspective the importance of each of many events that have played a part in the continuing evolution of managing the dollar.

Before embarking on a description of how monetary policy is made, a word about general economic policy making would be helpful. Millions of decision units in our economy—corporations, households, financial institutions, state and local governments, the federal government, foreigners, and others—interact to determine how much will be spent, how much produced, and how many employed at any given time. Each day billions of desires are expressed and fulfilled. These independent decisions are meshed together by our complex economic structure.

The form these transactions takes depends upon certain underlying relationships. Some relationships are legal, some institutional; others depend upon the behavior of firms, institutions, and individuals. From this structure of relationships stem the prices we pay, the incomes we receive, and the goods we buy.

Economic and monetary theory give rough indications of these relationships and the causal factors at work. Statistical and econometric estimations come closer, but still do not provide exact values. In a dynamic economy the relationships are constantly shifting. Consumers or businesses may alter their habits enough between two periods to cause major differences in the outcome of a given policy. Economic tools provide only an indication of probable movements, of the importance of particular magnitudes, of the direction of change, and of potential boundaries.

For purposes of analysis and prediction, economic activity is summarized in statements such as the National Income and Product Accounts (the GNP) and the Flow of Funds Accounts. They may be supplemented with additional price, employment, production, financial, and similar sector accounts. The possible groupings are limited only by time and available data.

Governmental policy makers use these accounts to make projections of the economy for future periods. The policy tools available to the government are used to move the nation away from undesirable situations such as slow growth, low output, idle men, or inflation and closer to desirable objectives. The available governmental policies are usually divided into three groups: (1) fiscal policy —changes in government taxes, expenditures, and saving; (2) structural or incomes policies—attempts to shift supply and relationships between supply and demand through price and wage controls, antitrust policies, imports, tax policy, farm policy, etc.; and (3) monetary policy—changes in bank reserves and other financial relationships. It is the last which is the special responsibility of the Federal Reserve.

A summary of the monetary process with a listing of the elements contained in it is outlined in Chart 1. This diagram shows that decision making for monetary policy follows the same form as that for economic policy in general. The first section of the chart shows the starting point for policy decisions. The state of the economy is examined and a forecast of economic and financial developments is made based on existing policy. As the decision making starts, the first two boxes on the upper left of the table show current operating instructions for monetary policy reflected in specific settings for the monetary instruments. (The variety of factors which have been used as operating instructions, the available instruments, and possible monetary variables, measures, or targets are all listed. These are defined and discussed in the remainder of this and the next chapter.)

Based on studies of how the propensities to spend and to finance are developing and shifting, a forecast is made of the status of the economy and of the monetary variables if monetary policy remains unchanged. The two-way lines between the propensities to spend and lend and the monetary variables show that their interactions mutually bring about a particular level of spending and financing. Included in the projections of spending and financial developments are such factors as expected movements of output, prices, balance of payments, money supply, interest rates, credit availability, and wealth.

The next section of the chart depicts the choice of goals and objectives. They are compared (as indicated by dotted lines) with the economic developments expected to result from current policy. If a gap between desired and forecast spending and financial outcomes appears probable, the Federal Reserve must then determine whether changing the monetary variables is likely to bring the economy closer to the nation's goals. The monetary variables influence many spending decisions. The relationships which depend upon money must be estimated and a path or target for money must be chosen which will bring the economy as close to its goals as possible. The Fed must also weigh the costs compared to the hoped for gains from such a change.

At the same time, decisions must be made as to what settings for the monetary instruments will keep the monetary variables moving along the desired path in the light of all the other forces interacting in the economy and financial markets. Operating in-

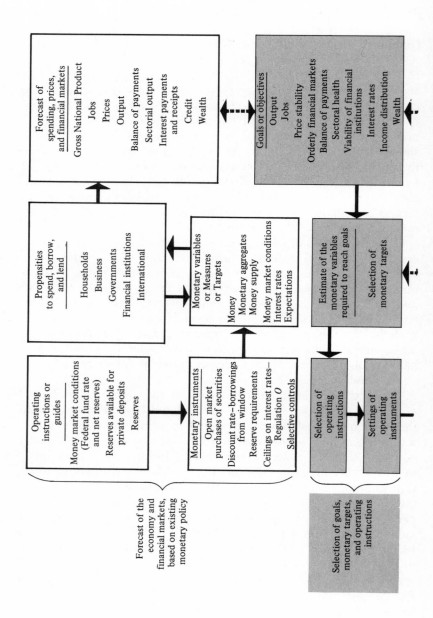

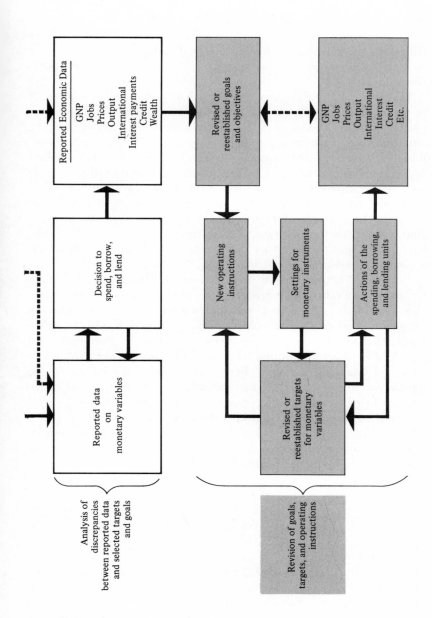

Reported Economic Data

GNP
Jobs
Prices
Output
International
Interest payments
Credit
Wealth

Decision to spend, borrow, and lend

Reported data on monetary variables

Analysis of discrepancies between reported data and selected targets and goals

Revised or reestablished goals and objectives

New operating instructions

Settings for monetary instruments

Actions of the spending, borrowing, and lending units

Revised or reestablished targets for monetary variables

Revision of goals, targets, and operating instructions

GNP
Jobs
Prices
Output
International
Interest
Credit
Etc.

structions or guides are selected to adjust the instruments in order that the movements in the monetary variables can be properly controlled.

The third section depicts the period of operations. As a result of the chosen settings for the monetary instruments and the constantly shifting decisions of households, businesses, governments, and financial institutions, spending occurs, with its related economic, financial, and monetary consequences. Our data-gathering system estimates what is happening. The reported economic data are compared to the chosen targets for the monetary variables and the desired goals for the economy. If, as is usually the case, the actual data diverge from the targets and goals, the possible causes for the divergence must be analyzed. Does the problem lie in the data, in errors in the estimated relationships, in unexpected movements in outside forces, in a shift in the structure of the markets? Depending on this analysis, decisions may be made to change operating instructions in an attempt to move the monetary variables closer to their previously set target; or the monetary targets may be revised to accord with actual events. On the other hand, the decision may be to accept the new developments and maintain existing operations while revising the goals for the economy and financial markets. These revised decisions, shown in the fourth section of the chart, interact again with new spending desires to bring about an altered and hopefully more desirable level of spending, output, prices, and financial impacts.

If we hold this framework in mind, much of what seems murky about the monetary process may be illumined and we can see how the various parts of the puzzle fit together.

Monetary Tools or Instruments

Just as any workman or business uses certain tools, so the monetary authority has its tools. Like those of other institutions or businesses, the Fed's tools are specifically designed to accomplish its particular business—namely, increasing or reducing the amount of money. For this purpose, the Fed has to have the special power (as do all central banks) of creating money and, equally important, of cancelling money.

Open Market Operations

Monetary policy is implemented chiefly through buying or selling government securities (bills, notes, and bonds). This is called an open market operation. (Operations also include foreign currencies.) To stimulate monetary growth, the Open Market Desk of the Federal Reserve in New York bids for government securities in the money market, as do other traders. The Fed pays for its purchases with its own check (or newly printed currency). When the sellers deposit the checks, the accounts at regional Federal Reserve Banks of the member banks receiving the checks are increased; their reserves, consisting of their vault cash and deposits at the Fed, have grown. The Fed has as a new asset the bond it has purchased and as a new liability the deposit it owes the commercial bank.

This open market operation accomplishes three things:

—First, by adding to the demand for securities, it bids up their prices and lowers interest rates. This is illustrated by thinking of a perpetual bond (so that we need not worry about amortizing any discount or premium paid) which has a fixed interest payment of $6 a year. If this bond sells for $100, it yields an annual interest rate of 6 percent, i.e., 6/100. If the price rises to $150, it yields an annual interest rate of 4 percent, i.e., 6/150. If the price drops to $50, its yield is 12 percent, i.e., 6/50.

—Second, the open market purchase increases the liquidity of the seller of the bond, who now holds noninterest yielding money in the form of a deposit instead of an interest bearing bond. This may either satisfy a changed desire for liquidity or lead him to buy more goods or securities.

—Finally, it generates an additional Federal Reserve deposit for a commercial bank, increasing the bank's reserves, thereby giving the banking system the power to make more loans and generate more demand deposits. Since the money supply consists of currency and demand deposits, the creation of deposits boosts the total amount of money.

The Discount Rate, Reserve Requirements,
Interest, and Credit Controls

Banks can also increase their reserves by borrowing from the Fed, which credits the amount borrowed to their deposit accounts. The interest rate they pay on such borrowings is called the discount rate. The discount window is an administered accommodation for use only under special circumstances (see Chapter 5, page 102). While a move in the discount rate is the most traditional, awesome, and newsworthy instrument in the Federal Reserve's portfolio, it in fact has a minimal real impact, since banks actually borrow very little from the Fed. A move in the discount rate can have a major impact, however, if it is intended to, and does, announce a shift in monetary policy and if it succeeds in changing expectations of future policy.

The level of potential bank credit, the money the reserves will support, can also be shifted if the Federal Reserve changes reserve requirements, or the legal reserve ratio. By regulation, the Fed can set the required reserves at between 7 and 22 percent for demand deposits and 3 and 10 percent for other deposits. When their reserves exceed the percentage required by law, banks can increase their loans or buy securities. When these excess reserves are used up, the banks can no longer generate demand deposits and money until they obtain more reserves.

Compared to open market operations, however, both of these actions, although useful, serve rather minor functions; except for their announcement effects on expectations, they can be neglected in most analysis.

How banks will act to expand deposits cannot be predicted with accuracy. They will be motivated to increase loans and investments to their maximum because they earn nothing on unused excess reserves. On the other hand, no bank wants to lose money on poor investments. Their profits may be higher if they hold idle funds until more profitable opportunities arise.

The maximum or ceiling interest rate that banks can pay on their savings and time deposit liabilities is set by the Federal Reserve under Regulation Q. At times, the ceilings may be removed or set so high as to have no effect on bank operations. When the ceilings are below short-term market interest rates, savers who want higher returns will purchase securities rather than make time deposits in banks. As deposits stop growing or fall, so does the credit banks can make available through loans or investments. Higher ceilings or their removal will, on the other hand, allow time deposits to be attracted.

Selective credit controls limit the amount of credit banks may make available for certain purposes. As an example, the amount that can be lent to a customer for the purpose of purchasing common stock on credit is set by regulating his minimum margin. The required margin is the difference between the market value and maximum legal loan which can be made on a stock, thus the cash a buyer must have as a down payment. Margin requirements have ranged from 40 to 100 percent; in the latter case banks could not lend at all against such collateral.

Other selective controls have been applied to consumer credit, mortgages, and international lending. These controls limit in various ways credit for specific uses, and individually have a minor effect on total bank credit.

The Decision-Making Bodies in Action

There are two prime decision-making bodies in the Federal Reserve System which may utilize these monetary tools. They are the Federal Reserve Board and the Federal Open Market Committee (FOMC).

The Board of Governors of the Federal Reserve System, with headquarters in Washington, consists of seven members appointed to fixed fourteen-year terms by the President of the United States, with the advice and consent of the Senate. The President designates one member as chairman and one as vice-chairman of the Board for four-year terms. The Federal Reserve Board has the primary powers and responsibilities under the Federal Reserve Act. The overall Federal Reserve System, however, operates in a decentralized manner. There are twelve District Federal Reserve Banks, each with a president and a local board of directors.

The FOMC, in addition to the seven members of the Board of Governors, consists of the president of the Federal Reserve Bank of

New York and an annually rotating panel made up of four of the other eleven Federal Reserve Bank presidents.

A review of the sessions at which the critical issues in the 1970 monetary crisis were considered will give some feeling for the types of decisions made and the discussions which occur at meetings of these two groups.

The Federal Open Market Committee

An unusual atmosphere of tension and excitement prevailed when the Federal Open Market Committee met at 9:30 AM on Tuesday, May 26, 1970. The news from the financial markets in New York was getting steadily worse. Stock prices had plummeted to their lowest levels in 6 years and interest rates for corporate and municipal bonds had reached their highest levels in over 170 years. The market for Treasury securities verged on the disorderly. Dealers had taken positions which turned out badly, forcing them to dump large amounts at considerable losses. The last Treasury financing had required much larger awards to bidders than expected, and the Treasury had barely obtained the funds it required. The Federal Reserve and the Treasury had had to offer massive support to the government securities market through large-scale purchases.

Seated at the thirty-foot mahogany table in the Federal Reserve boardroom were the twelve members of the Committee and also four other district presidents and two first vice-presidents without current votes. Staff members included the secretary and deputy secretary, the chief economist, two associate economists, and the manager and deputy special manager of the System Open Market Account. Behind the table sat twenty-nine advisers and consultants to the Committee.

During the previous week the Committee staff had prepared five major reports, totaling over 250 pages, which supplemented some scores of daily, weekly, monthly, and special reports also distributed to the Committee members since the last meeting. These reports conveyed the staff's views on what was happening to the economy, to money, and in financial and foreign markets. They also explained the staff's estimate of what would happen if monetary policy was maintained unchanged and an analysis of the probable effects of other possible policies.

Although monetary policy since January had been less restrictive, reserves were still being created grudgingly, in an attempt to lower inflationary expectations and price pressures so that more spending would go into real output and less into prices. Interest rates had risen because the increase in reserves had been inadequate to meet the demands of corporations and the Treasury for credit at stable rates.

The meeting opened with a discussion of the international monetary situation, which, in contrast to many other periods, was not bad. Nothing in the current foreign situation had to be given special weight in the decisions facing the FOMC. While foreign exchange markets were active and unsettled, the general situation was calm. Gold in the free market was selling under $36 an ounce and most demands for foreign currency were in good balance. The major exception was the Canadian dollar. Large inflows of funds into Canada were accompanied and reinforced by rumors that, instead of attempting to absorb the large inflows, Canada would allow its exchange rate to float.

At its previous meeting on May 5, the FOMC had decided to maintain conditions in the money markets and to create sufficient monetary reserves to support a policy of a moderate (4 percent) growth rate for money and credit. Staff reports had predicted that, with this growth for money, interest rates would stay high, with short-term interest rates around 8 percent. These rates and a moderate growth in money, together with other government policies, would continue to exert a deflationary pressure on demand and output. The projections, based on these conditions, were for a cessation for some time in real economic growth and a substantial rise in unemployment. This was consistent with the Administration's aim to slow inflation and was also acceptable to a majority of the FOMC.

The question now before the Committee was whether events since the Cambodian invasion threatened this plan. If so, how great was the danger and how should it be met?

The moves to improve stability in the Treasury market had increased bank reserves. Money supply and bank credit had grown far faster than appeared consistent with the 4 percent growth rate policy. Thus the FOMC would have to make a choice: To return to the 4 percent growth rate, reserves would have to be reduced. Even if the oversupply in reserves were not eliminated, the growth rate would still have to be reconsidered. Because of the unexpectedly large demand for money, if the money supply were held to a 4 percent growth rate, interest rates would continue to rise, perhaps at an accelerating pace, thus generating a still more rapid fall in bond and stock prices. Was this what the Committee wanted? Or, in order to avoid the unsettling effect of a more rapid increase in interest rates, would it prefer to allow reserves and money to grow more rapidly?

The economy had not yet experienced a serious setback, but the threat of one was present. A growing number of financial institutions, including stockbrokers, investment bankers, mutual funds, and some banks, were being squeezed. The demand for liquidity was surging. Failures were likely. A further deterioration of bond prices could escalate this development. Frightened by the specter of a few firms failing, other companies strove to improve their cash position. The proper action seemed clear to the FOMC's economists: If the Federal Reserve stayed with its prior decision and failed to meet the demand for liquidity, a true monetary crisis could develop.

As in many similar situations, the Committee was sharply divided in its views. Two hours were spent in lively debate. Some members supported the staff view, feeling that, when the 4 percent policy had been voted, the demand for money had been underestimated. Any policy causing interest rates to rise still higher could only endanger the entire financial structure. To leave the policy unchanged would be to move away from our goals for the economy. Since the money going into liquidity hoards would not be available to spend, output would decrease and unemployment would rise to at least 6 percent. However, a higher rate of monetary growth would save some of the firms and institutions bordering on insolvency and bankruptcy; the threat of a major liquidity crisis would be reduced.

Other members of the Committee took the opposite position. In their view, the demand for liquidity resulted from a lack of confidence in the determination of the Administration and the Fed to fight inflation. Interest rates were high because financial markets believed the government was not willing to accept sufficient sacrifices in output and unemployment. To add to reserves and money would only increase this distrust, pushing interest rates still higher. While some added reserves might be necessary temporarily to insure an orderly market, they argued that the policy should be to withdraw these new reserves as soon as possible, plus those already furnished which exceeded the amount needed to meet the 4 percent policy objective.

At a critical point in the meeting, Chairman Arthur F. Burns reminded the Committee of the duty of the Federal Reserve to support the economy by attending to its liquidity needs. A failure to do so might lead to a repetition of past monetary panics. The Chairman's statement swayed the members of the Committee who had not yet made up their minds. It also influenced somewhat those who believed in greater stringency. The debate continued. Finally, the FOMC agreed that it would not change its basic policy stand that monetary growth above 4 percent was not desirable. However, during the next month, the Open Market Desk would be allowed to furnish sufficient reserves to moderate pressures on financial markets arising from liquidity demands. A new vote would then be taken at the FOMC's next meeting, until which no attempt would be made to withdraw reserves which had been or might be furnished in excess of the 4 percent growth target. But, by the next meeting, the threatened Penn Central crisis dominated the debate and the vote.

The Board of Governors

Time and the slight ease injected into the money markets by the FOMC decision had somewhat calmed the financial situation. Nevertheless, throughout the first three weeks of June, planning to deal with a major crisis continued. In numerous regular and special meetings, the Federal Reserve Board discussed various possible actions. The previous meeting of the FOMC had shown it divided. Was the situation serious enough for the Board to use its own powers? Proposed regulations altering reserve requirements and interest rate ceilings were outstanding. Should they be the vehicle for a change in monetary policy?

The Administration and the Board had been informed of the growing cash shortage of the Penn Central Railroad, that it could not meet its financial obligations unless government aid was forthcoming. What role should the Fed play in this and similar cases?

Clearly the Fed's interest was not in Penn Central per se, but in the larger question of what effect its collapse, or that of other large and well-regarded companies, might have on the entire economy of the nation.

Under a provision of the Federal Reserve Act, the Fed can lend to individuals, partnerships, or corporations for short periods on satisfactory security, if they cannot obtain adequate credit from commercial banking institutions. The necessary money thus was either available or could be created.

Were the Federal Reserve to make funds available to meet demands for cash and to prevent a squeeze, what channels should be used? While it is axiomatic that a central bank exists to be a lender of last resort to avoid a liquidity crisis, the form the aid should take is less clear. The Fed could lend directly to firms unable to borrow from banks. It could authorize banks to lend to these firms. It could end the general liquidity squeeze by creating more reserves and money. Banks could be induced to lend by changed reserve requirements, loan requirements, or interest rate ceilings.

Finally, timing was important. What criteria should determine that the crisis had reached a point requiring action? How could the Fed act without raising fears of a further crisis? The possible announcement effects of any policy change had to be taken into account. Markets were skittish; borrowers and lenders were frightened. If the Fed announced major new policies, would the rush to liquidity be intensified?

It was decided not to use the Fed's own powers to lend to Penn Central. Although the situation was grave, it was not of a nature that fitted the legal authority for direct Fed action. A general financial crisis would have to be more imminent before emergency powers could be invoked and direct lending take place. Instead, the Fed urged the Administration and Congress to give special consideration to Penn Central in the light of its importance to the economy. For three weeks negotiations to ease the Penn Central situation went on. One possibility considered was for the Fed to guarantee an emergency loan to the railroad to handle its temporary needs. However, the Federal Reserve Bank of New York, investigating the credit situation, believed that the railroad would not be able to repay the loan and that the Fed—required by law to lend only on good security—should guarantee it on a temporary basis only and only then if Congress would pass a special law for this purpose. When Congress refused to do so, the railroad's fate was sealed.

On Monday morning, June 22, 1970, the Board of Governors of the Federal Reserve System met to work out a series of critical actions.° On Sunday, the Penn Central had gone to federal court for a receivership. Its collapse brought to a head all of the questions which had been debated for the previous six weeks. The major commercial paper market was threatened by a debacle. What should the Federal Reserve do? One step was obvious and had already been taken: to remind the banks that the Federal Reserve existed to lend in emergencies. Instead of turning away customers with outstanding commitments for lack of money, the banks should borrow the necessary money from the Federal Reserve discount window.

A vice-president of the Federal Reserve Bank of New York had called the top officers of the large New York banks on Sunday to be sure the message got through. Preceding its own meeting on Monday, the Board met with the presidents of all twelve Federal Reserve Banks. It was agreed that the same message should go out to all major banks throughout the country. But no public statement would be issued for fear that such an announcement might hasten a liquidity crisis.

However, increased use of the discount window was only a temporary palliative. It gave banks some cash, but increased their debts. The banks would not want to prolong this condition lest depositors begin to worry about the banks' liquidity. If the worry led to greater public demand for money, the effect of the added reserves would be offset. Because of public concern over bank liquidity, demand for money would rise faster than supply. Other action would be needed to halt the rise in demand.

Because money market rates were above the maximum ceilings that banks could pay on time deposits, corporations and individu-

° In order of seniority (important because in most debates members spoke in order of seniority followed by the vice-chairman and finally the chairman), the Board consisted of Chairman Arthur Burns, Vice-Chairman J. L. Robertson, Governors G. W. Mitchell, J. D. Daane, S. J. Maisel, A. F. Brimmer, W. W. Sherrill.

als had been purchasing commercial paper or Treasury bills instead of depositing money in banks. If these lenders now attempted to flee the paper market, the banks would have to lend to the borrowers on commercial paper the money they needed to pay off their debts on the paper as it came due. The increased demand deposits created for this purpose would need a large infusion of reserves. No one knew how much liquidity the paid-off lenders would want, whether they would hold the cash or not. One solution was to allow the banks to recycle the money through time deposits (with a lower reserve requirement) by raising the interest rate ceilings under Regulation Q. This would require much smaller open market operations.

Some board members had urged for months that the Regulation Q ceilings were harmful and ought to be removed. However, a majority still believed they were necessary to insure a better distribution of credit throughout the economy and to give the Fed leverage to halt overexpansion when credit was expanding at an undesirable rate. The Federal Reserve Board was now faced with the need for an immediate decision on policy questions that it had been debating for months.

At the outset of the discussion, on the morning of June 22, there were substantial differences of opinion among the members, including a difference as to whether the Penn Central failure and the threat it posed to the commercial paper market presented compelling reason to take action immediately on Regulation Q ceilings to assure liquidity in the economy. In other words, was there an emergency or was there not?

One view was that the fight against inflation, not a commercial paper credit pinch, was still the main issue; that, therefore, the Board should not act immediately to raise the interest rate ceilings. Another argument against raising the ceilings was that it might stimulate an outflow of Euro-dollars to foreign markets and worsen the United States' balance of payments. Yet another was that precipitate action by the Board might indicate an emergency to the public, thus initiating a money panic.

However, a solid core of opinion did exist on the Board that action was now needed. The argument was mainly over exactly what action to take, with exactly what timing. The debate was heated and acrimonious, partly because it was recognized that, if the Federal Reserve announced that it was badly split over policy and explained the reasons behind the split, any effects resulting from the Fed's show of concern over the monetary situation would be multiplied.

Finally a majority of the Board agreed that the regulation should be amended. The ceiling for some deposit and some maturity classes should be suspended. Banks would then be able to attract the deposits to cover the demand for loans from those who could not roll over their commercial paper. However, maintenance of some ceilings would indicate that, if banks expanded credit too rapidly or in undesirable spheres, the regulation could be reimposed.

By law the Federal Deposit Insurance Corporation (FDIC) and the Federal Home Loan Bank Board (FHLBB) had to be consulted about changes in interest ceilings. Even those on the Board desiring immediate action agreed that a failure to do this would signal too much urgency, so a meeting was arranged. The FDIC, which has the power to determine interest rate ceilings for the eight thousand commercial banks not members of the Federal Reserve System, agreed to act but preferred not to do so immediately; they wanted to suspend ceilings only on short-term deposits over $100,000. The Home Loan Bank Board was primarily concerned that the change not alter the competitive position of savings and loan associations.

With this background, the Board met again in the afternoon. A majority wanted to announce immediately the suspension of ceilings on all deposits of $100,000 or more with maturities of thirty through eighty-nine days. I argued strongly that while this decision should be taken, it should be delayed until the next morning when the FDIC would be willing to act as well. Also, the members of the Federal Reserve Board would be more unified and we would not be accused of acting in too great haste. This proposal carried. The Board acted, by a vote of 6 to 1, the next morning, Tuesday, June 23, before the previously scheduled regular meeting of the FOMC. The Committee accepted the action of the Board as a basic shift in policy. No attempt would be made to reduce reserves and return the rate of money and credit expansion to the 4 percent level. Short-term rates would be allowed to ease.

CHAPTER THREE

The Monetary
Decision-Making Process

THE MEETINGS of May and June 1970, thankfully, are not typical of the atmosphere in which the FOMC and the Board generally meet and make monetary policy. I chose this period as an illustration of unusual interest because of the important issues which dominated it. Most meetings do not focus on only one issue or spectacular development; they are more mundane. Policy changes evolve gradually through an orderly examination of the key factors in the monetary process: the state of the economy and of financial markets, the gap between their actual and optimum conditions, the changes in monetary variables and the instruments needed to close that gap, how to operate to insure that money will have a beneficial rather than harmful influence.

FOMC Meeting Format

The process through which the FOMC makes its decisions is not formalized, but during my seven years on the Board the agenda for its meetings hardly varied. Only on rare occasions did unexpected events disrupt the usual format. The framework described in Chart 1 allowed the staff to operate, discussions to be carried on, and operating instructions to be issued. It also made it possible for committee members to devise strategies and make plans.

The day before each FOMC meeting I carefully considered what the best monetary policy would be, and I tried to predict how the discussion would develop and what factors were likely to govern the final vote. I would then plan my own presentation and the best arguments to use in favor of the adoption of the policy I advocated.

The State of the Economy and Forecasts

Each meeting would open with a detailed discussion of the current state of the economy, money and financial markets, and the international situation. The accuracy of existing staff forecasts would be noted, together with the adjustments necessary to make them agree with current developments. Three or four times a year, the meeting would start with the presentation of a completely new set of forecasts. These reports were organized around the expenditure-financial market approach to monetary policy depicted in Chart 1. The dual label reflects the variety of Federal Reserve System objectives. Primarily monetary policy aims at expanding prosperity with stable prices. Secondarily, the Fed wants to minimize financial shocks that might cause sharp losses in the value of assets, imbalances in international payments, a haphazard redistribution of income, malfunctioning of financial markets, and acute fluctuations in credit availability.

The Federal Reserve has probably the best economic intelligence system in the world. Its staff surpasses all other agencies in its knowledge of the intricacies of the country's statistical system, in its detailed information on most special sectors of the economy, and in its ability to gather and rapidly analyze data on special situations. The staff's output consists of several hundred statistical series and studies per month. These are constantly refined into a basic series of weekly and monthly reports summarizing the latest information on the state of the economy and where it is expected to go. Even so, this material contains large gaps and many possibilities of error. The inescapable fact is that our economy is so immense and diverse that we are far from achieving accurate or complete measurement. Nevertheless monetary policy must be made, even with less than perfect information.

The projections presented to the FOMC also assess factors beyond the control of the Federal Reserve, such as anticipated policies of the rest of the government with respect to taxes, expenditures, income policies, controls, and so on, and the expected spending and pricing decisions of business, consumer, foreign, state, and local units. Parallel estimates are made of what will happen in money and financial and credit markets if the Federal Reserve does not change its policies. The projections of spending (the GNP) and financial markets must be closely synchronized. The growth of the money supply, credit, and interest rates will depend both on current policy and on the strength of the economy. The movements of the financial variables will in turn help determine the level of expenditures.

Because the System's objectives are more than a simple increase in current dollar GNP, projections must be quite detailed. Certain sectors such as housing, foreign trade, labor markets, and agriculture have a significant impact on expenditures. At the same time, their movements may be an objective or a guide to policy. In the same way, changes in spending must be related to prices, real output, and employment.

Goals and Objectives

Staff reports were followed by a discussion—sometimes heated—as to whether the forecasts seemed accurate and whether the path of the economy under current policies was a good one and likely to lead to desirable goals. Objectives other than the economy might then enter the debate. Sometimes individuals might be concerned about a sectoral problem such as low housing starts and climbing rents, a redistribution of income through higher interest rates, or a growing deficit in the country's international accounts. At others, attempts to influence the Administration or Congress to adopt a coordinated fiscal policy might be important determinants of votes. Yet again, members gave weight to Administration or congressional views as to current goals for monetary policy. Every Committee member based his votes on what he thought best for the economy. Having observed them in many meetings, I could rank the participants in order according to their views on how restrictive or accommodative monetary policy should be. Each one had an almost fixed position relative to the others, from a restrictive to an accommodative monetary policy. The rank order depended on personal philosophies and value judgments about the national well-being. Also significant were an individual's views on balance of payments, the importance of sectoral changes, movements in financial markets, and short- versus long-term goals. Although the absolute position on how tight policy ought to be might change from one meeting to the next, the rank order (from the member who always wanted to furnish fewer reserves to the one who favored somewhat greater expansion than the others) rarely varied.

There was a very high correlation between a person's view of a proper goal and his forecast for the economy. One who favored a low growth rate almost always saw a booming economy; thus both his goals and economic views would support tighter money. Conversely, those who favored greater expansion usually estimated the growth that would occur without monetary ease as very slight.

Although the value system of each member came into play during discussion, the actual goals and objectives being sought were rarely discussed. Frequently I played the devil's advocate by urging a more open discussion of objectives and proposed trade-offs, but I never succeeded in focusing the debate in this manner. Each member remained free to vote his own value judgments and prejudices without ever having to state or defend his objectives.

The Directive

The primary function of the Open Market Committee is to authorize the purchase or sale of securities and foreign currencies for the Open Market Account of the Federal Reserve Banks. This is one of the several tools available to the Fed to regulate monetary conditions (see Chapter 2, pages 34–36). These authorizations are large. In their Open Market Account, the twelve District Federal Reserve Banks own more than $73 billion of securities. In 1972 the Account purchased or sold more than $135 billion of Treasury and agency issues and acceptances.

While each of these transactions was authorized and approved by the FOMC, the actual day-to-day operating decisions were made by the Manager of the Open Market Account. The manager, with a staff of about eighty, operates the Open Market Desk in the New York bank. A similar staff is also engaged in foreign operations for the FOMC.

The authorization and instructions to the manager are contained in a directive. The formulation and adoption of this open market directive, which takes place at each meeting, is the key to Federal Reserve policy making. The directive enables the FOMC to focus its discussion and debate, to evaluate current and past policy, to agree on future monetary policy, to instruct the manager of the Open Market Account, and to hold him accountable for following instructions. It also is a vehicle for the Committee to report to Congress and the public on the Committee's policy decisions. Yet most directives contain fifty words or less in the operating instructions. For example, that of January 16, 1973 stated: "To implement this policy, while taking account of the forthcoming Treasury financing operations and possible credit market developments, the Committee seeks to achieve bank reserve and money market conditions that will support slower growth in monetary aggregates over the months ahead than appears indicated for the second half of last year."

The directive sets forth the objectives to be sought by open market operations until the next meeting (usually a month later). Together with the economic background and a very abbreviated statement of the debate, it is made public two to three months after each meeting. The published directive itself does not include specific numbers. However, in the supporting documents the manager is instructed to purchase or sell securities in order to affect the rate of growth in reserves or to maintain a range of rates in the money market. Usually these guides are given as a range, since it is recognized that the Desk cannot hit a specific number exactly, that conflicts may arise among the different series, and that attempting to achieve a given number might, in the manager's judgment, delay or weaken the desired policy. Typical guides might imply: a 5 to 5.25 percent rate for Federal funds, a $250 million to $350 million level of net borrowed reserves, or a growth for the month in reserves available for private deposits at an annual rate of 7 to 9 percent.

Included in and necessary for an understanding of the directive are all of the many projections and forecasts plus the economic and financial background data made available to the Committee. Also significant are the full discussions of the Committee, both recorded and nonrecorded. The fact that instructions must be issued forces the Committee to come to some agreement on an operating policy, even though individual members may have various estimates as to what effect the purchase or sale of more securities may have. Agreement is reached because a majority of the Committee believes that the policy contained in the directive will move the nation closer to its goals, although they may disagree about the method to use. For example, the Committee may vote to make no change in a directive. It would not be unusual to find two members voting not to change policy because they fear a balance of payments effect; two others who base their votes on the chance of getting a tax bill; two others who are concerned over a possible slowdown in the economy; another who desires lower interest rates; and still another who feels that the policy would lead to higher interest rates, but welcomes them. While in complete disagreement over the projection, goals, and policy results, they could concur on specific operating instructions.

Intermediate Monetary Variables, Measures, or Targets

While disagreements over where the economy is and should be headed are common in FOMC meetings, they pale beside the question of what monetary policy should be adopted to achieve those goals. Members of the FOMC often have different ideas of how added reserves affect the economy. Fierce debates among all those interested in monetary policy, the Federal Reserve Board included, have occurred over how best to measure the effect policy is having on the economy. When the Fed changes a monetary instrument, what will the consequences be? Will spending rise or fall?

The movement of an instrument causes a change in the intermediate monetary variables (money, money market conditions, interest rates, and expectations). Changes in these monetary measures influence spending and cause movements in financial markets. These are also called targets because, when the Fed adopts a policy, it picks a particular level for these variables as a target of operations. The term measure is used as well, because the movements in these variables indicate what is happening to monetary policy.

The variables are influenced, but not completely controlled, by the Federal Reserve. How they move depends upon what is happening in the economy and in financial markets (particularly banks and the Treasury) as well as upon changes in the monetary instruments. The variables do not move together and, at any given time, one may get a very different view as to whether policy has turned expansive or restrictive depending upon which measure one uses. Thus disagreements arise.

Let us briefly look at the four primary monetary variables which have been used as targets and some of the problems of interpreting them.

Money

Although most of us think we know what money is, it is actually quite hard to define. Money is frequently defined as whatever is generally accepted as a means of payment or a medium of exchange. This concept corresponds most closely to the stock of money or the money supply; that is, the currency and adjusted demand deposits in the hands of the public. This is also called money narrowly defined, or M_1. When time deposits at commercial banks (other than large certificates of deposit) are included, we have money broadly defined, or M_2. Money can be considered still more broadly as debts of the monetary and financial system whose prices do not vary but are fixed in the unit of account; i.e., deposits are considered money because $100 is always worth $100. On the other hand, a bond or note is not money because its value can vary; for instance, a $100 bond may sell for only $90 at times. In this book, when we speak of money we usually mean money in a broad sense. However, if we give an estimate of changes in money, we label it specifically as either money narrowly defined (M_1) or broadly defined (M_2). (For a full discussion of the different definitions and uses of money, see pages 269–73.)

Money Market Conditions

For most of the 1960s the Federal Reserve measured the influence of open market operations by looking at money market conditions. These are the combination of (a) the interest rate on Federal funds, the amount banks receive when they make an overnight loan of a reserve balance (deposit) at the Federal Reserve to another bank; (b) net reserves, the difference between the excess reserve balances of banks and the total amount banks borrow from the Fed through the discount window, and (c) at times, the interest rate on three-month Treasury bills. Early in the decade money market conditions also included the general atmosphere of the credit and banking markets as reflected in expectations and shifts in liquidity demands.

Interest Rates

Since monetary events often affect the rest of the economy through interest rates, many favor interest rates as a target or measure. Usually the interest rates meant are long-term rates, which primarily influence spending. Here, too, a major difficulty arises, however. One can easily find in the newspaper interest rates quoted in current dollars. But these are only the nominal rates; no one knows what is happening to "real" interest rates, rates corrected for changes in the value of money.

Expectations

Some members of the Federal Reserve have stressed the importance of changes in intangible forces such as expectations, desires, and feelings on lending and spending. They have attempted to gauge changes in expectations and the atmosphere of financial markets and business in order to determine the need for and effectiveness of movements in the monetary instruments.

Measuring the Effects of Monetary Policy

How to measure the effects of monetary policy continues to be a controversial topic because economists disagree over the relationships between money and spending. Everyone is certain that the Federal Reserve influences the monetary variables of money, credit and interest rates and that, in turn, these transmit the impact of monetary policy to the rest of the economy. But how this comes about; which measure can best predict money's influence; what target the Federal Reserve should use—all remain debatable points.

Open market operations increase liquidity—people have more money instead of other assets. Security prices are pushed up and interest rates down. But what then happens depends on how consumers and businesses react to being more liquid and to the lower interest rates. If no one altered his purchases, the only change would be that the amount of money compared to spending would be larger; in other words, the rate at which money was used (its velocity) would fall. While no one believes that increasing money will have no effect, major disagreement does exist as to how great the impact will be and how long it will take before all the effects are felt in the economy. This is called the lag between changes in money, spending, and prices.

People who have more money will usually spend some of it. Why keep idle money when you can use it for goods you need, or at least invest it in interest bearing or profit yielding assets? Consumers may spend even more when they find their wealth has gone up as lower interest rates and greater demand raise the value of their existing assets. Businesses will also spend. If interest rates fall, it will be more profitable to invest in plant and equipment, houses, and apartment buildings. Furthermore, if financial firms have greater liquidity, they will be more willing to lend, welcoming customers they previously turned away and searching out new ones. As the availability of credit rises, families and firms previously rationed out of the credit market can borrow to spend more for consumption or investment goods. Everyone will be more willing to spend if the cheaper, more available credit changes their expectations. Spending can be so great that the GNP rises faster than does money. Velocity increases. A runaway velocity is as dangerous as a sharp drop.

A failure to furnish reserves or money can, on the other hand, work in the opposite way. A growing economy needs more money to facilitate expanded transactions. Families or firms may fear the future and want to be more liquid. They step up their demand for money. If the Fed holds back and money grows more slowly than demand, interest rates rise, wealth falls, credit is rationed. Money is pressing to moderate the expansion.

The extent of disagreement over how much and when money changes spending is illustrated by the disparity between several of the more popular econometric models of the economy currently in use: that of Data Resources, Inc.; that of the St. Louis Federal Reserve Bank; and the Penn-MIT-FRB model. At one extreme, the first two models estimate that a 1 percent increase in the money supply above normal will cause an increase of 1 to 1.25 percent in spending (the GNP) in the following year, and that no further spending will be generated. The third model, that developed with the help of the Federal Reserve Board, says spending will grow by more than 4.5 percent if money is increased by 1 percent, but that it will take four years for this to develop. Obviously, differences of 300 percent (and over 100 percent even in the next year) in estimates of the effect of a policy action cause great differences of opinion on what action should be taken. Other models show an even greater variation in their estimates of what a change in reserves and money can effect.

While the key to monetary policy is to estimate how much and when movements in reserves will change spending, estimates of the ability of the economy to produce more goods must also be made. Depending on supply factors, increased spending may or may not be desirable. New demand which adds only to output and employment is good. But if it adds only to prices, it is bad. If it does some of each, as is usually the case, the policy makers face a difficult decision.

The FOMC Debate: How Much To Change Policy?

The main debate in the FOMC, as mentioned, is far more likely to be over whether a given set of instructions is stimulative or restrictive than over a conflict in goals and objectives. Generally there is rough agreement as to where the economy is and ought to go. A typical directive, for example, might allow for a growth in the GNP of 8 percent and a fall in unemployment of 1 percent over the ensuing year. But for the FOMC to decide how much to change money or interest rates in order for monetary policy to help achieve that goal is far more difficult. The Fed must first measure what the current monetary situation is doing to the economy and then by how much and when any change in policy will affect aggregate spending. Yet this is exactly where there is the least agreement among analysts and their equations and models.

To solve the problem requires untangling the influence of money on spending from that of spending and many other forces on the demand for money. We cannot simply look at the level or the direction of change of a variable to estimate what influence it is having. Prices may rise even as supplies are increased because demand is growing still faster. An all too familiar example is steak. Its price has gone up regularly in recent years, even as its supply has grown. The reason, of course, is that more people have higher incomes to buy steak, and thus demand more. The same situation exists for money. A rise in interest rates does not necessarily mean that the Fed has slowed the rate at which it is supplying money; the demand may have changed. Demand depends on many factors. For purposes of monetary analysis it is useful to separate the various demands or the desire to hold money, into two groups:

—The most critical is the demand relating money and income. As spending for the goods and services which make up the GNP rises, so does the demand for money. We then need to hold more money because one usually holds a regular portion of one's income in the bank to bridge the gaps between income and outgo.
—The remaining demands are lumped under the category nonin-

come (or non-GNP) demands. These include money held to meet
financial transactions, to meet our desires for liquidity or hoarding, held because we expect security or other prices to change,
and for similar needs.

In both cases, the amount of money desired at any particular
level of income or nonincome demand depends on interest rates.
The lower the level of interest the more money will be held, because when we hold money, we sacrifice less if interest yields are
less elsewhere. However, the rate of interest alone does not determine the amount of money held. If income rises, we will hold more
money at any given interest rate. And if the money supply is not
increased as income grows, interest rates will rise. (See the appen-
dix to this chapter for a diagram illustrating this point.)

While general agreement exists on the form of these relationships, there is considerable debate over how the various forces in
the market affect demand. Different theoretical estimates of how
closely and by how much a change in spending will follow one in
money supply depend upon how sensitive are people's demands for
money and how sensitive is spending to changes in interest rates
and credit. A rise in interest rates (if the money supply is not contracting) means more money is being demanded. If it is not supplied, there will be a contractive effect on the GNP because there
is relatively less liquidity and interest rates are higher. This relationship holds even if money is expanding rapidly. An increase in
money means spending can rise, but higher interest rates hold it
below the level it would otherwise reach if the increased demand
for money were accommodated by the larger supply needed to
hold interest rates stable.

When the FOMC discusses the best target and what path to follow, it is really dealing with the questions of what movements in
money or interest rates mean and whether they will aid the economy in reaching the desired goal. The crucial question is whether
pressure against spending is desirable or not. The answer depends
on what the cause of the shift in the demand for money was and
whether the economy is fully employed. Assume that, prior to the
shift, the level of spending has been moving properly. If the upward demand shift is due to outside forces (such as more govern-

ment spending), the failure to accommodate the new demand for money is desirable. Monetary policy would be exerting its force against an inflationary thrust in spending. On the other hand, if the increased demand for money is due to nonincome forces (such as money desired for financial transactions or to hold for purchases of financial assets in the future), the policy of not increasing money would be undesirable. With less money available for spending and higher interest rates, the GNP would drop toward a recession level.

Thus the stability of interest rates in and of itself is not a proper goal of monetary policy. When inflation threatens, allowing interest rates to rise because the income demand for money is increasing will slow down the rise in spending and is therefore a good policy. However, if spending is not excessive, allowing interest rates to rise because nonincome demand for money increases will be harmful. Higher interest rates and less money available for spending transactions will lead to lower spending, output, and employment. In this case, since the higher interest rates would have a depressing effect on the economy, they should be combatted by creating more money to keep them stable.

The label we put on monetary policy is not important. Some measure it in terms of interest rates. If they are higher than in the past, they call money tight. Others measure it by changes in the supply of money. If money is increasing at a slower or less than normal rate, money is tight. Rather than speaking of tight or easy money, I prefer to say money is more or less restrictive—a nonpejorative term. If the money supply is growing more slowly than its demand, even though more rapidly than in the past, interest rates will rise and exert a restrictive effect on spending. Holding back spending may be good or bad depending on whether the problem is inflation or recession.

Appendix

Figure 1A shows the demand for money related to spending (GNP), holding all other factors constant. Figure 1B shows the demand related to all other forces, holding the level of GNP or spending constant. In Figure 1A, the demand curve for money at a given time and a given income level (say $1,500 billion) is labeled Y_1. The demand curve slopes down to the right, indicating that the lower the interest that is lost, the more money will be held. If the level of income and spending rises, we will need and be willing to hold more money at each interest rate. This is shown by another higher demand curve for money labeled Y_2 (say $1,600 billion of GNP).

Figure 1B shows demand curves related to nonincome factors (assuming in each case spending remains at $1,500 billion). For example, if activity in financial markets shoots up, more money will be needed to handle the increased transactions. People will be willing to pay higher interest rates at the same income level (Y_1) to obtain the money they need to handle the greater activity. There is a move from N_1 to N_2.

The supply curve for money related to the amount of reserves the Federal Reserve creates is drawn as a straight line for simplicity. The total supply of money is divided between the two sectors. Thus the amount of money M_1 consists of M'_1 in Figure 1A plus M_1° in Figure 1B. The real situation is far more complex, since money may be used to meet different demands at the same time. Showing dynamic movements and adjustments requires far more complex charts, which are not necessary for our purposes. If, with a stock of money equal to M_1, income is Y_1 and the nonincome demand is N_1, according to the figure, the interest rate will be at 5 percent (as shown by the lower dotted line). If the stock of money were at M_2 and the demands for money stayed at Y_1 and N_1, interest rates would be at 6 percent (as shown by one higher dotted line).

Let us use this figure to illustrate the problem of selecting a monetary target, assuming we want to hold spending at the Y_1 level. For greater reality we might also assume Y_1 and all other factors on the figure expand at a normal growth rate. (This diagram is incomplete because it does not include the figure or equations which show the effect of changes in spending which result from the movement in money.) Does this mean that we ought to maintain the same interest rates and growth of money as in the recent past? The answer is, not necessarily.

We can imagine two cases. In the first, nonmonetary factors (such as a greater budget deficit) increase income and spending.

FIGURE 1.   *The Demand and Supply of Money*

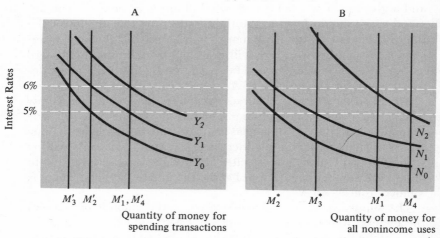

This shifts the economy toward the Y_2 curve. Interest rates start to rise. Should more money be furnished? If the aim is to maintain spending at the Y_1 level, the answer is no. The increased demand should not be accommodated by increasing the amount of money in an attempt to hold interest rates constant. If no money is added, the higher spending will push interest rates up and the higher rates will, in turn, cause some of the spending influenced by money and interest to decrease. The net effect of the greater deficit and higher interest rates will yield a GNP level somewhere between Y_1 and Y_2 instead of at Y_2. According to the diagram, interest rates would be near 5.5 percent. The exact rate would depend on how much money was shifted from sector B to A, because at these higher rates less money would be demanded for nonincome purposes, N_1. If deemed desirable, the stock of money could be reduced to M_2, which might completely offset, through monetary policy, the outside forces that had been pushing spending upward. In other words, the deflationary effect of higher interest rates could offset the push from the budgetary deficit. The diagram shows this would occur with an interest rate of 6 percent.

    In the second case, in which nonincome demand for money rises, more money should be furnished unless we want the level of spending to fall. In the table the failure to add money is shown by the lines M_3' and M_3''. The shift of nonincome demand to N_2 has caused interest rates to rise. Some of the stock of money shifts to this sector. The amount of money left for meeting income demands is now M_3'. With the higher interest rate, spending is restricted. This creates an undesired fall in income. It might go to Y_0 depending on how great is the deflationary impact of higher interest rates and less money available for transactions. The diagram shows interest rates would be 6 percent with income at Y_0 and nonincome demand at N_2. To keep monetary policy unchanged, the amount of money must expand to M_4. At M_4, with nonincome demand at N_2, the amount of money available for income purposes is the same as when nonincome demand was at N_1 and money at M_1. Interest rates with money at M_4 return to 5 percent and income to Y_1.

CHAPTER FOUR

The Age of Innocence
and Its End

JOHN KENNETH GALBRAITH once stated, "We have come to envisage the Open Market Committee as a group of men of excellent character and reassuring demeanor who meet to consider whether there is a good reason for tighter money." While most members of the Federal Reserve would attack this statement as an unfair caricature, like any good caricature it contains many elements of truth.

Every meeting of the Federal Open Market Committee decides whether money should be unchanged or more or less restrictive. From 1951 until 1966, the majority of the Committee did appear to seek "a good reason for tighter money." Many still believe in the doctrine that, irrespective of other factors, if prices are rising or if the United States is not accumulating international monetary reserves, the Federal Reserve should be seeking higher interest rates and tighter monetary conditions. Only rarely in the past twenty years have they felt that more restraint was not a good thing. Numerous financial observers believe that many of the economy's troubles started when the Federal Reserve began to take a broader view of the goals of monetary policy. Inflation, this view holds, stems from the failure of the Federal Reserve to maintain what bankers and traditionalists see as the eternal economic verities— opposition to growth in spending if prices are rising.

I call the pre-1966 period the age of innocence because it was possible at that time to think of monetary policy in very simple terms. Chairman William McChesney Martin summed it up in his statement of March 7, 1961, to the Joint Economic Committee:"The flexible monetary policy that has been in effect now for a full decade . . . as I have capsuled it before in the shortest and simplest description I have been able to devise, is one of leaning against the winds of inflation and deflation—and with equal vigor." This was a statement both of a simple and straightforward goal—to fight inflation and deflation—and of a belief in an uncomplicated technique of money management. If inflation threatened, accommodate only part of the demand for money; if the danger was recession, overaccommodate the monetary demand. Even today no one would quarrel with this statement as far as it goes; the problem was and is to make it properly operational.

The 1966 experience was a rude awakening. The degree of inflationary demand from the expanding Vietnam War was greater than United States monetary policy had attempted to cope with since 1920. The decision to fight inflation vigorously caused high costs elsewhere. A choice became necessary. It appeared that there was a limit to what traditional monetary policy could do. As monetary policy attempted to accomplish more, new techniques had to be developed. It was no longer enough simply to be less accommodative. The success of monetary policy in cutting back on demand now had to be measured.

The experience of 1966 led to a more sophisticated appreciation of monetary policy. Both goals and techniques had to be thought out more carefully. It was not enough merely to want to fight inflation. Actions had to be planned which could work in a dynamic economy. Changes in attitudes occurred:

—There was a recognition that the choice of a monetary policy also involved a choice among competing goals. The traditional concept that fighting inflation was sufficient to guarantee accomplishing the other objectives for the economy became much harder to rationalize.
—The balance of payments had been playing a significant role in determining monetary policy since President Kennedy, early in his term and on the advice of Treasury Secretary Douglas Dil-

lon, had designated it as a critical economic problem. But, as the need to pay for the war and to fight inflation became the dominating economic problems, the role of the balance of payments diminished.

—In 1966 it became apparent that the Federal Reserve could not neglect the side-effects of decreased money and credit, and higher interest rates. Three of these side-effects reached critical dimensions with relation to (a) the composition of demand and output, (b) the maintenance of viable financial markets, (c) the protection against large-scale failures of financial institutions.

—The markets in which monetary policy operated were examined with greater care and it became clear that these markets were not the idealized market of pure, perfect economic theory. Actual events occurred which differed widely from those in the abstract market of theoretical monetary policy.

The Goals of the Federal Reserve

"It is the policy of the FOMC to foster financial conditions consistent with sustainable real economic growth and increased employment, abatement of inflationary pressures, and attainment of reasonable equilibrium in the country's balance of payments." This or an equivalent statement appears in most FOMC directives. Only occasionally a phrase is left out, as, for example, if output or use of the labor force were deemed so high as to be inflationary. This statement reflects the general agreement, since the Employment Act of 1946, that it is the government's role to foster growth, high output and employment, and stable prices. It further expresses the virtually unanimous agreement that the Federal Reserve System has the responsibility of working toward these goals, in coordination with the rest of the government. Unfortunately, through constant reiteration, the goals of attaining maximum employment, production, and purchasing power—or optimum growth, stable employment and prices—have become clichés. Unless such questions as how the goals are to be achieved, how policies are to be implemented, and who is to pay and who is to gain from specific policies are answered, they become meaningless generalities. The need for the Fed to set specific goals and explain its techniques was expressed by the growing corps of critics in the first half of the 1960s. Many were concerned because they felt the Fed overreacted to events, usually on the side of tightness, and they wanted to know how the Fed selected its monetary goals and how it measured success or failure. There had been three recessions between 1953 and 1960. The last downturn had come well before output had approached capacity or full employment of the labor force. Why had the Fed tightened then? Did it believe the economy should always run with excess labor and plant capacity to avoid any price increases?

President Kennedy had campaigned against tight money and high interest rates. He had promised he would "get the country moving again." Money had become easier, but both his economists and those of the Johnson Administration continued to worry. How long would credit remain adequate? A recovery was under way. How far did the Fed think it should go? Would it jam on the monetary brakes as it had in 1957 and 1959?

In answer to such inquiries the Fed restated its general position: "Monetary policy focuses on the volume and availability of bank reserves in relation to the credit demand being generated by current economic forces and assesses whether the volume of such demands, given the share being satisfied by bank credit and monetary expansion, is making for inflationary or deflationary tendencies." This simply meant that at its meetings the FOMC decided to furnish a greater or lesser amount of reserves on the basis of a consensus as to whether the economy seemed to be experiencing inflationary pressures. There was no public attempt to define inflation or full employment, adequate or inadequate credit, or the amount of reserves to be supplied. In large measure, the public posture maintained by the Fed that it was not necessary to clarify its methods of selecting among competing objectives or to explain its operating procedures reflected the System's failure, prior to 1966, to face up to the problem in private as well. Its reluctance to specify what it hoped to achieve through monetary policy was based on the complexity of defining objectives and on the desire for flexibility.

The Objective of Stable Prices

While there has never been an official statement of Federal Reserve doctrine as such, a careful reading of Fed records and statements would show that it has traditionally placed more emphasis on stable prices as a goal than on any other objective. Prior to 1966, the potentially high costs of using monetary policy as the chief weapon to stabilize demand were not recognized. As noted in Chapter 1, the Fed was profoundly conscious of the high costs of inflation and deemed it its duty to push against general price increases. It rejected the concept of the trade-off, the notion that some sacrifices might be entailed in the effort to hold down prices in a period of cost-push or excessive demand from nonmonetary sources.

The assumption that the Federal Reserve ought to be more concerned about prices than output followed directly from the traditional concepts of central banking which hold that central banks were made independent both to guard against a tendency of governments to inflate the economy and to protect a country's international reserves. Central bankers believe that the public prefers a little inflation to a little unemployment, that they must, therefore, act as buffers against the political process in order to protect the value of money. Furthermore, since special interests always press for more public expenditures, and thus more inflation, it is argued that insulation from the election process allows the Federal Reserve more independence. It can thus make better judgments in the public interest than can the Administration or Congress as to the best levels of output and employment, as well as prices. Governments typically misuse money. For instance, politicians find it easier to finance expenditures by printing money or issuing debt to the central bank than by increasing taxes. The Fed traditionally has had to fight political inflationary pressures for such deficits, trying to make certain that government borrowing was financed through the private debt market rather than by the creation of money.

In addition to the battle for fiscal integrity and propriety, the

Federal Reserve has felt obliged to combat four other prime political heresies which the history of the System has demonstrated to be highly inflationary when implemented. Because these heresies have wide appeal, it was imperative to expose the dangers and educate the public to demand sound money.

—The first threat was that the Federal Reserve might be required to support the government securities market, as had happened during the 1940s. It was vital to make clear that any attempt to peg the price of government bonds for the purpose of bringing about lower interest rates would be self-defeating. Support of government bond prices creates an excessive amount of money and, consequently, inflation.

—A second insistent demand of politicians has been for the Fed to support particular sectors of the economy. For over 150 years there has been a demand for cheap credit for farmers, small businessmen and, in recent years, housing. Meeting these sectoral demands would interfere with the market. The results could be less efficiency, less output, and higher prices.

—A third popular issue has been a false belief in selective credit controls. Congress was concerned when "needy" sectors failed to obtain funds; it reasoned that, if some potential borrowers were removed from the market by selective controls, more credit would be available for the needy borrowers. The Federal Reserve had had unfortunate experiences in World War II and the postwar period with controls over consumer credit and mortgages. While maintaining that any selective controls would be harmful, the Fed's views were more ambiguous as to whether the existing law giving the System margin controls over lending on stock market securities ought to be abolished.

—A fourth constant threat is that the Fed might be asked to impose maximum interest rates on loans. With maximum interest rates the market would not be able to price credit properly, making for a greater need to ration that commodity.

The desire to maintain a fixed price for the dollar in terms of gold also heightened the priority of price stability over output. There were some, both within and without the System, who believed in the inviolability of the gold standard. To many, losses of gold were an evil in and of themselves, while to others the gold standard was a major automatic force to restrict the government's bias toward inflation. Monetary policy had to be restrictive so the United States would not lose gold.

The more sophisticated argument that perhaps a gold standard was not really necessary was also advanced. However, the United States and the world had prospered after World War II. No one could be certain how much prosperity was due to the fixed value of the dollar in terms of gold. Why take a chance? It was better to deflate the economy than to risk the unknown.

As time went on, most economists came to feel that this was an oversimplification. There was no evidence that a changed dollar price would not be better for all. The basic need, it seemed, was to measure the losses and gains from competitive exchange systems. Although economists became increasingly vocal in their arguments, their impact on Washington and on world policy makers was slight. Until 1965 maintaining the gold standard and achieving a balance of payments surplus were major concerns of the Fed. After 1965 the importance of these aims diminished, as it was recognized that international financial problems had to be treated in relation to far broader domestic and foreign policy goals.

It was also recognized that the government was not the only source of inflationary danger, but that speculative activity in the financial and business sectors also led to large and unfortunate booms. Since overspending in the private sector depends upon the creation of excess money and credit, the Federal Reserve must guard against excessive private as well as government credit. Although no one could be certain that the right amount of money was being created, the necessary and proper amount could be estimated by careful observation of events in the financial and credit markets. Such judgment could be based on specific studies of prices, the expansion of credit, and the expectations of both borrowers and creditors. People trying to borrow extra money to profit from a boom or inflation had to be stopped.

The philosophy that the Fed's proper functions are primarily restrictive has always had adherents in banking and financial circles and within the System, and until 1966 those who considered prices or gold as the real goals of the Fed were in the majority. Their attitude was paraphrased by the Fed's critics as "Do what can be done for employment as long as available credit threatens neither a rise in prices nor the balance of payments." The Fed, however, believed its philosophy was more positive. When it was holding interest rates stable, it was accommodating increases in demand. When the Fed was no longer willing to continue accommodating the full demand of the economy, it signaled a change in policy by raising the discount rate. Such decisions were made, however, without any estimate of how far the economy was from full output potential nor of what impact monetary policy was expected to have.

The Discount Rate Change, December 3, 1965

It was against this background of a simple concept of goals that the discount rate was changed in December 1965. The action was one of the more dramatic incidents in Federal Reserve history. Of far more importance, it marked a true watershed: It was the end of the age of innocence; the Fed would not be the same again.

For four years there had been a widening difference of opinion within the Federal Reserve Board and the Open Market Committee over the issue of how soon and how much to tighten monetary policy. This was a contrast to the situation which had prevailed during the Eisenhower Administration when, even on most of the critical votes, there had never been more than one dissenting member, and even that had been rare. Recent appointees of the Kennedy and Johnson Administrations, however, had brought new value judgments and theories to the Board which often differed considerably from those of earlier members. Split votes became more frequent. In addition, the clamor of outside critics was increasing.

From 1962 to December 1965 three permanent FOMC members —President Alfred Hayes of the New York Bank and Governors Canby Balderston and Charles Shepardson—based their votes primarily on the price and balance of payments doctrine. In any vote

on greater or lesser restraint, they always voted for greater restraint. They were usually joined by two of the rotating bank presidents on the Committee. On the opposite side, Governors George
Mitchell, J. L. Robertson, and I favored a policy of furnishing the
funds necessary for full employment. We, too, were usually joined
by two of the bank presidents.

Thus there was a basic five-to-five split in the FOMC, which
meant that, on any divisions, the deciding votes were held by
Chairman William McChesney Martin and Governor Dewey
Daane. Since on the whole they, too, subscribed to the price and
balance of payments goals, a majority of the Committee generally
favored the more restrictive targets. However, because a strong minority stressed broader objectives, as did the Administration,
moves to restrict credit were less frequent and more moderate;
those in the middle had to be sure of themselves before they joined
the restrictivists.

The need for and possibility of a discount rate change had been
discussed in general terms since September 1965. In October
Chairman Martin and Governor Daane announced that they favored further tightening and a rate change. From then on, the
question was when and how the Federal Reserve would act. In
November I raised some questions with the staff and the rest of the
Board which, it seemed to me, still required answers if the decision
were to be made logically.

In accordance with the Federal Reserve Act, a discount rate
change is normally preceded by a request for a rate change from
one of the District Federal Reserve Banks before it comes officially
before the Board. I assumed that the receipt of such a request
would be the signal for the necessary consideration by the Board of
the problems involved. I expected first to receive a thorough documentation of the pros and cons of the move, a summary of what
impact it was expected to have on the economy, and where those
impacts would be felt. I then thought there would be enough time
to study these facts and to marshal my views to be presented during a discussion before the vote. In short, I expected a far more
formal procedure than was followed.

I was dumbfounded when I appeared at a special meeting of the
Board of Governors called to deal with a minor regulatory matter,

on the afternoon of December 3, to find that a request from the New York Bank for a discount rate change had been added to the agenda. No staff studies were before us; no statements by the Board; no opinions from other government agencies were available. In contrast to the reams of paper and studies that accompanied most actions of the Board, this crucial step was handled informally and without documentation. True, there had been several months for Board members to formulate their opinions individually after the question had first been raised, but it was a shock to me to find that a decision of this magnitude would be disposed of with little or no documentation. So much stress was laid on intuition that the question was considered to be primarily one of the timing of the move. What it was expected to accomplish or what target would be sought was not part of the discussion.

I urged that we put off any decision until the following day so that we would consult with other government agencies which were vitally concerned. We would then have time to consider new information and think about the decision in a less hurried and calmer atmosphere. Since the next day was Saturday, there could be no harm in the delay. The suggestion was rejected. The decision to raise the discount rate from 4 percent to 4.5 percent was made on the afternoon of Friday, December 3, with Governors Mitchell and Robertson dissenting along with myself. It was announced on Sunday, to be effective on Monday, December 6, 1965.

The discount rate move was widely publicized because it was a direct confrontation between a majority of the Board and President Johnson. Congressional hearings were called immediately, with wide coverage in the press and on television. The question everyone asked was whether a basic split had occurred between the Federal Reserve and the Administration. If so, they wanted to know, why had it happened and what would it mean for future policy?

During the congressional hearings, I testified before the Joint Economic Committee of Congress: "I felt it [the discount increase] was wrong for three reasons: (1) it was done at the wrong time; (2) it was done in the wrong way; and (3) it was done for the wrong reasons." Obviously feelings ran high or I would not have been so vehement.

In retrospect, both sides proved to be right on some issues and wrong on others. Whether a longer and more careful consideration would have led to a better decision is not clear. As aggregate demand was rising rapidly, quick implementation of a policy of greater restrictiveness was in order. However, a move which was better coordinated with those of the Administration could have led to an improved package of economic policy. Even if only monetary policy changed, better techniques could have reduced considerably the shock to the economic system and the strain on monetary policy during the next year.

The Issues behind the Discount Rate Rise

During our discussion three principal areas of disagreement emerged. They concerned inflationary pressures, the question of coordination with other government agencies versus the independence of the Fed, and the method of tightening money to be used.

The Inflationary Pressures

The basic economic reasons for the move were (a) the increasing threat of excess demand pressures arising from the war and (b) the continued unsatisfactory state of the balance of payments. The first was a legitimate reason for the move; the second, which received most of the emphasis, I still believe was wrong.

In the previous six months, unemployment had dropped from 4.8 percent to 4.3 percent while consumer prices had increased by 1.4 percent. In my view and that of a majority of those in the government, the economy was delicately balanced. Progress toward full employment had been great; in fact, the expansion might well become too rapid. Whether this occurred or not would depend primarily on Vietnam spending and overall governmental fiscal policies. The continued success of the price-wage guideposts was also necessary. (These guideposts were the Kennedy and Johnson Administrations' attempt to meet the cost-push problem so that jobs would expand without inflationary price rises.) If any of these factors became more unfavorable, more tightening would be needed to maintain the balance. However, there had already been a considerable tightening of monetary policy. Reserves furnished by the Fed, total credit, and business loans had all slowed sharply. Both short- and long-term interest rates were up about .25 percent over the start of the year. The only indicator showing less tightening was the narrowly defined money supply, which had spurted in the last several months. Monetary policy was already offsetting some of the outside pressures toward further expansion.

On the other hand, I was not willing to accept the balance of payments as a legitimate reason for the change. It seemed to me that there were other and better techniques than a tight money policy to alter the balance of payments. An attempt by the Federal Reserve to offset speculative international capital flows by raising interest rates was a misuse of monetary policy. Taxes and the existing voluntary program to control such flows would be far better.

With hindsight, it is clear that Chairman Martin was right in his estimate of the demand pressures. The staff and I had underestimated war spending. The time was ripe for a change. In fact, it might have been better if the still greater tightening had started earlier. On the other hand, with time there has come to be greater agreement that the balance of payments should not dominate policy.

Coordination or Independence

The most dramatic split within the Board concerned the Fed's relationship to other agencies of the government. The traditional aloofness of the Board had mellowed somewhat. Chairman Martin, as a member of the Quadriad (the group which coordinated economic policy within the government) met with the other three members—the secretary of the Treasury, the chairman of the Council of Economic Advisers, and the director of the Budget. Although the need for coordination of policy was recognized, it seemed to me that some of the majority preferred dramatic and independent action. Their rationale was that because the Fed had to blow the whistle on the Administration from time to time, if its independence were to remain an effective force it must not get overly entangled with Administration policies. If it did not occasionally demonstrate its powers by using them, it might lose them.

It seemed clear to those of us in favor of coordination that the major danger of overexpansion was coming not from spending dependent on a monetary expansion, but rather from Vietnam expenditures. Since this was the case, in any change of economic policy greater weight should be put on a tax increase and on fiscal policy in general than on monetary policy. A new budget and economic message were being prepared; they seemed the proper place to insure a coordinated monetary-fiscal policy. I felt that, because the President basically preferred a mix of cheaper money and tighter taxes, he would have moved farther and faster in the fiscal area if the Board had given him a chance to tighten through fiscal instead of monetary restraint.

We were further concerned that the Board's action threatened the Administration's price-wage guideposts. We believed in them, although it was clear that some members of the Board did not. The latter wanted to shift the burden of resisting inflation to monetary policy; we wanted it to stay where it was with informal guideposts fighting cost-push pressures. Interest was a critical price. If the Federal Reserve took the lead in raising this or any other price, one of the death knells of the whole price-wage system might be sounded. Many firms would use the rationale of higher interest payments to raise their own prices; it was important that this not occur.

I was also concerned that we were acting without any knowledge of the Administration's views or possible programs. Although the staff of the Quadriad had been considering the problem in detail, none of their information or any Administration analysis was made available to us. That the Administration opposed the action was all we knew.

Because I had talked to Gardner Ackley, chairman of the Council of Economic Advisers (CEA), and to the people at the Treasury prior to the decision, I knew that they strongly opposed the action for fear it would weaken overall economic policies. In the week following the move, I was particularly disturbed to learn that both the Treasury and the Council had offered to coordinate monetary and fiscal policies, in an attempt to make certain the decision of the Board met the overall needs of the government. Yet these offers had not been reported to the members of the Board.° One of the arguments given for haste was that future needs of the Treasury to borrow in the market would make it impossible for the Federal Reserve to act because it might upset a Treasury borrowing operation. But the Treasury had stated that this fear should not be a factor; they would make room in their borrowing schedule for any future discount rate action if it were postponed at this time. However, this fact too was not divulged.

The day following our meeting Chairman Ackley told me that he too was becoming convinced that increases in demand ought to be slowed up. And he had also concluded that it would be preferable to use fiscal rather than monetary policy. He and Secretary of the Treasury Henry Fowler had stated that, if fiscal policy were not tightened, they would urge President Johnson to call for a tighter monetary policy in his State of the Union message. Thus it would be clear that all were agreed on the need for a policy change.

Obviously we will never know which view was right. Although all agree that fiscal action would have been preferable, the majority of the Board and many outside observers as well felt that the President simply would not have moved along fiscal lines and that, even with a delay, the Board would have arrived at identical results, but action would have been further postponed.

The Method of Tightening

When it was determined that a change in monetary policy would be voted by a majority of the Board, another debate ensued over what form the tightening should take. Robertson and I argued along a line introduced by Daane at the previous FOMC meeting:

° Chairman Martin later told me that the disruption due to President Johnson's operation had made coordination both with the Quadriad and within the Fed extremely difficult. Given the developing situation in Vietnam and the President's penchant for secrecy, Martin never felt sure how much of what he was told was in confidence, or what positions taken by members of the Quadriad reflected positions acceptable to the President. In the critical period prior to the Fed's move, no meeting of the Quadriad with the President took place.

that we ought to avoid an announcement effect. Although we were willing to go along with the majority in tightening, since we now had no choice, we felt it important that the more restrictive position be brought about by furnishing fewer reserves through the open market rather than by using the discount rate. Let interest rates rise. As banks became squeezed against the Regulation Q ceilings, they would obtain fewer deposits. This would curtail the creation of money and credit, which we saw as the way to fight inflation. Once interest rates were clearly out of line with the discount rate, it could be raised. This would cause less of a shock to the entire system and it would retain the good will of the Administration and the Congress.

A majority of the Board, however, wanted an announcement effect. Those who believed in tightening for balance of payments purposes felt that the announcement would have a favorable overseas impact. Foreign central banks would welcome the fact that the Federal Reserve had listened to their pleas for tighter money.

But a more critical factor was the desire to aid the banks in breaking President Johnson's stranglehold on the prime rate. As part of his general desire for lower interest rates and his guidepost policy, President Johnson had forced the banks to maintain a low prime lending rate. Since the banks wished to avoid a political battle with the President, some Board members felt that it was up to the Federal Reserve to oppose him in order to avoid a threatened inflationary increase in bank credit. They argued that the President's policy was creating major distortions in the money markets. At the low prime rate, there was an inflationary demand for credit. The Fed was furnishing the reserves to meet this demand. But the vicious circle had to be broken. If interest rates were no longer held down artificially, they would rise so that the market could balance supply and demand. Some Board members clearly did not want a delay in raising the discount rate. And they saw the announcement impact as a way of freeing the market to do a better job of credit allocation.

While releasing the market from one constraint, it seemed an opportune time to free it from another. The law required the Board to fix maximum interest rate ceilings. But it could not remove them. It was, therefore, decided to raise them so high that they would be inoperative. The market would be free to set whatever rates were logically called for. An increase in the Regulation Q ceilings of a full percentage point on all time deposits was voted. This seemed a large enough increase to prevent the ceilings from having any effect on the market for the present and far into the future.

Implementing the New Policy

By January, after the dust from the increase in discount rates and interest ceilings had settled, there was unanimous agreement that monetary policy should take the lead in the battle against inflation. Excess demand in the economy was expected to be generated by the superimposition of Vietnam expenditures on rising private demands. When President Johnson failed to ask Congress for a tax increase, most of his economic advisers, including the Council of Economic Advisers, the Bureau of the Budget, and all members of the Federal Reserve Board, wanted monetary policy to play a maximum role in cutting back spending. Now, however, a new debate arose within the Federal Reserve over how to implement policy.

At this point, after being on the Board for eight months and attending twelve open market meetings, I began to realize how far I was from understanding the theory the Fed used to make monetary policy. Policy was formulated in meetings where the form, language, and decisions followed an oral tradition. As in any specialty, words took on special connotations and nuances were extremely important. Further, I was struck by surprising gaps in the arguments and presentations.

When I arrived at the Federal Reserve in 1965, I was handed volumes of documents and descriptions of what the Fed did. I searched through them carefully, expecting to find an outline of the basic operating procedures for formulating monetary policy. I was disappointed. Nowhere did I find an account of how monetary policy was made or how it operated. The lack of a precise description of procedures did not seem important at first because the issues being debated had been evident. Those seeking a tighter monetary policy and those wanting money and credit to grow at normal rates had understood what was at issue. Arguments had been strong and quite clear because they were based primarily on ideological views of the economy. Only in rereading the minutes for 1965 do I now note how often positions were based on semantic confusions. Frequently, members of the FOMC argued over the merits of a policy without ever having arrived at a meeting of the minds as to what monetary policy was and how it worked. These problems were, and still are, neither recognized nor clarified.

The divergence in views as to what monetary policy was and how it worked was brought more clearly into the open by a side-effect—one not intended or desired—of the discount rate increase which created a rush for credit (the announcement effect). Borrowers stormed into banks to obtain money before its price rose too high or before others used up the available funds. Banks increased their lending. They were able to do so because the Fed created more reserves through open market operations. Money and credit expanded rapidly. It seemed to me to be a case of "let not thy left hand know what thy right hand doeth." The Board was divided as to the significance of the added credit in the fight against inflation. Four members held that the Fed was aggravating, not decreasing, inflationary demand. Three felt that the banks had to be given time to adjust, even if credit expanded rapidly in the interim. The surprising fact was that the Board members, within a month, appeared to have reversed their positions completely: Three of the four who had pushed for rapid action now wanted to go more slowly, while all those who had wanted to delay action until the federal budget was fixed now wanted to tighten faster.

Why had the Board members reversed their positions? To understand, one must examine the theory used by the Federal Reserve to set policy and measure its impact. It was a simple procedure, proper for an age of innocence, and another victim of 1966.

A Money Market Strategy

Federal Reserve doctrine was based on a money market strategy. The Fed used money market conditions simultaneously as a target, or measure, of monetary policy and as a guide for the manager of the Open Market Desk. This meant that the Desk operated by buying and selling securities so as to force the banks to maintain a particular net reserve position. The desired position (within a range) was set by the FOMC at each meeting, but the manager was also given some leeway depending on the tone and feel or atmosphere of the market.

The level of net reserves forms a simple operating guide. For example, the manager may be instructed to hold net borrowed reserves at $250 million. This means that the amount member banks are borrowing at the discount window exceeds the unused (excess) reserves of the nonborrowing banks by $250 million. If the target were net free reserves of $100 million, the reverse would be true— the excess reserves would exceed borrowings by that amount.

Commercial banks determine the reserves they require by creating deposits to buy securities or make loans. If the Fed does not create an equivalent amount of reserves, banks must borrow them at the discount window. Thus net borrowed reserves increase when banks create deposits faster than the Fed creates reserves, or when the Fed cancels reserves faster than banks pay off deposits. The manager of the open market account has little difficulty in carrying out his instructions. He knows the Federal funds rate minute by minute and can control net borrowed reserves on a weekly basis easily. Because of movements in currency, deposits, and Treasury operations, total reserves required by banks do shift frequently; but such movements can be forecast. Together with its forecasts, the Federal Reserve has a feed-back system through which it receives daily information on movements of required reserves within the banking system, and adjusts its operations accordingly. Under this system it furnishes and contracts the assets required to support the deposits of the Treasury, foreign central banks, and other uses which subtract from the reserves of member banks. The Desk's errors arise only during the final day of the week or as a result of reporting or computer mistakes.

From week to week there is a relative consistency between the Federal funds rate and the level of net borrowed reserves. Although small fluctuations do occur as reserves move through the banking system, resulting in shifts in the regional and interbank distribution, such changes in the relationship are minor. Over longer periods, however, the simple relationships among net borrowed reserves, interest rates, or any other monetary variable disappear since they are affected by many other forces in the economy. Furthermore, as bank borrowings increase, interest rates do not move up along a simple linear path.

The use of net reserves as an operating guide has been widely criticized because, at any level of net reserves, the Fed has no control over the total amount of reserves, money, or deposits created. If banks lend more money and create more deposits, their required reserves rise. They borrow more from the discount window. To keep their net reserve position constant, the manager must create the added reserves they need. The situation has been compared to that of a strainer. The amount coming through the strainer depends both on the size of its holes and on the pressure with which the material is forced through. As pressure (demand) increases, even with net reserves held at a fixed position, more reserves will be created.

Under a money market strategy the level of net reserves was also regarded as a measure of monetary policy. If prices were rising or credit was expanding rapidly, a decision would be taken to tighten monetary policy. This was done by firming money market conditions, by raising the amount banks had to borrow at the discount window. Pressure was thus applied to the banks, either because the discount rate they paid to the Fed on their loan was above market rates, or because the Fed as a creditor could insist that banks reduce their deposits in order to have their loan renewed. Potential spenders who wanted more credit would have to pay higher rates. If the market continued to demand too much credit, rates could be raised again. Money market conditions could grow tighter and tighter until rates were so high that the creation of new credit would come to a halt.

Monetary policy operated by varying the degree to which the money demanded at a particular interest rate would be supplied. If there was a sufficient supply of goods and labor, policy would be accommodative. All reserves necessary to maintain money market conditions unchanged would be furnished. If prices were rising and it was decided to tighten monetary policy, not all demands for reserves would be met, money market conditions would be firmed,

net borrowed reserves and money market interest rates would go
up.

The Problems of the Money Market Strategy

When does tightening fail to tighten? This can happen when monetary policy is measured by money market conditions alone, as it
was in the spring of 1966. As the spring progressed, it became increasingly clear that an inflationary boom was getting underway
and that monetary policy should have been working to curb it.
But, despite the higher discount rate and higher prevailing interest
rates, the demand for funds had gone up even faster. Banks were
finding it profitable to lend money, create deposits, and borrow at
the discount window. In accordance with the FOMC directive, the
manager was holding net reserves at the desired level; but to do
this he was obliged to purchase an ever-larger number of securities, and thereby was raising the level of total reserves rapidly.

To those who adhered to the traditional doctrine and saw money
market conditions tightening, the Fed was doing its part to fight
inflation. But to those of us who saw the fast growth of the monetary aggregates and the rapid creation of money and credit, it
seemed that the Fed, far from combatting inflationary forces, might
even be adding to the inflation.

Governors G. W. Mitchell, J. L. Robertson, Charles Shepardson,
Andrew Brimmer (who had replaced retiring Governor Canby
Balderston), and I urged that the manager be instructed to slow
the growth rate of reserves, in order to cut back on the expansion
of money and credit and thus curtail demand. Chairman Martin,
Governor Daane, Presidents Alfred Hayes and Watrous Irons,
usually joined by Presidents Karl Bopp, George Clay, and W.
Braddock Hickman, felt that the instructions to the manager to operate in accordance with money market conditions and the tone
and feel of the market were adequate. In their view, there was a
further reason to retain the money market strategy: It avoided the
need for measuring magnitudes. Monetary policy was thought to
work through a gradual application of the brakes. To attempt to
set a target in terms of money supply or credit could lead to too
activist a policy and to distortions in the flows through the mar-

kets. One of the reasons for raising the discount rate had been to smooth out the flows.

For the past decade economic literature had been calling attention to the difficulties that the use of money market conditions as a target could lead to. In addition to the creation of an unknown and unwanted quantity of reserves, there was a further problem. Money market conditions cannot measure the degree to which markets should be tightened or for how long the restraint should be retained. There was no direct or known relationship between money market conditions and spending; no theory to show how much tightening was necessary or when conditions ought to return to normal. It was known that a lag exists between monetary action and its impact on spending, but money market conditions did not measure lags any more than magnitudes. Many economists believe that the last two recessions occurred because the Fed had tightened too much and too soon. Critics did not accept on faith the Fed's claim that use of money market conditions allowed it to accommodate a proper growth in jobs and output; they wanted to know what measure the Fed used to show that this was true.

As I gained more insight into the way monetary policy was being made, I began to suspect that the Fed might be committing some of the errors our critics accused us of. Those of us who wanted to change the measure of policy argued that both the problems of magnitudes and of lags could be attacked by introducing a target that could be used to measure the degree to which monetary policy was tightening. We wanted the FOMC to adopt monetary aggregates, reserves and bank credit, as a measure of policy. Our problem was to convince the others that the level of net borrowed reserves was not, by itself, an adequate measure of policy; that it had to be supplemented by another measure.

The problem of picking a proper target came to a head during the spring. In December and January System operations had aimed at calming the markets after the discount rate increase. In these two months, reserves had increased rapidly and interest rates had risen about .5 percent. Once the transition period had passed, the question asked was, Was the desired tightening taking place? The answer depended on which measure one used—money market conditions or monetary aggregates. Net borrowed reserves had averaged about $110 million before the discount rate increase. After falling to $40 million in December and January, they were averaging $230 million by April. To those who used this measure, tightening had been sharp. Three-month Treasury bills had sold at about 3.85 percent in the third quarter of 1965. This rate was 4.65 percent in February and was just over 4.50 percent at the April meeting. Even though the market had eased somewhat in the preceding month, this measure too confirmed the desired tightening in pressure on the money markets.

But the monetary aggregates painted an entirely different picture. In the four months prior to the discount rate change, bank credit had grown at an annual rate of 7.2 percent. Between December and the April FOMC meeting, the annual rate of growth had gone up to about 15 percent. The money supply had spurted from a rate of increase of about 5.9 percent to one of 8.3 percent, or by more than 40 percent. However, the most dramatic movement was seen in total reserves, the one measure completely controlled by the Federal Reserve. In the four months prior to the discount rate change, they had grown at less than a 1 percent rate. Since December 3 their rate of increase had been above 10 percent. This occurred despite the fact that a literal reading of the FOMC's records would seem to have directed that they be reduced.

At the February 1966 meeting of the FOMC, the directive had been changed to instruct the manager of the Open Market Account to operate "with a view toward a gradual reduction in reserve availability." Those of us who were anxious to slow the rapid increase in credit thought the Committee had come around to our view. It turned out we were wrong. The manager continued to furnish reserves, even more rapidly than before. He believed he was following the directive because the amount of net borrowed reserves had gone up. Money market conditions were tighter. We failed to see how, by increasing the rate at which reserves were furnished, he was obtaining a "gradual reduction in reserve availability."

At the opening of the April 17 meeting, Robert Holland, the secretary of the FOMC, attempted to reconcile the discrepancy. He pointed out that even though the directive had called for reduced "reserve availability," in the traditional parlance this did not refer to the total reserves furnished by the System. The Committee appeared to use the term to refer primarily to the level of net borrowed reserves and total borrowing through the discount window. Mr Holland called particular attention to the increase in reserves, money, and credit which had taken place, saying this showed "how accommodative of changes a net borrowed target can be." The larger borrowings and net borrowed figure raised the cost of marginal reserves; however, if the banks were willing to pay a somewhat higher rate, the Fed would create all the additional reserves they wanted.

Governor Mitchell and I agreed that if one accepted this interpretation, the manager had acted properly; but the Committee had nevertheless failed to bring about the desired reduction in reserves and bank credit. The Committee had given the manager poor instructions, both on measures of policy and on the real degree of tightness that should be applied and, as a result of a poor directive, the Federal Reserve was not really battling inflation.

"It is clear from this experience that the Committee's directive has been 'formulated improperly," I stated. "We ought to put less stress on the marginal measures. . . . In place of primarily a money market instruction, we should make certain our directive is interpreted in terms of a desirable rate of expansion in total reserves and in bank credit. . . . The rate of increase in reserves and bank credit should be cut back from the recent five-week rate of nearly 16 percent to an annual rate of 5 per cent or less . . . even if this means considerable increase in net borrowed reserves and money market rates." Governor Shepardson agreed.

On the other hand, Governor Daane commented that he thought it necessary to gauge the degree of pressure that was being exerted in broader terms than the movements in reserves and bank credit. Considering the fact that a bite of undetermined proportions was being achieved with the existing degree of restraint, he would align himself with those who favored a net borrowed reserve target of $250 million.

President Hayes urged that the manager be instructed to maintain net borrowed reserves in the current range, which was a considerable degree of pressure. Mr. Irons agreed with him, as did Mr. Clay. Mr. Hickman believed that "monetary policy in the past three weeks had followed the last directive." However, he favored

"letting net borrowed reserves rise slowly against that demand."
Mr. Bopp, the last president to state his position, indicated "he
would be reluctant to move toward further restraint at this time."

Chairman Martin stated that it was clear the Committee did not
want to relax monetary policy. In his view no relaxation had occurred. "A process of cautiously and gradually increasing the degree of pressure" should be continued.

Modification of the Money Market Strategy: The Proviso

No action was taken to change the directive at the April meeting;
the difficulties of managing monetary policy persisted. Finally a
compromise suggested by Governor Robertson was adopted in
June. Under the new procedure, the Committee continued to instruct the manager to operate to achieve specific conditions in the
money market. However, a secondary set of targets was also
adopted by the FOMC which was based initially on reserves and
later on growth in bank deposits at member banks (the bank credit
proxy). If these targets were not being hit, the manager was instructed to shift to a new set of money market conditions.

As an example, the FOMC might set as a target for the month of
July net borrowed reserves of $250 million and a Federal funds
rate of 5 percent. The secondary target (expected to be consistent
with this level of net borrowed reserves) would be for a growth
rate in bank deposits of 8 percent. If, in the course of the month,
bank deposits were expanding at, say, 12 percent, the manager
would have to alter his primary target. Instead of net borrowed reserves of $250 million, he might, by selling in the open market,
force banks to borrow (net) $350 million of reserves. This might be
expected to raise the Federal funds rate to 5.25 percent.

This type of secondary target is called a proviso because of the
way in which it appears in the directive. It is a special clause in-
structing the manager as to what action to take "provided that" another condition arises. The first new directive containing the proviso, or secondary target, read,

> To implement this policy, System open market operations until the
> next meeting of the Committee shall be conducted with a view to
> maintaining net reserve availability and related money market condi-

tions in about their recent ranges; provided, however, that if required reserves expand considerably more than seasonally expected, operations shall be conducted with a view to attaining some further gradual reduction in net reserve availability and firming of money market conditions (Board Report, 1966, p. 151).

How much difference did the adoption of the proviso make? As far as actual operations were concerned, it did not come into use at this time because the situation had changed substantially. The Board had decided to use other instruments of monetary policy, and large excesses of reserves were no longer furnished. The proviso remained in the directive, and there were later periods when it could have been useful had it been well implemented.

In this instance, as in many future ones, it was apparent that it was not sufficient simply to adopt a new philosophy or theory. Finding the operational techniques to implement new ideas was as great an obstacle as winning adherents to the new concepts had been in the first place. The real significance of the proviso lay in the fact that a majority of the FOMC had agreed that some improvements in operating procedures were necessary. One part of the doctrine of the age of innocence—that of measuring monetary policy only by a feel for the degree of accommodation of demand gained by looking at money market conditions—had been recognized as inadequate.

At the same time, the second part of the doctrine—that goals were simple and primarily to fight inflation—was being challenged by the course of events.

CHAPTER FIVE

A Testing of
Monetary Doctrine

HISTORIANS, REVIEWING THE YEAR 1966, might wonder why there was so much excitement in economic and financial circles in that year. Nothing very startling is revealed in the annual statistics. Although interest rates climbed somewhat above previous levels, in comparison with later periods, they remained low. The discount rate stayed at 4.5 percent and commerical paper rates topped at only 6 percent, compared to 9 percent in 1969–70. Income, output, spending, and jobs all grew rapidly. Prices rose more than they had in recent years, but far less than in subsequent periods. The historian would have to extend his search to more detailed data. He would note that the principal differences between this and a normal expansion were that the money supply (M_1) averaged hardly any growth for the first nine months and that the growth rate of all deposits in financial institutions was far below previous periods. The expansion of industrial production halted and then dipped slightly in the last few months of the year. A sharp fall in housing starts and production for construction was not quite offset by a rapid rise in war output.

A Reevaluation of Federal Reserve Policy

The economic importance of 1966 must not be underestimated. It was an extremely difficult period for all engaged in economic policy making, especially for those at the Federal Reserve: The situation presented a basic test of the ability of monetary policy to halt an inflationary rise in demand. Although, in terms of overall central banking responsibilities, the Federal Reserve's actions during this period could be considered no more than its duty, it was a radical departure in the United States. Since 1920, this country had not attempted to use monetary policy to the degree that it was employed in 1966.

The financial institutions which had to bear the brunt of the fight against inflation were totally unprepared for it. Most of their leaders had only experienced years of growth and prosperity; few of them remembered the Great Depression. Although they believed in the use of monetary policy to fight inflation, they were shocked to discover how much it cost. I remember a visit from a man who had built a savings institution from nothing into one holding several hundred millions of dollars. He was in despair because he had no defenses against this new form of pressure which was destroying his entire institution.

How successful the Fed actually was and how its performance could have been improved have been the subjects of many an argument among economists and business and financial men. In the opinion of Arthur Okun (a senior fellow at the Brookings Institution and a former chairman of the President's Council of Economic Advisers), an eminent economist who was in the thick of the action,

> Judged by its performance in getting GNP on track, the Federal Reserve in 1966 put on *the* virtuoso performance in the history of stabilization policy. It was the greatest tight-rope walking and balancing act ever performed by either fiscal or monetary policy. Single-handedly the Fed curbed a boom generated by a vastly stimulative fiscal

policy that was paralyzed by politics and distorted by war. And in stopping the boom, it avoided a recession. . . . What more could anyone want? Yet, you won't find the 1966 Fed team in the hall of fame for stabilization policy. In the view of most Americans, the collapse of homebuilding, the disruption of financial markets, and the escalation of interest rates were evils that outweighed the benefits of the nonrecessionary halting of inflation.°

Just as the period following the December 3 discount rate action required that the Fed rethink its simple concepts of measurement, so, too, it occasioned a necessary reexamination of its goals and views as to the use of monetary instruments. The first nine months of 1966 witnessed a major test of traditional Federal Reserve doctrine in all spheres and resulted in a definite shift in emphasis. The way in which economic events and political pressures caused the Board to change its ideas is a good example of the general relationship between theory and the "real world." In the light of new economic experiences, it was recognized that the previous theories had been greatly oversimplified, that they had paid too little attention to sectoral problems. They had also failed to take into account the fact that the Fed's need to function as a lender of last resort imposed limits on the amount of tightening it could effect through monetary policy.

A major factor in the raising of the Regulation Q ceilings had been the philosophy that the market ought to be allowed freely to determine the distribution of credit. Raising the ceilings was regarded as correcting a structural imbalance in the banking and credit markets. The action would free them. The Board's philosophy further included a strong determination not to give any consideration to the needs of particular sectors when monetary policy changed; the Federal Reserve's concern ought to be only with the total amount of credit. The market would distribute it properly.

Shortly after I joined the board, I was surprised to learn that, in 1963 and each year thereafter, the Federal Reserve had recommended that Congress amend the Federal Reserve Act to remove

° From "Rules and Roles for Fiscal and Monetary Policy," in *Issues in Fiscal and Monetary Policy: The Eclectic Economist Views the Controversy*, edited by James J. Diamond (Chicago: DePaul University, 1971), pp. 57–58.

the special lending powers granted to it in the Great Depression. These recommendations followed from a major System study which had placed great emphasis on not interfering in any way with the market. The System should not, therefore, be in the lending business, and the idea that a time might arise when the Federal Reserve would have to step in and lend on an emergency basis was forgotten. In fact, the entire concept of a lender of last resort to the financial system had virtually disappeared.

Policy Results Depend Upon Institutional Structures

The pre-1966 theories underlying monetary policy were too simple because they failed to give sufficient weight to movements which resulted from the institutional structure of financial markets. A tendency to neglect these forces in analysis continues to plague monetary debates. In constructing a theory solely as an aid to understanding, it may be proper to disregard the legal and institutional structure of the economy in order to study its basic tendencies. In formulating policy, however, the economy's true behavior cannot be treated so cavalierly. Analysis for policy must consider the channels through which economic forces actually move. Policies do not sail the calm seas of theoretical assumptions; they must steer their course among the rocks and shoals of laws, regulations, market institutions, and market imperfections. The theoretical marketplace, wholly governed by the laws of supply and demand, does not exist. Perfection is rare in the working of credit markets. Shifts in demand due to changes in interest rates or in the availability of credit are neither smooth nor efficient. The imperfections that characterize markets act to reallocate credit with seriously destabilizing results. If each sector of the economy had equal access to all capital markets, as it does not, everything might work through the price mechanism and allocational goals might be well served. If markets were truly impersonal, as they are not, those with the projects promising the best return might get the credit.

The truth, however, is that forces other than prices play major roles in the marketplace.. When credit is tight, this fact becomes glaringly apparent. For example, there is really little in a long-standing customer relationship to tell a bank how meritorious a prime depositor's project may be compared to those of other applicants for loans. Yet, in times of credit stringency, the old customer is given credit on favorable terms while other would-be borrowers with excellent projects are rationed out of the market. If markets functioned with perfect economic efficiency, this would not happen.

For the economy in general, the most important effect of high interest rates has been to restrict the funds flowing into the housing market. At such times, the bond market attracts funds that in times of lower interest rates are deposited in mortgage lending institutions which, because of legal constraints and the slow turnover of their assets, cannot compete when interest rates rise.

Rapid shifts in credit flows also have serious effects on stabilization. A reallocation of real resources such as labor, plant capacity, and materials, takes a long time. It is difficult to move labor geographically or to retrain a bricklayer to be an engineer; unions can and do impede the entry of new businesses. Reallocation is neither perfect nor cheaply accomplished. Given this lack of real factor mobility, a temporary shift of credit may cause structural unemployment. It may also, in the case of housing, lead to an inflationary rise in rents and the cost of living if the supply of residences lags behind demands. While it may be true that the resources would move eventually, by the time such movement gets under way, credit may be flowing back into that sector again. Specific policy proposals must take into account such real imperfections.

Problems of the Thrift Institutions

As soon as the December 1965 change in Regulation Q was announced, the Federal Reserve began to hear from other groups, particularly the thrift institutions and those concerned with their operations. Both the Federal Home Loan Bank Board (FHLBB) and the Federal Deposit Insurance Corporation (FDIC) raised questions, as did numerous congressmen. These agencies had coordinate responsibilities with the Fed for deposit institutions. The FDIC set interest rate ceilings similar to Regulation Q for insured nonmember banks. The Home Loan Bank Board was responsible for the regulation of savings and loan associations (S and Ls). Under normal circumstances the changes in the ceilings would have been coordinated with these agencies. However, because of the rapidity with which the discount rate and the ceilings had been raised, this coordination did not occur.

John Horne, then the chairman of the Home Loan Board, was greatly concerned over the safety of his institutions, which were in a most unenviable position. Congress and state legislatures had insisted that their deposits be very short term, while their assets were limited largely to fixed-interest-rate mortgages. With rising rates, the savings and loans institutions were already subject to sharper competition from the market; the Federal Reserve had now created further competition from commercial banks, which could and would attract household time deposits by use of savings certificates, savings bonds, and certificates of deposit. And they could pay rates up to 5.5 percent on deposits whose only restriction was that they were payable only every thirty days.

Horne was concerned that thrift institutions would be unable to raise the interest rates they paid on deposits by as much as the banks, which lend primarily on a short-term basis and thus have considerable flexibility to raise their charges and income. The portfolios of thrift institutions are invested primarily in mortgages. Mortgages have a fixed yield and a very slow turnover; the institutions would be fortunate if they could invest 20 percent of their assets at the new higher rates during a year. Consequently their income was primarily fixed, based upon the rate of return on their existing portfolio. Nor could the institutions raise funds through portfolio sales. The value of a mortgage with a fixed interest rate falls as rates rise. Any attempt to sell mortgages would mean large capital losses, and reserves for safety would disappear.

The reactions of the Fed to Horne's and similar congressional complaints were almost completely negative: The Federal Reserve was simply allowing the free market to work. The complainants were suggesting that a noncompetitive situation be maintained, one which could only result in a distortion of credit flows and a less efficient economy. Further, members of the Federal Reserve Board believed that the S and Ls had used their freedom from interest rate ceilings to expand in a most dangerous way. This was particularly true of associations in California. Most were profit-making institutions which had recently discovered the joy of rising price-earning ratios on their common stock.

There were indications that some institutions had been taking undue risks in order to show increasing profits. The associations had advertised widely on a national basis, attracting deposits because of interest rate differentials over other areas. Many of the California associations had as much as 50 percent of their deposits from out of state. Some had up to 80 or 90 percent. These funds had been attracted from interest-sensitive depositors. As such, they were "hot money," likely to be withdrawn suddenly and invested in higher-yielding securities. The efforts of the Home Loan Bank Board attempting to deal with the situation had been singularly unsuccessful. The Federal Reserve felt that it would be a salutary development if lifting the Regulation Q ceilings slowed deposit flows into S and Ls.

It was recognized that most of the monetary constraint would initially be felt in housing. Commercial banks were only minor lenders to housing. Most lending to the housing industry was done through the thrift institutions. And as their mortgage funds dried up, a fall in new construction would be inevitable. Nor was this projection of great concern to the Fed, which concurred in the fairly general belief that the recent rate of house building had been faster than the economy could sustain. Partly because of the large flows into savings and loans and their speculative activities, more mortgage money had been made available than the housing industry could absorb. Many apartments were started, not because they were needed, but simply because builders could obtain 100 percent financing. As a result of the large number of houses started, vacancies were growing rapidly. Thus, given the excess supply of housing, what more reasonable area was there to be cut back?

The Inflationary Flows of Funds

The squeeze on the thrift institutions and housing starts developed as predicted during the spring of 1966. Because they were expected, these events did not cause too much concern. What caused the Federal Reserve its main difficulties, however, was the fact that inflationary credit continued to expand rapidly in other spheres.

As a result of the increase in Regulation Q ceilings, the largest banks appeared to be gaining funds rapidly. They, in turn, were lending the money to their major corporate borrowers. In consequence, spending for physical plant was expanding at an accelerating pace. While a depression was approaching in building, extremely sharp inflationary pressures were affecting machine tools and similar types of equipment. Overall deflationary pressures were far weaker than desired. The most critical figure that the Federal Reserve had to face was that, in the first half of 1966, business loans by the large banks of the country were 37 percent higher than they had been in the first half of 1965, even as other users of credit were being squeezed. These opposing flows raised serious questions as to whether the market was providing the best distribution of credit for the economy. The situation was not at all clear. Banks were getting more money to lend to corporations to spend in the spheres of tightest supply.

Were real resources able to transfer freely from one sector of the economy to another, this might not be harmful. All of the added plant and equipment might be needed and would help to fight later price increases. However, if the corporations were expanding too soon and too rapidly, the effect would be inflationary. What was good for General Motors was not necessarily good for the country.

Further difficulties arose from the inflexibility of labor. Problems of both geography and skills restricted the transfer of resources into the expanding sectors. It is true that resources and labor made idle could be deflationary if the result were a decrease in their purchasing power, because their decreased spending would free resources for other uses. But there was little indication that such adjustments were taking place.

By May, the majority of the Board still felt that its actions had eliminated some of the distortions from the market—the Federal Reserve's chief concern. Funds should now flow freely to the potential credit users who could pay the highest rate. But no one knew whether the new flows were those that would be brought about by a freely competitive market. Along with at least one other member of the Board, I stressed that this was a long-run theory that assumed perfect knowledge. As a matter of fact, the flows were distorted by institutional factors, such as the way in which government policy had set up differentiated deposit institutions and the limits to competition which statutes and regulations had imposed. The ability to lend and the customers selected grew out of the existing portfolios of the institutions and particularly from the customer relationships which had developed over the past. There was no assurance that the loans made would correspond to the needs of the economy. The question was whether the operation of the market tended to increase or decrease inflationary pressures, and whether the loans were in line with the aims of monetary policy.

Responses to the Growing Squeeze

All during the spring, the squeeze on the thrift institutions got worse, and it also spread to life insurance companies which had made advance commitments based on an assumed cash flow. As credit became tighter, policyholders found it advantageous to borrow on their policies at rates lower than those being charged by other lenders. Policy loans mushroomed, cutting into the available funds of the insurance companies. In the case of a few companies, the amounts falling out through these loans disrupted their entire operations and raised questions as to their continued liquidity and solvency.

Washington was suddenly filled with delegations of house builders and executives of savings and loan associations, mutual savings banks, and insurance companies. Most of them headed directly to the White House to meet with its staff and with advisers from the Treasury and the Council of Economic Advisers. I was asked by the White House and by the Federal Reserve to sit with the committees of the Administration that were meeting with these delegations.

Since inflationary pressures were growing, we attempted to convince these groups that their problems were simply part of the free market mechanism. Some borrowers had to be cut off in order to make money available for the increased war needs. If demand were not curtailed, they would be even worse off, for there would be inflation and the level of savings would fall, perhaps drastically. We urged them to accept the market mechanism and to adjust their operations as rapidly as possible to the new situation. We assured them that conditions were being watched carefully, that the government and the Federal Reserve were aware of what was happening. We would not allow the situation to become so critical that financial institutions crashed. Few of the delegations were won over. Instead, they hurried down Pennsylvania Avenue to lobby with their congressmen to force the Federal Reserve to rescind its December 3 decision.

The House Banking and Currency Committee

During May, as a result of these pressures on Congress, the Regulation Q ceilings became a political problem for the Federal Reserve. At least a majority of the House Banking and Currency Committee appeared to have been persuaded by the builders and the savings and loan associations that the only way to stabilize the situation and to allow the housing industry to function at a normal level was to insure a greater flow of funds into the thrift institutions. They believed that this could be done by returning the ceilings to the December level. Chairman Wright Patman of the House Committee, always one of the strongest advocates of lower interest rates and, therefore, lower ceilings, introduced a bill which would have required that all interest rate ceilings on time deposits be rolled back from their current 5.5 percent to a 4.5 percent maximum.

The Federal Reserve took the stand that any such rollback would be disastrous, if not impossible, and that money would not flow from banks to thrift institutions. Instead, all institutions would lose funds to the market and the deflationary impact on the economy would be drastic. The probability of maintaining viable financial institutions would almost disappear unless inflationary credit were greatly expanded.

After the introduction of this legislation, it appeared that the

Federal Reserve faced three critical problems. Two were economic: How could the Fed insure a minimum flow of funds into certain sectors in order to avoid a crisis and to insure that production would be maintained at an acceptable level? Secondly, how could it slow the rate of credit flowing into the most inflationary sectors of the economy? Finally, on the political side, how could the Fed convince Congress that it recognized the problems and was taking appropriate action? What type of legislation should it support in place of that which had been introduced?

Reviewing the situation, I saw four related possibilities. The first was to make certain that the Federal Reserve was prepared to act as a lender of last resort. A cascade of failures of financial institutions had to be prevented. Secondly, the Board needed to look into the histories of World War II and Korea to see what lessons they furnished for controlling credit, since special efforts might be needed to use credit as a method of channeling resources toward the war effort. (I was charged with the responsibility for the Board's defense planning. Prior planning had been concerned only with the maintenance of the economic system in case of atomic attack. I now shifted the emphasis to a reexamination of the policies which would be best for the Federal Reserve to follow in case of a limited war.) The third possibility was to recognize the congressional pressure for moving the Regulation Q ceilings, but to recommend workable amendments to the proposed bill and to prepare the regulations that would accompany any new legislation. Finally, I raised the question of whether existing Federal Reserve powers, particularly those of the discount window, could be used to influence the allocation of credit to various markets.

Insuring the Liquidity of Financial Institutions

The problems of the thrift institutions and of some insurance companies were the most worrisome to the Board. Most thrift institutions were getting along because they depended upon deposits from small savers, whose incomes were rising. But in the most critical areas, such as California and New York, many large institutions were losing funds. By offering higher rates than those on Treasury bills or commercial paper, they had attracted sophisticated, short-term depositors from the money market. But, as rates rose, these deposits flowed back into the market.

Some institutions attempted to hold their deposits by offering still higher rates, but this started a vicious cycle: Paying higher rates made many of the associations unprofitable, since they were paying more on their deposits than they were earning on their mortgages. On the other hand, if they did not offer higher rates, they would lose funds and would have to sell assets at a loss. Insolvency would follow sooner if they did not raise their deposit rates than if they did.

In theory, action had been taken to forestall these problems. Most depositors would not lose any money because the institutions were insured by the Federal Savings and Loan Insurance Corporation (FSLIC) or the FDIC. Furthermore, the Federal Home Loan Banks existed to lend to S and Ls so that they would not be forced to sell assets in the market and take losses. However, by the start of the summer, both the Home Loan Bank Board and the FDIC were greatly worried. Although the Bank Board was increasing its loans to the S and Ls that were losing deposits, it feared it might not be able to borrow the money it needed as the securities markets verged on the disorderly. Also, because its charges had to cover its costs, its lending rate might rise even higher than deposit rates, thus rendering the associations even more unprofitable. Further, if many of the several hundred shaky institutions went under, funds available to the FSLIC might not suffice to pay off all borrowers; its accumulated reserves were quite small compared to its potential liabilities.

The fears of the FDIC were different. It could meet the losses of the depositors in mutual savings banks, albeit at a sacrifice; but the mutual savings banks had no lender of last resort; the FDIC was primarily an insurer. It could not lend funds simply because the banks were losing deposits. Only after the banks had lost capital in an attempt to find the liquidity necessary to meet a deposit outflow could it step in to protect the depositor. That, of course, would be too late to save the bank.

This situation focused attention on the Fed's function as a lender of last resort, a responsibility which had not been used in over twenty years. The Fed could not limit its attention to total money or credit entirely; it had to concern itself with the impact of shifting flows of credit on financial institutions as well. In July the Federal Reserve Board granted authority to the Federal Reserve Banks to provide emergency credit facilities to nonmember depository institutions. These included mutual savings banks, savings and loans, and, upon further request, insurance companies. It turned out, however, that the point at which loans were to be granted was not reached.

At the same time, a significant decision was made by the Treasury. The Treasury had the right to deposit funds in the Home Loan Banks, but had never used it. It was now agreed that, if the crunch became critical enough, this authority would be activated; the Treasury would insure the liquidity of the Home Loan Banks at rates which would make lending feasible for their associations.

However, guaranteeing liquidity for deposits flowing out would not solve all the problems of the thrift institutions. Those that were losing money could become insolvent; their reserves against losses would be adequate only if they maintained or gained deposits. Furthermore, the problem of the housing industry would not be solved merely by insuring that the institutions could meet deposit demands. As the thrift institutions came under pressure, they had drawn back mortgage money and virtually disappeared from the new construction market. Many builders found mortgage money unobtainable, even when they offered rates considerably above the market. Housing starts, which had been at an annual rate of 1,770,000 in December 1965, dropped steadily. By October 1966 the rate was under 850,000.

If starts remained at or below this level, a single sector of the economy would be making a major sacrifice, while most other parts of the economy were reaching new heights in income and profits. Even with only the brief drop in starts which occurred, in many areas a majority of builders and subcontractors went out of business. Unemployment in the building industry rose rapidly. Losses were severe. Most important from the national point of view, an extended period of low housing starts threatened to be inflationary, with expanding demand and contracting supply driving up rents. There would also be a major decline in housing standards and family welfare. Furthermore, a decimated industry would experience much higher future costs. Such a situation would not be acceptable either politically or as a matter of policy.

In fact, later studies have shown that the housing industry accounted for up to 90 percent of the deflationary impact of monetary policy during this period. The effect was equivalent to a high tax on one industry for the purpose of cutting spending. Congress would never have chosen this type of fiscal policy to pay for the war. Even when accomplished through monetary policy, it became a major political issue.

Differentiated Ceilings

When, in May 1966, Congressman Patman introduced a bill to roll back the interest ceilings on time deposits, the Board unanimously called attention to the tremendous potential damage that such a statute could cause. Nevertheless, there was a need for authority to differentiate among deposits in setting interest rate ceilings. Under the existing law the Board could set separate rates for deposits based on the time required before the deposits could be withdrawn, but not for those that differed in size or some other feature. The markets for investments of different sizes were separate; ownership, transaction costs, liquidity needs, and similar factors fostered a variety of types and sizes of deposits. It, therefore, made sense to me for the Board to differentiate by size in imposing interest rate ceilings. A logical division seemed to be between deposits over and under $100,000. At first Governor Andrew Brimmer, the most recent appointee to the Board, was the only other supporter of this position.

Two members of the Board opposed the proposal as unfair to smaller consumers. Why should banks pay less simply because a saver had less? The best answer was to look at the market. It functions through demand and supply, which is not necessarily fair. Those with more money could exercise more choice in their investments. Since they had alternatives, they had to be paid more if financial institutions were to attract their funds. Smaller savers had fewer alternatives so would be willing to deposit at lower rates.

Numerous congressional hearings ensued. The Board was split so badly that each member was asked to testify personally in an attempt to help clarify congressional views. The political heat increased as the crisis of the thrift institutions became more apparent. By the middle of June, all members of the Board agreed that the authority to set ceilings based on the size of deposit would be useful. They were also unanimous in their opinion that it would be disastrous for Congress to attempt to impose an interest rate ceiling by statute. Regulations could be changed as market conditions indicated, but legislation of actual ceilings would freeze all deposit institutions in an untenable position. The Johnson Administration supported the Federal Reserve point of view. It also agreed that any amendments to the ceiling law should apply to savings and loans as well.

Congress delayed action. A major split developed within the savings and loan associations and their lobbyists. Some still believed they had enough political muscle to force through the lower ceiling for banks while avoiding any ceilings on savings and loans. Some preferred the existing situation to new legal ceilings over their own rates. Others supported the Administration and Federal Reserve point of view. As more and more associations began to feel greater and greater pressure, the latter view became predominant.

Meanwhile, recognizing how distorted credit flows were becoming, the Federal Reserve Board implemented policies it could apply with its existing powers. It attempted to hold back bank credit expansion by raising required reserves from 4 to 6 percent on all certificates of deposit (CDs) a bank held in excess of $5 million. The object was to decrease the profitability of the CDs while tightening reserves directly. The $5 million exemption freed smaller banks which were no problem. This action marked the first time since 1951 that the Federal Reserve had used its power to raise reserve requirements. Banks dislike reserve increases because it raises their costs, and they had lobbied strongly against the use of this device. Many had assumed that the Federal Reserve doctrine developed during the 1950s insured that this power would not again be used.

The Board also attempted to restrict banks' efforts to attract more volatile household deposits. It defined a new category of deposits, the so-called multiple maturity certificates, which could be renewed automatically. For deposits with automatic renewal dates of under ninety days, the ceiling was 4 percent; for those of ninety days and over, it was 5 percent. This regulation aimed at halting payments of high rates on certificates of deposit whose owners considered them to be savings deposits.

The Use of the Discount Window for Differential Support

In June the search for ways to influence the flow of funds away from inflationary sectors speeded up. The Board agreed that the staff should look at Regulation A, which controlled borrowing at the discount window. If the regulation could be helpful, proposed amendments should be drafted.

Traditionally the Federal Reserve allowed member banks any funds necessary to meet unexpected demands. They were given money from the discount window without question, provided they did not have weak assets and had adequate security. If such borrowings went unpaid too long (four to thirteen weeks, depending on circumstances), the bank in question would be asked to discuss its loan with a discount officer. As a rule, it would be requested to pay off its loan in an agreed-upon period by either decreasing outstanding loans or by selling securities. This policy has sometimes been stated as, "We help them make up their minds not to apply again."

In the middle of August the need for action appeared imminent. An exceedingly rapid expansion in business loans was being financed by liquidation of other banking assets. Pressure spread to other markets. Some banks borrowed from the discount window for longer than normal periods in order to avoid liquidating their securities. Others began to dump municipal bonds and other securities. As a result of bank selling, the securities market became somewhat disorderly. Apprehension grew that a full-blown crisis was in the making, that people trying to achieve liquidity by selling bonds would find no market for them or would find prices so low that they could not afford to take the capital losses.

The Board met with the twelve District Bank presidents to consider possible actions. The concern was with both the expansion in business loans and the disorderly functioning of the securities market. The Board believed it would be advantageous to act through the discount window, since it could not raise the Regulation Q ceilings again. To allow banks to borrow more in the market would cause further distortion of the already tight credit. The conference of presidents was unanimous in opposition to a change in Regulation A. They did not want to alter the way they dealt with their member banks through the discount window. But as the situation grew more critical, the Board felt that action was necessary, and obtained the presidents' agreement to act in a less formal manner without amending the Regulation. This was a clear example of the power of the Board to act when it felt the situation required it, even in the face of opposition from the District Banks.

The action took the form of a letter from the Federal Reserve to all member banks on the use of the discount window. While the letter marked a major break with the precedents of the past twenty years, it was worded in a typically diplomatic manner. The key paragraph read,

> The System believes that the national economic interest would be better served by a slower rate of expansion of bank loans to business within the context of moderate overall money and credit growth. Further substantial adjustments through bank liquidation of municipal securities or other investments would add to pressures on financial markets. Hence the System believes that a greater share of member bank adjustments should take the form of moderation in the rate of expansion of loans, and particularly business loans.

The letter was sent on September 1.

While greeted as a major change, no one was certain whether the letter meant that policy was tighter or looser. Through speeches, we tried to make it clear that money would be more available at the discount window for everything but business loans, that we were concerned over their rapid expansion. Banks which continued to expand business loans rapidly could borrow from the Federal Reserve in a normal fashion, but they could not expect extraordinary accommodations. They would be expected to repay their loans within a month or two.

Initially the banks reacted sharply to the letter. They objected that the Federal Reserve was attempting qualitative controls over credit, which would destroy our economy. At the same time, however, a general feeling of relief was felt in the security markets. Interest rates stabilized and began to come down. Confidence was much enhanced. It is also interesting that, while the banks denounced this policy in 1966, when the crunch came in 1970, many large banks came to the Board and suggested that we ought to reissue a similar letter.

The End of Tight Money

The letter of September 1 was followed in rapid order by other actions aimed at correcting some of the distortion in the flow of funds. The credit crisis was recognized as a paramount national issue. Action had to be taken to calm the financial markets.

On September 8, the President asked Congress to suspend the 7 percent tax credit on investments in machinery and equipment, and also the accelerated depreciation provisions for new buildings. Both measures were designed to decrease the excess flow of demand from these sources. At the same time, the President announced that, in order to curtail government demand, he would reduce nondefense spending. A rapid increase in agency borrowing and their market competition had been factors threatening to bring about disorderly markets. New presidential regulations were issued to cover these borrowings by government agencies in the securities markets: The White House would regulate the intervals at which the agencies came to market.

In addition, Congress was urged to pass the amendments which the Board had proposed to the Federal Reserve Act in order to allow regulation of interest rate ceilings by deposit size as well as by time. Given the near-crisis that existed, the new act was passed almost at once (September 21, 1966). The lobbying pressures which had stalled the bill evaporated. The President signed it into law immediately. The same day, the Board acted to cut back the maximum ceilings on time deposits of under $100,000 from 5.5 to 5 percent. The FDIC and the Home Loan Bank Board passed coordinated ceilings for the thrift institutions, which gave them a slight advantage over the commercial banks, thereby removing the critical pressure on them.

A decision had also been made to halt the contraction of total money and credit. The September 1 letter opened by noting the System's belief that an orderly expansion of bank credit would be appropriate. By October, it became evident that the economy now faced the probability of a slowdown rather than an excess expansion of demand and output. Monetary policy became less tight. The problems of 1966 were past. Planning could now begin on what action to take if similar events occurred in the future.

The July and September actions marked a watershed in Federal Reserve policy. Blind faith in the market as a method of properly distributing funds was discredited. Doctrine became more flexible. It was recognized that, while it may be desirable to free markets for a more efficient distribution of funds, this must be based on the market's actual operation, not a theoretical abstract of it. Traditional channels of lending exist which cannot be overturned in short periods. For such reasons the Federal Reserve has to be in touch with what goes on within the market and the resulting flows of credit. It cannot neglect the impact on the economy if certain flows are cut off. Its analysis cannot be confined to the growth in money or credit, but must be concerned with the continued orderly operation of the financial markets and the way in which they distribute money and credit.

CHAPTER SIX

The Makers of Monetary Policy: The Chairman

A DISTINGUISHED GROUP gathered in the East Room of the White House the morning of January 31, 1970. Headed by the President and his family, the cabinet, and the senior White House staff, it also included some who had been on the White House staff under President Eisenhower, the entire Federal Reserve Board, and many of the country's most prominent bankers. The working White House press and national television were there in full force. The occasion was the swearing-in of Dr. Arthur F. Burns as the tenth Chairman of the Board of Governors of the Federal Reserve System.

No one was quite certain how to act. It was nearly nineteen years since a new Chairman had been sworn in. At that time, William McChesney Martin had taken over what was then a far less prominent post. For the past month the financial press had been filled with praise of Martin, both as an individual and as Chairman. (The Federal Reserve Act precluded his reappointment.) Some, however, expressed reservations about what they considered to be his conservatism and penchant for tight money. As the end of his term approached, some feeling of coolness and dissatisfaction toward him had emanated from the inner White House staff. Now all wondered what would happen as the result of the change.

The President made it clear that he expected a new Chairman

106

would mean a new Federal Reserve policy. In a news conference the preceding night, the President had indicated that he thought an immediate easing of monetary policy was necessary. At the swearing-in ceremony, President Nixon publicly greeted the new Chairman with some pointed, joking-in-earnest comments about easing credit and lowering interest rates: "I respect his independence," said Mr. Nixon, "However, I hope that independently he will conclude that my views are the ones that should be followed." After a burst of applause, the President added, "You see, Dr. Burns, that is a standing vote of appreciation in advance for lower interest rates and more money."

It did not take a very close observer to see that both the incoming and the outgoing Chairmen were extremely uncomfortable with the President's jokes. Both knew that the Fed had acted to ease credit and lower interest rates several weeks earlier. When it would become obvious in future weeks that easing had occurred, the President's words on this occasion might cause the press to raise questions as to the reasons for the change. Was it due to the change in Chairmen?

Much of the public's awareness of the Federal Reserve System comes through the Chairman and his public statements. He personifies the System, and monetary policy is seen as a reflection of his ideas and personality. His role in monetary decisions is paramount. Since 1934 the Federal Reserve had had two strong Chairmen: Marriner Eccles and William McChesney Martin, with only a brief interval between their terms. Their dominance is illustrated by the remark current in Washington during much of Eccles's and Martin's tenures that the Federal Reserve Board consisted of the Chairman and six nonentities.

With a new man taking over, what effect would the change have on the economy? Would the influence of the White House be increased at the Fed? Obviously, the fact of a new Chairman was important to estimates of future financial conditions. Monetary policy does not merely reflect monetary doctrine; it is strongly influenced by the personalities in the Federal Reserve System and by their interaction, as well as by their responses to external suggestions and pressures.

The Interactions of Influence

Many pundits agree that "The Supreme Court follows the election returns." But they wonder what drum sets the pace of monetary expansion at the Federal Reserve. The power of semiautonomous agencies has long been a subject of fascination to political scientists. Many, fearing that the political process may overrespond to popular pressure, believe it useful to have nine or seven "wise men" who can take a longer, more dispassionate view of the national welfare, immune to special interest groups or large contributors. But the problem then arises, Who will guard the guardians?

Hard as it tries, the Federal Reserve cannot make monetary policy in a completely unbiased manner, free from all background influences and generalized business and professional pressures on the individual Board members. Each time a new governor is appointed and confirmed, the stance of the Board shifts to some degree. The critical question is how much freedom and independence from the political process should be granted any small group, given the existence of these biases and special influences.

The question of the Fed's power and its use was vividly illustrated in January 1971 when members of the Federal Reserve, both as individuals and as a Board, were publicly explaining the dangers of expanded prices and reduced output the economy could incur if no price-wage or incomes policy were adopted. In articles and speeches, the press and prominent economists began to predict a new confrontation between the Federal Reserve and the Administration, suggesting that, unless the Administration adopted a price-wage policy, the Fed might slow the creation of money, with the result that output would not rise in accordance with the Administration's plans.

I became concerned that the public was getting a false picture of the Fed's power. When Hobart Rowen, financial editor of the Washington *Post*, wrote in his nationally syndicated column that the Fed was wielding a big stick in threatening to hold monetary policy hostage if the Administration failed to act, I called him to say that I believed he was leaving an incorrect impression of what the Fed could or would do. He expressed surprise at my statement, pointing out that his columns reflected the views of many informed observers, including his own experience of over fifteen years. I said perhaps the situation had changed gradually, but enough so that the past experience no longer applied. We agreed that he ought not to take my word for this change, but ought to investigate the best possible opinions from different sources as to the real situation, which he did. Shortly thereafter his column reported what I considered to be a correct evaluation of the situation, "The internal view at the Fed of its own proper role does not call for it to veto the official stance of the Government in any significant way. . . . The Fed can not and will not hold its ability to be 'liberal' as hostage for White House acquiescence to a wage-price restraint program." Although this statement accurately expresses the predominant attitude within the Fed, the opposite view continues to be widely held. Again in 1973 stories almost identical to those of 1971 were current, to the effect that the Fed would tighten unless the government reduced its deficit.

In short, both individuals and the structure of the Federal Reserve System influence the monetary process. In answer to the question of what drum is heard when policy is made, I have drawn up Chart 2. It illustrates my estimate of the relative monetary power of various groups, both within and without the Federal Reserve System, during the time I served on the Board. The length of the line after a group's name indicates its impact on policy in relation to the others in the same section.

One cannot estimate the relative importance of internal as opposed to external pressures. The comparative impact on monetary policy of the President of the United States, the chairman of the House Banking and Currency Committee, the secretary of the Treasury, or the Chairman of the Federal Reserve Board varies widely from one situation and one period to another.

The first section of the chart shows the power relationships within the Federal Reserve System. It is here that individual perceptions might show the largest divergence in the weights assigned. Other knowledgeable persons would certainly draw charts

DEGREE OF MONETARY POWER 1965–1973

THE FEDERAL RESERVE SYSTEM

The Chairman	45%
The staff of the Board and FOMC	25%
The other governors	20%
Federal Reserve Banks	10%

OUTSIDE INFLUENCES

The Administration The President The Treasury The Council of Economic Advisers The Office of Management and Budget All other nonfinancial	35%
The Congress House and Senate Committees on Banking Joint Economic Committee Senate Finance Committee House Ways and Means Committee	25%
The public directly Unorganized The press Economists Lobbyists	20%
The financial interests Banks S and Ls Stockbrokers Etc.	10%
Foreign interests	5%
Other regulatory agencies FDIC Comptroller FHLBB SEC	5%

with different weights; in fact, if I were to chart another period, it would not be the same. No one would question that the Chairman of the Board of Governors holds the most monetary power, as explained in the remainder of this chapter. The second most important group is the staff of both the Board of Governors and the Federal Open Market Committee, including the two managers of the Open Market Desk in New York and their assistants. The third group is made up of the six other members of the Board of Governors. Finally come the Federal Reserve regional banks, within each of which the power is divided, depending upon personal and historical relationships, among the president, the staff, and the board of directors.

The second chart section is "Outside Influences." These are the groups whose speeches, phone calls, letters, memoranda, articles, and so forth are likely to be heard in monetary policy decisions. The most significant influence on the Federal Reserve comes from the President and other members of the Administration. Within this group the greatest force emanates from the White House staff and the other three Quadriad members, the Treasury, the Council of Economic Advisers, and the Office of Management and Budget. The remaining nonfinancial agencies in Washington have only a minor impact.

The relative power within the Administration has varied greatly depending upon the President, how he organizes his advice, and who occupies the various chairs. At times the weight of the Treasury has been greater than all the others. In other periods, either the CEA or OMB has been most significant. In recent years the White House staff has dominated.

The next most important influence is the United States Congress. While some pressure emanates from individual congressmen, most of the actual influence is wielded by the committees with oversight in the banking and economic fields: that is the Committees on Banking, the Joint Economic Committee, the Senate Finance Committee, and the House Ways and Means Committee. Within a committee, power tends to be concentrated in the hands of the chairman, the staff, and a few members who have either seniority or the personalities and abilities to use the press to publicize their economic views. Novices on the Washington scene often assume that congressional power is somewhat evenly divided among the 100 members of the Senate and the 435 members of the House. In fact, the Federal Reserve sees almost all of the oversight concentrated in the 10 to 20 members of Congress on the committees; their effective power far surpasses that of all the other congressmen together.

Another group is labeled "The Public Directly." Both the public and financial interests carry a great deal of indirect as well as direct weight, through their influence on the Administration and Congress. I divide the public into four primary groups, each with a roughly similar impact. They include the unorganized voters who write and speak out; the press; economists who criticize, evaluate, and suggest new or better policies; and finally, organized interests, including business, labor, and consumers, whose impact varies with the effectiveness of their Washington lobbies. The Federal Reserve listens carefully to the public, since each governor is primarily a public representative. How well messages are received, however, varies with the ability of a group to be heard above the general clamor, and with the understanding and clarity with which positions are presented.

The fourth category includes the financial interests recognized as having a special concern with monetary policy. It comprises the commercial banks, the government security dealers, other financial institutions such as savings and loans and insurance companies, and stockbrokers. All of these groups constantly make their presence felt in Washington through official committees, individual calls, letters, and publications aimed specifically at the Federal Reserve. They are important as a source of information on what is happening in the financial spheres and as the medium through which monetary policy influences the economy. On the other hand, they are recognized as special interest groups; their views and statements are carefully analyzed in that light.

The fifth line shows "Foreign Interests," which are foreign governments and central banks. They influence international monetary reserves and the exchange rate of the dollar. Again, as explained in Chapter 9, their influence varies greatly, depending upon the importance attached to international reserves by the President and upon the strength or weakness of the dollar in international exchanges.

The final category shows the other financial regulatory agencies, which include the FDIC, the Comptroller of the Currency, the Federal Home Loan Bank Board, and the Securities and Exchange Commission. All of these agencies have certain coordinate powers with the Federal Reserve.

Two Chairmen: Contrasts in Style and Approach

The reaction to the change in the Chairmanship illustrates two conflicting views on how to predict Federal Reserve action. One assumes continuity. What the Federal Reserve will do tomorrow can be predicted by referring to actions taken ten, twenty, or thirty years ago. The other holds that tomorrow's acts depend on the views and personality of the current Chairman. Clearly both views are extreme. The Chairmen both affect and are affected by the System itself. If the Federal Reserve primarily reflected its Chairman, each change in the Chairmanship would bring major shifts in policy. Policies and operations in the past ten years would have shifted more than they actually did.

Both Chairmen, Martin and Burns, have been dominant public figures. For nearly nineteen years, Bill Martin *was* the Federal Reserve to most of the public. After he took over, Burns also moved from backstage at the White House to the center of news interest. A comparison of the two men gives some idea as to how individual ideas, beliefs, and personalities create changes in monetary policy and doctrine.

Were Federal Reserve policy closely correlated with the physical characteristics of its Chairman, the replacement of Martin by Burns would have caused a complete about face in the Federal Reserve's actions. Outwardly the two men are opposites. Martin is slight of build, quick in speech and attitudes, athletic, an ex-champion tennis player who still plays an excellent game of tennis or squash almost daily. Burns is larger, stolid, stocky, giving the appearance of a determined man; he is slow in speech and movement. Martin is a nonsmoker. Burns is rarely seen without a pipe in the corner of his mouth. He appears always to be in the process of preparing his pipe or lighting it, actions which give more time for careful preparation of his thoughts, allowing ideas to emerge in a logical, constant flow, although spoken so quietly as to be almost inaudible.

Martin likes people and has the ability to put others at ease. His interest in individuals he felt to be a significant part of his job. He enjoyed talking to people in depth, trying to obtain a better feel for the economy and an understanding of the problems faced by people in every walk of life. In addition, he believed his job required interpretation of the Federal Reserve to others. One can truly say, in a slight alteration of Will Rogers's statement, that no man who really knew Bill Martin disliked him. Whenever I traveled throughout the world, people would make a point of meeting me in order to be remembered to Bill Martin. They wanted to express their great fondness for him.

Contrasting Views of the Function of Economics

While physical differences are interesting, they do not, of course, play a major role in monetary policy. However, the sharply contrasting views of two consecutive chairmen as to how the Federal Reserve should function are important in understanding the development of monetary doctrines and operations.

In many of his public statements, Chairman Martin made clear his view that the primary function of the Federal Reserve Board was to determine what was necessary to maintain a sound currency. This required, primarily, judgment as to whether the economy was in danger of inflation or deflation. The press frequently reported Martin's dismay over the number of economists appointed to the Board. He felt that the economy was too complex to explain in detail; intuition would be lost and false leads followed if too much stress were put on measurement. It was stated that he had opposed the nomination of Burns as Chairman on the ground that he would bring to the job too much of an economist's viewpoint instead of the necessary broad vision of a generalist.

Burns's view was almost diametrically opposed to that of Martin. He sees the Federal Reserve as primarily an economic agency which cannot function without a clear view of where the economy is and of what economic policy is necessary to move it closer to the best possible track. While he does not underestimate the difficulties of measurement and analysis of the current and future situation, he still makes it clear that good monetary policy requires good economic knowledge and judgment.

William McChesney Martin

Bill Martin has aptly been described as a fun-loving Puritan. He has a high sense of personal integrity. He is convinced of the need and advantages for both individuals and the country to maintain high economic standards. Among the many attempts to characterize the position of Chairman Martin, I think most apt is that which describes him as a "money moralist." Through speeches and writings over many years, his doctrine on money has become widely known. Money as Martin sees it is a basic moral force. Throughout history it has been misused by governments creating too much of it and depreciating its value. This is an immoral act. It is as immoral for a country today to allow the value of its currency to fall as it was for kings of old to clip coinage.

Martin has been almost universally described as the "symbol of monetary integrity." The Federal Reserve has the critical function of seeing that there is not too much money. The dollar must be protected from constant attacks, either from the government or from corporations or promoters seeking a free ride in financial markets. Martin's experience on Wall Street left many scars. He made it clear in speeches that he was concerned when elevator girls or shoeshine boys began to buy stock, fearing that this signaled irresponsibility and a possible return to the 1929 situation of uninformed speculation.

Martin's Federal Reserve was inward-looking in its relationship to the Administration and other groups in the economy. The importance of monetary policy made it vital that the Fed avoid entanglements with other groups which might, at critical times, restrain it from making its necessary moves. The fact that the Fed was governed by a board of seven members with terms spread over a long period enabled it to make independent judgments as to the cost of inflation for the future. It was given political independence so that it would be able, when necessary, to point out that the public interest required a halt to inflationary pressures.

While it was agreed that the Federal Reserve must cooperate with the Administration, great tension was sometimes produced by the conflict between independence of views and the necessity to coordinate policies. I would judge that an important shift occurred in Martin's position on this subject during the course of his eighteen-year tenure. For much of the period he apparently felt that the Federal Reserve should not be represented in Administration policy making unless it was absolutely necessary. Such discussions by the Federal Reserve with the Administration could lock the Federal Reserve in at times when it might feel that policy shifts were necessary. During most of the Eisenhower Administration, particularly when George Humphrey was secretary of the Treasury, even the relationships between the Federal Reserve and the Treasury were formal. At critical times the Federal Reserve took action which the Administration opposed, clearly a reaction to the previous period when the Treasury had dominated Federal Reserve actions.

When Robert Anderson became secretary of the Treasury, he met more often with Martin, and the isolation of the Federal Reserve began to end. President Kennedy made it a matter of policy to meet frequently with Martin, both out of a personal liking for the Chairman and apparently out of fear that the Federal Reserve, unless handled properly, would not cooperate in the desired economic expansion.

The insistence of both the Kennedy and Johnson Administrations on a coordinated fiscal and monetary policy led to greater emphasis on the Quadriad to advise the President. While Chairman Martin sat with the Quadriad and offered the Federal Reserve's views with respect to specific policies, he made it clear that the Fed retained the right to dissent from the views of the Administration or of the other members of the Quadriad when they were sent to the President. In addition, the right was maintained to disagree with the President's decisions if necessary.

Many people are surprised that Martin, appointed originally by

Truman and reappointed by Eisenhower, Kennedy, and Johnson, was a Democrat and continued to consider himself one. But his politics remained in the background because he felt so strongly that the Federal Reserve had to be completely nonpartisan. This did not mean that the Federal Reserve could be completely nonpolitical. On the contrary, it could operate freely only if it maintained a firm base of political support throughout the country. It was important, though, that the political support be nonpartisan.

Martin felt it vital to build up sufficient local strength, particularly among those with power and the interest to use it, to insure that the Federal Reserve would be free of domination by the President or Congress. He wanted it known that the Federal Reserve stood for the public interest and that it was one of the few bodies that did so. Thus, when unpopular positions had to be taken, there would be a base for popular support, or at least support among those in the Establishment with the ability to make themselves heard. Consequently one of Martin's major efforts as Chairman was to promote the image of the Federal Reserve throughout the country. He did this by direct example, by speeches, and by the use of the Regional Banks and their boards of directors.

In line with this posture, Martin avoided taking stands or expressing views in areas outside the monetary field. He was concerned that if the Federal Reserve offered advice, advice would be thrust upon it in return, causing it to lose some of its freedom of action in the critical monetary field.

In the same way, the Federal Reserve had to be sensitive to the political pressures on Congress and the Administration. It had to remain as free of politics as possible so that when it acted it would not embarrass those who had to act for political reasons. As a matter of policy, the Federal Reserve avoids attacking individual politicians and their ideas; even when under bitter attack from particular congressmen or segments of the Administration, the Federal Reserve has attempted to answer in a restrained, factual manner.

As another example of its nonpartisanship, Federal Reserve policy has always been to avoid, if possible, taking any major monetary actions as elections approach. This follows from the view that the Fed can better perform its long-run functions if its does not become the focal point of political battles.

Since Martin's philosophy played such an important role in the development of Federal Reserve doctrine during his tenure, it is significant to discussions of the Federal Reserve's approach to monetary policy and operations. Martin often characterized himself as a man skilled in the interpretation of financial markets. He pointed out again and again the inability of everyone, including himself, to explain movements in the money supply—a fact which led him to put his faith in the tone and feel of financial markets as opposed to specific measurements.

Believing in the importance of psychological reactions, Chairman Martin had very little faith in the value of attempting to quantify Federal Reserve policy. In his opinion, measurement was dangerous, if not impossible: Numbers obtained would not accurately reflect real conditions and the Fed could do best by carefully evaluating events in the financial markets. He consequently spent a great deal of his own time in this pursuit. Through a wide network of friends and meetings with bankers, he was always extremely well informed as to what was occurring in financial circles. The Federal Reserve had to be concerned with the impact of its operations on market psychology. Its moves, even if made gradually, would create announcement effects. Dealers and others intimately involved would recognize that Fed policy had changed and would adjust their operations accordingly. Market psychology would spread to the banks, whose loans and loan commitments would be affected.

On the basis of its knowledge of the markets, the Federal Reserve acted to adjust the degree of ease with which money could be obtained. One might picture the Federal Reserve as operating like a giant rubberband: As the markets became too ebullient or expansionary, they would have to push harder and harder against the restraining action of Federal Reserve policy. If the markets or the economy were becoming too deflationary, the Federal Reserve would attempt to ease the pressure.

Banks could also be influenced directly through moral suasion. It was assumed that the major banks recognized the importance of their roles in fighting inflation and would, therefore, operate in accordance with the public interest. One of the principal functions of the Chairman of the Federal Reserve was to make clear to the banks, through speeches and private meetings, what the public interest consisted of and how they could cooperate in protecting the dollar.

In 1969, the largest banks were expanding credit rapidly, contrary to general monetary policy, by borrowing dollars in Europe and relending them in the United States. These funds, in so-called Euro-dollars, were not subject to reserve requirements. In fact, through a subterfuge, some of the largest banks were using these transactions to reduce sharply their normal reserve requirements. As a result, each Euro-dollar transaction caused a double increase in credit. This appeared to be a case in which moral suasion might work. The primary activity in the Euro-dollar market was concentrated in less than a dozen banks. The Federal Reserve could issue regulations covering these transactions; but, if banks cooperated voluntarily instead, they could retain a good deal of flexibility. They would have a safety valve which they could use in emergencies. Consequently, Chairman Martin asked them to restrain voluntarily their importation of Euro-dollars. However, the voluntary program collapsed rapidly. As individual banks came under pressure, they ceased to cooperate and, instead, met their desired credit expansion by continuing to borrow funds abroad. Banks which were cooperating complained bitterly that they were being unfair to their stockholders; they could not continue unless their competitors did. As a result, the Federal Reserve had to issue a rather complex regulation. Its effect and policing caused constant problems for both the banks and the Fed.

While the public view of Chairman Martin was certainly that of a deflationist, one who, on the whole, sought tighter money throughout his chairmanship, I do not think that this is a correct reading of the record. In the spectrum of the Board and the Open Market Committee, during most of the 1960s he was either on the expansionist side or in the middle. His own personal views of the economy favored maximum possible growth and a financial structure that made this possible.

He was, however, probably less expansionist than the Administration. His belief that most currencies lost value because of budget deficits made it difficult for Martin to accept the new economic view that fiscal policy was based on a relative rather than an absolute standard. It was hard to believe that whether budgets should be in surplus or deficit depended on whether or not aggregate demand in the economy was excess, and not on some arbitrary concept of balance. As a result, Martin occasionally issued strong statements on the need for a balanced budget. However, the Federal Reserve did not operate so as to attempt to offset budgetary deficits. On the contrary, many academic critics have argued that it gave too much support to budget deficits. I believe, however, that the Fed was primarily neutral with respect to the budget, although the last half of 1968 was perhaps an exception.

On the whole, Martin believed that the Federal Reserve ought to accommodate normal growth. However, the amount of attention paid to financial markets meant that too little account was devoted to how the overall economy was performing in relation to its potential. This led, at times, to a tendency to tighten credit too soon.

Arthur F. Burns

Chairman Burns approaches monetary policy as a trained economist who is also one of the country's foremost experts on the business cycle. In contrast to Martin, in policy making he has sought more and more information and better and better measurement.

Burns started out with the reputation of a semimonetarist, placing considerable emphasis on the money supply. For the year prior to becoming Chairman, he had been a special counselor to President Nixon in the White House. During that period, numerous monetarist statements issued from both the White House staff and the President himself. However, experience with the problems of operating the Federal Reserve has deepened Burns's understanding of monetary policy. Never doctrinaire, his views have become increasingly eclectic. Policy is made in the real world, not the abstract world of theory.

Burns has been more involved than Martin with the political process in Washington. He has devoted more effort to relations with Congress. His concerns have encompassed the entire scope of the Administration's economic programs, while Martin primarily considered their impact on the Federal Reserve. In their relationships to the President, Burns has been a general economic adviser;

Martin's role was more largely limited to monetary developments. While attempting to be nonpolitical as Chairman of the Federal Reserve, he could not fully suppress either his ideology or his personal relationships: His strong belief in President Nixon's policies was frequently visible. While Chairman Martin hesitated to intervene in Administration plans, this has not been the case with Chairman Burns. As a former head of the Council of Economic Advisers and White House adviser, his concern has been with overall macroeconomic policy. Monetary policy is only a part of the total picture. Because its success or failure depends on the budget and other governmental activities, monetary policy must be coordinated with other government programs.

In addition to his awareness of his own value as an economic adviser, Burns recognized the excellence of the Federal Reserve's economic staff. Given these two factors, he saw the Fed's role as one of innovator, supporter, and public pleader for good macropolicy. The Federal Reserve, if successful in this role, could influence economic policy as much as or even more than through its direct actions in the monetary field.

Burns spends much time on general economic policies not necessarily related to those of the Federal Reserve. In addition to being an adviser to the Cost of Living Council and a frequent adviser to the President, Burns was appointed chairman of the Committee on Interest Rates and Dividends in 1971. He played an active role in convincing Congress to pass legislation allowing the government to guarantee loans to major corporations such as Lockheed.

An illustration of the new activist role of the Fed Chairman is evident in the events attendant on the birth of the new economic policy in August 1971. Had Martin still been Chairman, he probably would have participated in some of the planning of the new economic program, or at least would have been called in to help obtain agreement on the international aspects, but Burns was present from the beginning as a personal adviser to the President. He played a major role in planning the program, helped to determine its initial shape, and then, as a member of the Cost of Living Council, monitored new programs as they developed. Only a few of these functions could be considered responsibilities of the Federal Reserve.

Another interesting contrast between Martin and Burns appears in their attitude toward Wall Street. Martin, coming from the stock market, was well aware of its problems. He was concerned that the market not become a speculative danger to the country. He feared a repetition of 1929 and was always on guard lest too rapid a rise in stock prices lead to a future sharp fall and deflation. Burns, on the other hand, shares the view that the stock market is a critical determinant of the country's economic future. It is necessary to treat the market delicately and to feed its concerns and ego. Success in this effort will increase confidence and improve the level of spending and output in the country.

Burns remains at heart a National Bureau of Economic Research business cycle economist. He supplements the Fed staff work with his own sources of information and a personal evaluation of the current status of the economy and of optimum macroeconomic policy. He increased the emphasis of the Federal Reserve on the problems of recession and stressed its functions as a lender of last resort. He was one of the strongest advocates in Washington of attempting to keep the Penn Central from going bankrupt and, failing that, to minimize the secondary reactions of the financial markets to the bankruptcy. His approach is pragmatic. More importantly, however, he knows from history that monetary policy has to prevent the secondary credit liquidation that caused severe depressions in the past, even though furnishing the liquidity to avoid such crunches reduces the impact of monetary policy on inflationary expectations.

Most of those who experienced the change of chairmen were extremely thankful that Burns was a trained economist. 1970 and 1971 were successful years for the Federal Reserve because Burns assumed the Chairmanship with an understanding of the economy and a knowledge of past recessions, depressions, and crises. Learning to understand the operations of the Federal Reserve System alone is an immense and time-consuming task. If, in addition, an incoming Chairman had to bone up on fiscal policy, monetary policy, and the role of the Fed therein, a disastrous hiatus or impasse in monetary policy could occur.

Watching this transition, I was repeatedly struck by the thought of how dangerous it would be for the economy if, in the future, a new Chairman of the Federal Reserve was not well trained in economics. A *sine qua non* for the position is a thorough understanding of the economy in general and of the role government economic policy plays in its functioning. The need for this knowledge is so great that it probably could not be acquired quickly enough and completely enough by anyone who has not spent at least part of his career as a professional economist.

The Sources of the Chairman's Power

The length of the bar marked "Chairman" in Chart 2 illustrates the paramount role that he plays in the monetary process. What are the factors that give him this power?

On some regulatory boards and commissions in Washington the chairman wields little more power than the other members. This is far from the case in the Federal Reserve, however, even though the Chairman has only one vote out of seven and legally there is little difference between him and the other Board members. The Federal Reserve Act states, "The Chairman of the Board, subject to its supervision, shall be the active executive officer." At many times in the past, most of the power of the System has been concentrated in the Chairman.

The Chairman's power arises from five major extralegal sources: First, his appointment makes him the titular head of and the spokesman for the Federal Reserve System. It is assumed that the Chairman's voice reflects System policy. But, even if this were not the case, it is often true in fact because of announcement effects. Second, the Chairman represents the System and he participates in many decisions which never come before the Board. The acts of representation and participation carry power per se. Third, any chairmanship carries certain inherent powers, such as the selection of the agenda and the leadership of meetings, which at times influence decisions. Fourth, the Federal Reserve Board has delegated much of its supervisory powers over the staff and the System to the Chairman, thus increasing his actual strength. And, finally, a less tangible strength is his ability, because of his other powers, to attract extra votes at Board and FOMC meetings.

While the influence of the Chairman is indeed great, he does not make policy alone. At times he may even feel that he is a prisoner of the staff, the other members of the Board, or the Federal Open Market Committee. The limits on his time and energy force him to depend on others for advice and for operations. While any policy he believes in strongly is likely to be adopted in the end, the influence of his colleagues has a great deal to do with its form and timing. Thus, to make his power effective, the Chairman must spend considerable time in negotiations. He cannot issue orders and must use his powers carefully. The Federal Reserve Act has wisely given the power to manage money to a group rather than to an individual.

There are some policies which Chairmen have opposed but found they could not change, since a majority of the Board members must concur. A good example is the use of interest rate ceilings on deposits (Regulation Q) as a monetary constraint. Martin at various times was unhappy about ceilings. Burns made his opposition clear both within the System and in public. Still the policies remained in effect until mid-1973 because the majority of the Board felt that ceilings were a lesser evil than other alternatives. Despite the Chairmen's opposition the regulation stayed on the books.

The Chairman As Official Spokesman

A major function of the Federal Reserve Board is to testify before congressional committees on Board policy, on general economic conditions, or on proposed legislation which affects the Board or upon which it has expertise. For most testimony the Chairman will, if possible, represent the Board. Other members do appear when the Chairman cannot or when a member has a particular expertise. However, in the three years from 1970 through 1972, Chairman Burns presented twenty-three statements; the other six members together testified ten times. In many of these cases, they appeared as personal experts rather than as spokesmen for the Board itself.

Although the policy statements read by the Chairman are voted on by the Board as a whole, his personal judgments can, and frequently do, dominate a statement. While statements reflect the Chairman's own style and current views, the Board as a whole frequently changes some positions, inserts other ideas, and may deemphasize certain points important to the Chairman but not acceptable to a majority. Nevertheless, in my experience, most final statements follow closely the Chairman's original draft.

Most testimony is followed by a question-and-answer period during which the Chairman speaks for himself, although with limited responsibility to the other Board members. He can and often does stress his own personal points of view, many of which may never have been considered as Board policy. Frequently the questions and answers dominate the hearings and the press reports, rather than the original statement.

It is not always recognized, however, that other speeches of Board members, including the Chairman, reflect individual points of view rather than general policy. It is often assumed that a speech by any member, and particularly by the Chairman, is an expression of Board policy. Since the Chairman's views get wide publicity, they may lead to major changes in expectations and, as a result, to changes in actual policy even though they initially reflected a purely personal viewpoint.

The Chairman As Representative of the System

Probably more important than the Chairman's role as public spokesman is his representation of the Federal Reserve in meetings with other governmental and important private organizations. The Federal Reserve sits on many government committees which formulate and coordinate economic policies. Important committees of this type deal with balance of payments problems, international monetary negotiations, the cost of living, and many other areas. On these, as well as on *ad hoc* government committees established to consider particular questions, such as credit controls or credit shortages, the Fed is usually represented by the Chairman.

If individual congressmen or community leaders have ideas or want information about Federal Reserve policy, their automatic contact is the Chairman. Similarly, when the President seeks spe-

cific economic advice, he calls the Chairman, asks for the view of
the Quadriad, or asks his staff to obtain the view of the Federal
Reserve on a particular policy matter. In most such cases, although
he may delegate the responsibility to other members of the Board
or to the staff, the Chairman represents the Board.

It is most difficult to insure that the views expressed in outside
meetings reflect Board and not individual positions. In theory,
when problems involve Board policy, the Board as a whole is consulted. However, in fact, few requests are made to the Board for its
advice. As a result, the input of the Federal Reserve into governmental policies frequently depends upon its representative at a
meeting. An individual's particular knowledge, his willingness to
speak, and how he handles himself may have a greater impact than
does the official Board policy or the System's legal rights.

The Powers of the Chair

The right to select the agenda and to chair meetings can be powerful tools in any committee system. The Chairman's ability to shape
debate at times increases the effectiveness of his position.

The power to control the agenda has not been used frequently,
although in several cases both Martin and Burns, uncertain as to
the advisability of proposed new regulations, caused long delays
and consequently the failure to adopt policies which a majority of
the Board appeared to support by not putting them on the agenda.
Regulations for changing discount operations, for adopting reserves
for importing Euro-dollars, and for changing the form of reserve
requirements were postponed this way. While the reasons for these
delays were never clear, the Chairmen apparently believed that
their added responsibilities as the System's spokesmen and representatives made it proper to hold off the desires of the majority
until they were personally convinced that a change was wise.

Related to his control over the agenda is the Chairman's prerogative in chairing a meeting to call on members in a particular se-
quence, to interject personal views, and to formulate the way in
which decisions are put for the Committee. This enables him, wit-
tingly or unwittingly, to use his position to influence System policy
by shaping the debate. The Federal Reserve operates under flexi-

ble parliamentary rules and Board tradition attempts to insure for each member his say on a policy.

The powers of the chair have been particularly important in the Open Market Committee, where the number of speakers is large, the decisions are complex, and the range of debate is wide. Both Chairman Martin and Chairman Burns used their position in somewhat the same way: If no critical questions threatened or if decisions seemed fairly cut and dried, they would act in a relaxed manner, allowing discussion to wander and calling the question only when everyone was completely talked out. On the other hand, when a matter was critical or when they were in doubt as to how the final decision would go, they did not hesitate to state their views early in the meeting and to interject them strongly as the debate developed. They used such a tactic only occasionally, but when they did the impact was considerable. A strong statement by the Chairman early in the meeting is influential and transforms the debating atmosphere.

In cases they considered important, both Chairmen felt free to use their position and the lack of formal parliamentary procedures to put votes in a form most likely to promote their own position. For example, if they preferred a broad rather than a narrow range of interest rates, they would put the broadest range first. In this way they would avoid the possibility that, if a narrower range was voted upon earlier, it might achieve a majority. Similarly, on occasion, each Chairman used his prerogative to sum up the discussion, thus making certain that the manager carried away an interpretation compatible with his own. While individual members could object to the summation, it is difficult under normal procedures to achieve a new vote. But, since the manager usually heard the entire debate, he could also be asked for his own summation.

This type of maneuvering is probably no more, and possibly a good deal less, prevalent in the Federal Reserve than in many similar committee situations. Certainly it appears to be far less frequent than what is reported in the committees of Congress. In any case, it does increase the Chairman's influence in determining System policy and it helps to insure that the position of the Federal Reserve does not differ too much from that held by the Chairman.

The Chairman's Administrative Reponsibility

The Federal Reserve Act gives the responsibility for administration, hiring and firing, paying and controlling the staff, to the Board as a whole. The Board has delegated these duties to the Chairman, aided by the executive director and a member of the Board, because the time required to administer the Board staff of more than twelve hundred individuals would be inordinate. However, the Board continues to approve budgets, all salary increases, and all appointments to official positions, and the Board members receive a weekly report on all actions taken under delegated authority. They may also request that any particular action be delayed and voted upon by the Board as a whole, but such actions are rare.

The staff gives the highest priority to the Chairman's needs and projects. Because top advisers must work closely with the Chairman, the Board is agreed that they must be personally acceptable to him. Any advisers whose ideas constantly conflict with the Chairman's will naturally move or be moved. On the other hand, divergences from the views of individual members of the Board are frequent. Both the Board and the staff take great pride in the fact that the staff is urged to, and does, take an independent view of the state of the economy, where it is going, and what changes in policy may be necessary. They have the right, which they frequently exercise, to present dissenting opinions from those of the Chairman or a majority of the Board. But it is also true that subtle pressure is put on the staff when the Chairman takes a strong view contrary to their opinion.

The Chairman's Ability to Attract Votes

Because the Chairman has special responsibilities and prerogatives, he attracts votes from members of the Board or the FOMC to his position simply by virtue of his office. According to my rule of thumb, when the Chairman cast his vote, he automatically carried with him at least one other vote at any meeting of the Board and two other votes at any FOMC meeting. The members who make their decisions primarily on the strength of his opinion are not necessarily the same from meeting to meeting. Such influence of votes can be attributed to the fact that in recent years, in most debates, the Chairman has been close to the center of the spectrum of opinion, which has meant that voting with him has not required much, if any, shift of views.

Continuity

Although there are indeed rather sharp contrasts between the personalities, economic beliefs, and views of the Federal Reserve's role held by Burns and Martin, it would be appropriate to conclude by mentioning some of the major areas where they were in substantial agreement. Basically both Martin and Burns maintained a strong faith in the importance of monetary policy as a means of achieving the nation's economic well-being. They believed that the Federal Reserve had a major role to play in formulating and operating national economic policy. They saw the job of Chairman as a vital one of insuring that the Federal Reserve pursued the policies necessary to achieve the nation's economic goals. They felt that every channel ought to be used to gain the widest possible acceptance of necessary policies to maximize their impact on actual events.

Both men were extremely pragmatic and nondoctrinaire. While maintaining strong beliefs and confidence in their own judgments, they were willing to compromise and deal flexibly with pressures emanating from the White House and from Congress. The fable of the great oak uprooted in the strong wind while the smaller trees which bent survived holds a pertinent lesson for the Federal Reserve.

Because even minor suspicions could impair the Federal Reserve's basic mission, constant vigilance is necessary to insure that the System operates in the most ethical manner possible. No monetary policy should be endangered by personal shortcomings. This also means that the Federal Reserve has to have as clean a regulatory record as possible. Any suspicion that a lobby or an individual bank has been able to sway the Federal Reserve Board must be avoided.

The record in this sphere has been excellent. Even Congressman Patman, while generally critical of the policy decisions of the Federal Reserve, has frequently commented on how fortunate the country has been that the large and, to his mind, undue powers granted to the Federal Reserve have been exercised by men of undoubted probity. Because of the reputation which the Federal Reserve has gained in its regulatory capacity, it constantly has to urge Congress not to add to its regulatory powers and oversight.

When decisions had to be made on the trade-off between price and output pressures, both Burns and Martin were usually very close to the center of the Federal Reserve System opinion, although they leaned somewhat more toward expansion and full employment than the average member of the Federal Open Market Committee, and probably slightly more toward contraction than the other members of the Board. But this also meant that they were less active proponents of expansion than a typical congressman or member of a Democratic administration. Because they were close to the center and because they could influence strongly one or two other votes, their position tended to coincide with that of the Board and the Open Market Committee as a whole. This was not always the case, however. Some splits were so sharp that even their added votes were insufficient to carry the day. When they failed to get the votes, they settled for the best possible compromise.

At times both Chairmen have found this inability to control the System frustrating, begrudging the time spent in the negotiations to carry their views. On the other hand, since they accepted the concept that joint decisions are preferable to those made by an individual, these efforts were inevitable. Both probably would agree, however, that the Open Market Committee is too large for the most efficient discussions and decisions.

Finally, in their views of the Board's role in the international monetary sphere, Burns and Martin were also close. Both were internationalists, believing that a stable international situation would have a major favorable impact on the internal economy of the

United States. Consequently, to a greater degree than the majority of the Board, they favored maintaining the *status quo,* even when to do so was difficult and expensive. On the other hand, while emphasizing the advantages of international cooperation and trade, they were not willing to sacrifice very much in the way of domestic output in response to pleas for international cooperation.

These areas of agreement are common to most members of the Federal Reserve Board. They form part of a body of tradition that lends continuity to policy, even as individuals come and go, and makes it possible to generalize about Federal Reserve policies on the basis of decisions made in the past.

CHAPTER SEVEN

The Makers of Monetary Policy: The Board and Other Influences

DURING THE PAST DECADE, there has been a steady development of the role played by the Federal Reserve in economic policy making. In the light of the many controversies and confrontations of recent years, it is now possible to draw a clearer picture of how the Fed interacts with other groups in this pursuit. Awareness has increased that monetary policy is only one among many policy tools which must be coordinated for maximum effectiveness in the effort to achieve our national goals.

While there are still no formal policy statements as to how the Federal Reserve sees its function, I believe that there are three primary responsibilities that the Fed ought to and does implement in the field of economic policy making:

—Operating monetary policy in a dynamic economy in the fairest, most efficient manner

—Analyzing the economy and coordinating monetary policy with other policies to insure the maximum likelihood of achieving the nation's economic goals

—Taking action, if necessary, to thwart attempts by the government to abuse the power to create money for mistaken purposes, such as reducing the cost of the public debt at the expense of growth or stability

Many press reports and speeches by Federal Reserve officials between 1950 and 1965 give the impression that the Fed had another responsibility, namely the duty to seek price stability even at the expense of growth, output, and employment.

The Fed has often been pictured as an independent referee, ready to blow the whistle on economic decisons made elsewhere in the government; however, it is hard to find any direct expression of this philosophy in official Federal Reserve statements. The Federal Reserve Act and the Employment Act of 1946—the two basic congressional directives to the System—do not suggest this role; nor is it evident in legal or constitutional theory. The Federal Reserve Act contains a delegation of authority to act specifically with respect to money and credit with a limited set of objectives: "to furnish an elastic currency," "to accommodate commerce and business," and to act "with regard to their bearing upon the general credit situation" and so that no "injurious or undue credit expansion" occurs. The Employment Act is a broader statement of goals for the federal government as a whole, specifying that the government should "coordinate and utilize all of its plans, functions and resources . . . to promote maximum employment, production, and purchasing power."

In any case, it seems evident that some officials in the System and some of its supporters saw the Fed's role as one of a counterweight to any government tendency to seek economic goals with which the Fed disagreed. It is hard to estimate how widespread this belief was because the Fed's actions were so often clothed in secrecy and mystery. My guess is that there was a confusion among policies, actions, and goals. The Fed did not explicitly try to move the economy away from the goals sought by the rest of the government, but it does not seem to have been recognized that monetary policies used vigorously to control credit creation did play a major role in determining whether the national goals could be achieved. In the 1950s the Fed was correctly criticized for not allowing the economy to achieve the goal of full employment, for instance.

Because its own history, as well as that of other central banks, had taught it to beware of government abuse of the privilege to create money, the Federal Reserve overemphasized the need for independence, at the expense of coordination. This led to an insufficient emphasis on nonmonetary tools and on the duties and policies of other government agencies in the economic sphere. As the government's major responsibilities to promote prosperity and avoid recession, to stabilize prices and curb inflation have become more widely accepted, monetary policy has been recognized as only one of many instruments to be played in the economic ensemble.

The Sources of Federal Reserve Influence

Since 1966 there has been increased emphasis on the Fed's external role of attempting to insure the proper coordination of monetary policy into the overall package of economic policies, in addition to its own internal monetary operations. The experiences of the sixties and seventies (the Vietnam War, the balance of payments problems, and the inflationary crisis) showed that, for successful achievement of national goals, it was not enough for monetary policy simply to be added onto or used to offset other governmental policies. It gradually became apparent that the overall decision-making process of the government would be improved if Federal Reserve input occurred all along the line rather than only at the final level, when it was often too late to influence policy. As a result, the Federal Reserve presence became common in numerous governmental working groups. For instance, significant contributions were made by the Fed in formulating the new policies for gold and special drawing rights in the International Monetary Fund, for post-1966 housing policy, wage-price controls, and many other programs.

Despite this more frequent collaboration, relationships between the Fed and other government bodies remain delicate. It is much easier to work with someone who ultimately has to agree than with an independent voice, and there is always a reluctance to share information without being able to control its use. Sometimes I have wondered whether the more recent secretaries of the Treasury and the chairmen of the CEA, when they were defeated on certain policy questions, might not have felt they had lost by their efforts to get the Fed involved; they may well have wished they could return to the days when the Board was treated like a foreign sovereignty.

The Federal Reserve learned that it had other problems far greater than protecting the coinage from secretaries of the Treasury. The tendency to overwork monetary policy or to use it as an excuse for avoiding other action was clearly more serious. It has become obvious that nonmonetary methods may be cheaper and more effective means to economic health than monetary policy. The Fed is now only slightly reticent in speaking out for changes in taxes, expenditures, or incomes policies when economic conditions seem to warrant it.

One of the principal values of the Federal Reserve's independent position is that it can speak out and be heard at the highest levels. Sound, independent voices in Washington are important.

Because of its special relationship with Congress, which has been criticized for its inferior economic staff work, the Fed is able to assist with analysis and with its best opinion on pending bills, legislation, and programs, even at the risk of embarrassing its relationships with the Administration. By the same token, however, the Federal Reserve can go directly to the President, if necessary, to express its views on economic matters. Because of its structure, the Fed's decisions are free from immediate political implications. Such independent advice may be extremely valuable to the President, who does have political responsibilities and sometimes needs wider options than those he gets from his staff, which may have any number of biases. The Fed provides well-informed opinion that at least gives the President the opportunity to look at an alternate view of the economy.

The extent to which the Federal Reserve should present its views to the public before the President has made a decision or after he has rejected them is less clear. Should the Federal Reserve as a System or Board members as individuals try to convince the public that current economic goals are wrong or that existing policies will fail to achieve them? Although the matter is a delicate one, on the whole the Fed has been willing to speak out, attempting to make clear that any disagreement with the Administration is based on a different analysis or interpretation of the national interest, not on partisanship.

In this spirit, Chairman Martin spoke out frequently with respect to budget policy, and Chairman Burns called for an incomes policy. As a Board member, I gave speeches on the problem of gold and the need for reform in the international monetary field. Other Board members have discussed foreign credit restraints, credit controls, and similar matters related to Fed interests, but not its direct responsibility. Fed members as individuals have made many important contributions to economic discussions.

I have sometimes speculated as to what makes the pronouncements of Fed officials important. Perhaps it is the unique features of the Fed's position: People believe that it is independent, concerned with the national interest, and has the power to support its position. The amount of power may be overestimated, however. Although no legal method exists for the President to issue a directive to the System, its independence in fact is not so great that it can use monetary policy as a club or threat to veto Administration action. The System's latitude for action is rather circumscribed, as I believe it should be. In any showdown, no nonrepresentative group such as the Fed can or should be allowed to pursue its own goals in opposition to those of the elected officials.

The Federal Reserve's ability to maintain its influential position rests on four cornerstones: its budgetary freedom, the long terms of and immunity to removal of Board members, its ability to hire an excellent staff, and its long-standing nonpartisan reputation for seeking the public interest. The importance of nonpartisanship has already been discussed in Chapter 6. A brief expansion of the other three points follows.

To an outsider, an unexpected feature of Washington is the degree to which he who holds the purse strings, whether in the Administration or in a congressional committee, calls the tune in theoretically semi-independent agencies. Valuable programs have been emasculated and critical public policy measures and regulations have been poorly implemented because agencies were denied funds to perform their legal functions well. The Federal Reserve, however, utilizes a minor part of the earnings of its open market operations for its expenses and is thus not dependent upon either the Administration or Congress for appropriations. (Most of the remainder of its earnings is turned over to the Treasury.)

While fourteen years is a long term of office, extended tenure, plus the fact that they can be removed from office only for cause and not at a political whim, allows Federal Reserve Board members true independence in their decision making. It is quite another case when members of a regulatory body are concerned over their reappointment or possible removal.

If the Federal Reserve lacked analytical capacity and creativity, the freedom it enjoys could be harmful rather than constructive. But the Fed's independence, flexibility, and nonpartisan reputation have enabled it to hire and retain one of the finest staffs in Washington. The only other economic group which has compared over the years in quality of staff is the Council of Economic Advisers.

In listing the factors which give the Federal Reserve its voice, I have not mentioned one which many in the System believe most important, but which I do not: the idea that the regional Banks and their numerous directors provide a significant grass-roots political base. Federal Reserve policy states that Reserve Bank directors are in a position and have a duty to interpret monetary policy to interested people in their respective districts. It is important that System policies and the reasons for them be understood by businessmen, bankers, and others in order that the sound features of such policies be accepted and supported. Conversely, defects will be pointed out. Chairman Martin in particular often stressed to the directors and to business groups that enlightened self-interest would insure that sound monetary policy had major political support throughout the country. The regional Banks were thought of as a major base for such support.

The Functions of Federal Reserve Board Members

In my travels around the country, meeting with a variety of groups and individuals, I was often asked to describe what I did as a governor of the Federal Reserve System. No one seemed to have a very clear picture of what functions a Board member performed.

There are three basic ways in which Board members can influence economic policy:

—By their debates and votes they shape the decisions which daily come before the Board on the current agenda.

—They influence future monetary policy through such debates and, more significantly, through any ideas, new concepts, doctrines, and procedures which they help to develop.

—They have an impact on economic events in general through their speeches, their consulting with Congress, and their relationships with other parts of the government.

There have been times when the powers of the individual members of the Federal Reserve Board have been squeezed between those of the Chairman and the staff. While each member has an equal vote on all issues that come officially before the Board, if many questions are handled through negotiation with other agencies, or if the Board functions primarily to vote on staff proposals, the power of the vote may not carry much weight in itself. As an example, I note in Chapter 9 (see pages 222–27) that because of the way in which international issues reached the Board during my tenure, individual governors had very little input in that field. On domestic issues, in contrast, while I was on the Board, because most of the individual members were extremely able and hard working, their contributions to policy were significant and were greater than was true of many Boards of the past. However, in general, as shown in Chart 2, I judge the power of the Board members, not including the Chairman, to be less than that of the staff.

Allotment of Time

In reviewing how my time was actually spent, I find that in a typical month I attended twenty-three meetings with formal groups, lasting from one to three hours each.

—The Federal Reserve Board itself met eleven times.

—The FOMC met once.

—The Board met three times with other bodies, such as bankers' representatives, the academic consultants to the Board, or other advisory groups.

—I attended five committee meetings concerned with the operations of the Federal Reserve System. Two of these were system-

wide committees, composed of some Board members and some of the Federal Reserve Bank presidents. Three were meetings of Board subcommittees, such as personnel or budget.
—Three meetings were with other governmental groups; for example, a committee of the Senate and intergovernmental committees on credit policies or housing.

In a typical month I also gave two or three speeches to civic, financial, banking, and academic groups throughout the country. And sprinkled throughout the month, in addition to the formal meetings, were numerous encounters with individuals and the staff of the Federal Reserve.

While the number above seems large, I believe members of the Federal Reserve probably spend less time in meetings and have more time for reading, writing, and thinking than most high-level officials in Washington. For instance, I spent one-third to one-half of my time with others or on the phone and had one-half to two-thirds of my time available for concentrated thought and research on Federal Reserve problems.

Another and perhaps more important perspective is how time is apportioned among responsibilities. Between 50 and 60 percent of my time was spent on monetary policy, including an ongoing review of the economy, the financial markets, and the international sphere, as well as a study of current monetary policy. Other time in this primary category was spent on intermediate- and longer-term projects concerned with trying to clarify and improve Federal Reserve monetary operations. The regulation of bank holding companies and banks was my second most time-consuming function, occupying 15 to 20 percent of my time. Operations of the Federal Reserve System was a third responsibility, occupying about 10 percent of my time. The System has twenty-three thousand employees, mainly engaged in operating the economy's payments mechanism, although some also perform monetary and regulatory functions. The Board oversees them in a general way, attempting to improve the System's functioning.

As the need for a coordinated economic policy became more evident, the Federal Reserve began to spend more time consulting with other governmental agencies, the Administration, and Congress. We advised on economic policies in areas such as fiscal policy, the operations of financial markets, general credit policy, the impact of federal borrowing on money, and similar matters. Such consultation requires not only meeting with others but, more importantly, preparing position papers or reviewing the papers presented by other participants. Such activity occupied 10 to 20 percent of my time. Finally, there was the need to provide public information and to make speeches explaining the operations of the System, what monetary policy was about, what monetary policy was attempting to do, and so forth. This took up the final 10 percent of my total time.

It is sometimes suggested that the Federal Reserve Board should be relieved of responsibility for bank regulation or the operations of the Federal Reserve System, on the assumption that these functions interfere with the making of monetary policy. I think these suggestions are based upon a misconception of the time available to the Board. I found that it took only one-half of my total time to prepare fully for all matters requiring current decisions. Included in this time, in addition to the regulatory and operating functions, were the preparation for and debate on the FOMC's directive as well as consideration of the use of the monetary instruments within the control of the Board. Each week a complete review of the economy, monetary developments, and possible monetary action takes place. In my experience there was always adequate time to prepare fully for this Board discussion, as well as for the required decisions in the regulatory and operating fields. (I might note, however, that, because of his much broader responsibilities, the Chairman does have difficulty in freeing the time for these functions.) Beyond the day-to-day decisions, the other half of my time was available for developing in-depth concepts, theories, and new ideas, both in the monetary sphere and in the other areas of Board responsibility.

Measuring the time one spends on individual topics gives no real indication of what one is accomplishing. Performance depends upon what decisions are actually made and how good or bad they are. I considered it my responsibility as a Board member not only to discuss and vote on current issues, but also, and most importantly, to try to influence future monetary and economic policy.

Both while serving in Washington and in reviewing the record subsequently, I felt that influencing the future was more significant than most current votes.

Providing New Ideas

It is vital to sit back to examine current and future problems in quiet without being interrupted. Many top officials in Washington attend so many meetings and are so busy coordinating and administering that they have little time to reflect. As I arrived in Washington, a close friend, who had held a key position in the White House, announced he was leaving. He explained that it was because he had used up all his good ideas and the level of new ones was deteriorating daily. He said, "The rewards of this job are tremendous. I can pick any of innumerable problems that come across my desk every day and feel that when I finish with them, I have made a real contribution. But now I worry all the time because good ideas to deal with these problems are harder to come by.

"Everyone in Washington lives off his intellectual capital—the concepts, knowledge, and understanding he brings with him from the outside world. There is no time to read, think, and recharge the batteries. My intellectual batteries are run down. I am leaving before I start doing harm."

The inability to get recharged is not a problem at the Federal Reserve. With only about half of one's time required to prepare competently for the day-to-day decisions of the Board, each member can spend the remainder of his time on other projects. I chose to use this time to develop new ideas, concepts, and doctrines, both for monetary policy and for broader economic and credit policies in areas where the Federal Reserve's responsibilities were less evident.

Government, like every other organization, needs new ideas. Often too much time is spent reacting to crises rather than creating new programs. But, as elsewhere, new ideas are not easily accepted. They tend to be automatically opposed. Only in emergencies or as a result of considerable effort will they be welcomed.

Federal Reserve members enjoy a strong position in trying to put forward new ideas. They have both the time and necessary staff assistance to provide background. They also have access to the fertile ground of the academic world and form a useful bridge from it to the government.

When the Federal Reserve Board must make decisions, as, for example, concerning projects on the payments mechanism, monetary doctrine, discount theory, or operating procedures, a Board member can introduce new solutions directly into the Board's debate. On the national economic and financial scene, Board members may either sit on intergovernmental committees or at least be in touch with those who will make the decisions, and thereby be able to supply them with new ideas. A Board member can also carry his ideas directly to Congress or to the public, through his speeches before financial, business, labor, consumer, or academic groups.

Because a major function of the Board is to explain policy problems and their background, channels exist for a wide dissemination of ideas. All speeches can be issued as news releases, sent automatically to the wire services, TV networks, and the financial reporters of the major newspapers and magazines, as well as to over five thousand individuals on the distribution list of the Federal Reserve Board. Any newsworthy statements will be carried nationally, reprinted in full in the banking and financial press and discussed in more detail by the financial reporters.

I personally found the attempt to introduce new ideas and economic theories at once the most rewarding and the most frustrating part of my Federal Reserve service. Many were debated, and quite a few were adopted. But which ones received consideration, which were adopted, and which neglected seemed almost a result of chance. Some Federal Reserve operations changed readily as new ideas were introduced, while in other areas, movements were glacial. My influence on credit techniques and institutions in the housing field was probably more important than any other function I performed in Washington. On the other hand, closely related ideas which I thought were better and equally significant fell with a dull thud, attracting only slight attention or interest. As an example, after much work on international monetary problems, on the assumption that the Fed had a specific function in this sphere, I was forced to retreat in frustration.

Participating in Decisions

Jokes about decision making by committees are legion. When an individual makes policy, decisions come sooner and the process is less cumbersome. I have no doubt, however, that the Federal Reserve's decisions are better because they are made collectively. The decisions the Board makes differ greatly from the management problems which have brought committees into disrepute. They are improved by the process of give and take. Collective decisions, furthermore, require an orderly process and provide a record. And because a group is involved, each member is less susceptible to pressures than he would be as an individual decision maker.

The process of decision making by the Board is orderly. Decisions do not have to be made rapidly. There are only a few critical decisions per week, and they thus receive the ample deliberation they require.

A question which used to occur to me frequently in the midst of debates and which I have rarely seen analyzed is the problem of "boardsmanship." What techniques should be used in debate to move the final decision as close as possible to one's own point of view? To be able to influence other members was particularly important in meetings of the FOMC, where both the debate and the concepts under consideration covered a wide spectrum. With views on such questions as reserves to be furnished or the level of desired interest rates spread over a broad range, a number of possible strategies were possible. One could take an extreme position, in the hope of gaining leverage in working out the final compromise. One could move closer to the center in an attempt to find a position that the majority would accept readily. One could stand without compromise, hoping either that a majority would move to a compatible position or that, failing this and entering a minority dissent, one would have a salutary effect on future decisions.

Dissents create another problem. Chairmen dislike them, apparently since they may appear either to weaken the force of a policy or to expose a lack of leadership. As a result they strive diligently to obtain a consensus. At times in our meetings this search for a consensus went too far, resulting in decisions so broadly phrased as to be weak. When the FOMC fails to resolve a question and the range of a directive is too broad, the manager must make the real decision in the course of his operations. A broad consensus takes the pressure off Committee members to formulate a precise policy. Furthermore, at times when the directive was broadened to include a minority opinion, the actual operations shifted so close to their position that the views of the majority were in fact disregarded.

The ability to dissent and to publicize their actions is an important protection for individual Board members. Whenever a member feels strongly enough, he can write a dissent and publicize it widely. The weight given a member's views will depend upon the strength with which his position is developed and on whether it strikes a responsive chord among groups on which the Federal Reserve depends. And, further, the split vote itself may have some impact, since it may raise questions as to the soundness of the majority decision. If the minority position appears to have merit, it will be given weight in estimating future policy.

While recent years have not witnessed a major controversy between a single member and the rest of the Board, such a possibility always exists and helps to determine the power relationships among them. The fact that all Board members are presidential appointees in their own right and are approved by the Senate is at the back of everyone's mind in negotiations over particular issues. A member cannot be removed merely for stating his policy views loudly, clearly, and publicly. In fact, the Public Information Act makes it the duty of each Board member to make known his dissenting views. Such an appeal to the public could certainly be made if an individual member of the Federal Reserve Board felt that he was not being treated fairly or that his colleagues were acting in bad faith with respect to the public.

I believe that criticism of the System for seeming to speak with different voices when individual members publicize their own minority policy views is ill-advised. Collective bodies exist so that the maximum number of views may be brought into the decision-making process. Further, individual ideas can be tested by the public. A recycling of ideas from the public back to the Board will result in better decisions which are closer to the public interest than those taken without this input.

The Functions of the Staff

Most actions of the Federal Reserve are based on memoranda prepared and distributed by the staff before each meeting. In the regulatory and operating spheres, this is completely the case. It also tends to be so in the monetary area. In addition to reams of reports and analyses, the staff prepares drafts of specific directives, regulations, and regulatory decisions. Each one is accompanied by an analysis of the background, the arguments for and against the suggested decision, and its expected impact. The staff's importance and power originate in this duty to prepare the basic documents that appear on the agenda, which is why its power, as shown in Chart 2, exceeds all the governors combined, except the Chairman.

A member of the Board can deal with staff documents in two ways. If he feels major errors have been made in the analysis or important alternatives neglected, he can discuss his views with the staff in advance of the meeting and request that his proposed alternatives be analyzed. Such discussions can lead either to a change in the staff documents or to an informal agreement that the question will be taken up in the Board meeting. If no agreement is possible, the staff will aid him in preparing his own position paper, including the necessary analysis and justifications. At times, since the staff is considered an independent professional body serving the public interest, even the Chairman may have to present such an alternative presentation.

A second course of action for a member is to wait until the Board takes up the document. Each member may then ask clarifying questions, express his opinion, and offer alternative proposals. By such give and take in debate the individual member can make his most important contribution, either by altering the decision under discussion or by laying the groundwork for a future policy change.

The Federal Reserve is aware that its successful functioning depends upon the ability to recruit an outstanding and independent staff and to utilize its work effectively in policy formation. Both Chairmen Martin and Burns recognized the importance of making sure that the Fed not become hidebound and fail to examine and adopt new ideas. Thus, the staff has had virtually unlimited freedom to develop new concepts, and most position papers reflect the staff's independent views.

When I sometimes disagreed with the staff it was usually in cases when I thought they had made some specific error. When I was critical, it was for a failure to develop rapidly enough new concepts of doctrine and operations. As in any bureaucracy, it is difficult to discard existing programs and to adopt new ones. But I believe the Fed suffers less from a hardening of the mental arteries than most large organizations.

The Influence of the Administration

Chart 2 includes my estimate of the relative influence of outside groups on monetary policy. The fact that the weight of the President and his principal advisers is the heaviest of these by far arises from the need for a unified economic policy. Monetary policy cannot run counter to national policy in either the domestic or the international sphere.

Although no conscious policy decision was ever taken, I believe the Fed gradually came to understand that it could carry out its direct responsibilities for monetary policy better if it interacted more completely and at more different levels with the rest of the government. This tendency grew steadily under Chairman Martin and has accelerated under Chairman Burns. Coordination, however, means less freedom for all. For instance, if the Fed helps to plan a wage-price or credit policy, it is more difficult to adopt a conflicting monetary policy, even though, in the course of debate on the final overall program, Fed representatives may have been overruled at many crucial points and even though the Board as a whole was not sufficiently integrated into the decision process.

Nevertheless, I believe the freedom lost is more than compensated for by better coordination. As a matter of fact, the Fed's actual ability to act contrary to the rest of the government was never very great.

Economic policy is a critical political matter. President Kennedy was elected primarily on an economic platform. Until Vietnam, President Johnson was building his historical record on his domestic achievements. President Nixon was defeated in 1960 largely because of a recession, and he did not want to have it happen again. In each case, the President concerned believed that monetary policy could help him reach his goals. Recognition of the importance of monetary policy did not mean that the President issued orders to the Federal Reserve on what policy should be followed. In fact each President has made it clear that if he had his "druthers" the amount of money and interest rates would be somewhat different from those prevailing. Instead, monetary policy is arrived at through the accommodation which takes place because all concerned recognize the President's ultimate responsibility and authority.

In time any president can make certain that his views prevail. Even if he did not have the power to appoint new members to the Board as vacancies occur, it is clear that no body—even a private one—can continue to function well under an all-out attack by the Administration. The White House holds too many cards in any direct showdown. Such an attack, however, could be costly to the Administration, which would have to justify the policies it was attempting to impose as well as the techniques it was employing to congressional committees eager to investigate any attacks on traditional institutions.

The President could also proceed more subtly and attempt to reorganize the Federal Reserve Board out of existence. But Congress could veto his actions and the committee hearings could become embarrassing. For example, even a White House statement critical of Chairman Burns and suggesting a possible reorganization of the Fed was enough to cause the stock market to fall and heavy pressures to arise in the foreign exchange markets.

Chairman Martin held an even stronger position. While many of President Kennedy's and President Johnson's advisers would have preferred a new Federal Reserve Chairman, Martin was a symbol of monetary responsibility in business circles both in the United States and abroad. It was frequently said that Martin was worth a billion dollars in gold to the Treasury, at a time when the Treasury considered gold an extremely critical item. As a result, whatever the views held by their staffs or their own predilections, both Kennedy and Johnson pleaded with Martin to remain in office. Obviously Martin gained considerable leverage in policy debates from this situation.

On the other hand, the same factors that lead a President to select, perhaps unwillingly, a particular Chairman can also limit the Chairman's freedom to bargain, for he has the same concern for the national welfare as the President. He can threaten to resign, but must recognize that if he does so, he cannot ask for an all-out investigation or unburden himself in the press because of the possible monetary consequences.

It was the recognition of this symbiotic relationship which caused the Federal Reserve to move away from its basic tenet that its role in critical times was to blow the whistle on the President or to attempt alone to hold back inflationary pressures. To be a staunch anti-inflationary voice, the Fed's effectiveness lies in its ability to work with the Administration.

Relationships with the Treasury

The most misunderstood relationship in the monetary field is that between the Federal Reserve System and the U.S. Treasury. The relationships concerned with operations and policy advice between the Treasury and the Federal Reserve are not complex, and they generally run smoothly. Only in the area of debt management have real problems arisen. Admittedly, at times in the past these have been critical, and conceivably they may become so again in the future.

In my reading of current financial analysis, I constantly find statements to the effect that the Federal Reserve will have to increase the money supply because of the size of the federal deficit or the amount of required Treasury borrowing. These statements are based on an erroneous idea of how monetary policy is formulated. It would be much more accurate to work on the opposite assumption.

The Federal Reserve in recent years has given no special consideration to the Treasury's demand for funds when selecting its monetary targets. (An exception is "even-keeling," explained on page 152.) In general the Federal Reserve policy is that the government must pay going market interest rates. Any attempt to peg the market to insure lower rates can have no more than a temporary effect. Too many reserves furnished in an attempt to hold rates down would lead to inflationary price rises and higher interest rates for all. The Federal Reserve is far more concerned that interest rates may affect other borrowers adversely than it is about the U.S. Treasury. Because it can tax or can increase its borrowing, the federal government is able to raise the money to pay market interest rates no matter how high they may be. For analysis, one should assume that the rate of interest on government securities per se affects the Federal Reserve no less and no more than any other interest rate.

The origin of this misconception about the influence of the Treasury on monetary policy can be found in two correct facts:

—During the period of World War II and after, the Federal Reserve did attempt to maintain low rates on government securities by means of a peg; that is, it set a maximum interest rate in the government market by buying as many securities as needed to keep interest rates from rising above the peg.
—It is a major concern of the Federal Reserve that the government securities market operate with maximum efficiency and that the Treasury get the best possible market price when it sells securities.

Debt Management

Earlier in this chapter I listed as the third primary responsibility of the Fed the need to protect against government attempts to abuse the power to create money for the purpose of reducing the cost of the public debt. Countries in which the central bank is controlled by the minister of finance or the treasury have frequently found public debt problems dominating their monetary policy. A short-sighted desire to reduce the cost of the public debt leads to higher costs for the economy as a whole. While in the past the Federal Reserve has at times been subservient to the Treasury, no such problem has existed since 1951.

The magnitude of the Treasury's borrowing problem is hard for the ordinary man to conceive. Each year the secretary of the Treasury must borrow or reborrow over $130 billion, which explains why any secretary would emphasize the advantages to the government of lower interest rates. However, only about 7 percent of the total budget is paid to the public in interest in any case.

Magnitude is the core of the problem: How much emphasis should economic policy place on the possibility of saving $1 or $2 billion for the Treasury, when monetary policy's primary concern is with the gross national product of well over $1.3 trillion? Both the Administration and the Federal Reserve agree that whatever technical action is possible to minimize the cost of the public debt should be taken. On the other hand, no risk of upsetting the economy or starting an inflation should be incurred for debt management purposes.

Even when the Federal Reserve supported the government bond market through open market purchases, the underlying concern was not primarily the government's interest burden. Rather, the policy was undertaken to prevent the government's financing from driving the general level of interest rates up to an unsatisfactory level. Such broader considerations could, of course, arise again. Monetary and credit policy must be concerned with movements in interest rates as well as with their impact on the distribution of credit. The Fed may want to alter policies if it fears that a government deficit will create imbalances by increasing the demand for funds.

Although the use of inflation as a method of taxation is not unknown, it was not the policy in this country in the 1960s. Throughout that period, policy was based upon the desirability of allowing the financial markets to set the interest rates needed to equate supply and demand without an excessive increase in money. The Federal Reserve set its targets in order to avoid having debt management increase the supply of money beyond that deemed necessary on other criteria.

Maintaining Efficient Markets

Some observers, however, remain convinced that the Federal Reserve does support the government bond market because they assume that Federal Reserve technical operations in the market are a part of a general pattern of support for the Treasury. But what the Fed is really trying to do is to maintain as efficient a market as possible, and thereby also to minimize the government's costs.

The question has been raised as to whether these attempts to improve market efficiency do not conflict with general monetary policy. Some believe that concern over the government securities dealers tends to exert a strong influence on monetary policy. (These dealers are the twenty or so commercial and investment banks which operate the principal over-the-counter market in government securities. They have a special relationship with the Open Market Desk, which trades with them almost on an hour-to-hour basis.) My own view is that this does not occur. Except in cases of disorderly or even-keel markets, I can recall no debate in which, even by implication, the status of the government securities dealers entered into a decision as to what monetary policy ought to be established or how it should be operated.

The same cannot be said with respect to how government securities are bought and sold, the capital and profits of the dealers, and the general relationship maintained with the dealer group. The Federal Reserve feels a technical responsibility for the government securities market. It is an extremely large market, handling daily purchases and sales of over $3 billion. It is an efficient market, with an extremely low spread between buying and selling prices, distributing the federal debt at a low cost.

Technical efficiency is due mainly to the fact that dealers carry large inventories with low equities. If prices change radically, the dealers could easily be wiped out. Consequently, the Federal Reserve does, in effect, guarantee the market during an underwriting or on other special occasions against unusual price changes which might arise as a result of wars, international crises, or a sudden change in government policies. One form the guarantee takes is called even-keeling, which simply means that the Federal Reserve refrains from making any major changes in monetary policy (whether shifting the Federal funds rate drastically or announcing a new discount rate) during the periods of major Treasury financings. The periods of even-keeling include the time between the announcement and approximately the settlement dates of major new security offerings or refunding by the Treasury. The idea behind even-keeling is, not to support the Treasury, but to insure that market forces rather than Federal Reserve action actually determine rates in this period.

Another part of the implicit guarantee is that the Federal Reserve stands ready to step in and purchase inventories if the market becomes disorderly. However, it specifically does not guarantee the dealers against normal market risks. If the Treasury sets an incorrect price or the market takes too many securities in an auction, or if dealers' inventories become large through a misspeculation, bond prices can fall. In such cases the Treasury may help out by purchasing for trust funds or other special accounts when the prices seem ready to break sharply and large losses to dealers as a group are threatened, but there is no attempt to save individual dealers from their personal errors. Normally, the Federal Reserve will not step in unless the degree of general loss becomes unusual or unless some outside event occurs that is completely unexpected, as, for instance, the Cambodian invasion in 1970. When the market begins to drop in a disorderly manner, the Federal Reserve will put in a bid below the market to take over most of the inventories of the government dealers. Usually such actions are taken at prices which do not prevent the dealers from incurring losses, and there is no set limit for such losses.

The debate over even-keeling centers around whether or not the Federal Reserve remains overly accommodative during a financing period. When money market conditions have been used as a target, such overaccommodation can occur because reserves are created to meet whatever demand arises in banks, and much of a new issue may be bought by banks or by dealers with bank loans. Thus the purchases create a demand which is then supported by the infusion of new reserves.

When the Federal Reserve uses monetary aggregates as a target, such overaccommodation does not take place. A minor fluctuation in reserves and the money supply may occur, but this is due primarily to problems in making seasonal corrections. Such a temporary reserve creation would have little or no intermediate term effect or economic significance.

Nothing in the policy of even-keeling guarantees any particular interest rate or leads to the creation of reserves beyond those required by a target which ignores Treasury activity. I believe it is the failure of observers to recognize how Federal Reserve policy making has changed that accounts for the persistent belief that the federal deficit or Treasury financings are important determinants of monetary policy.

Other Functions with the Treasury

When the Federal Reserve System was established, it assumed certain major responsibilities for the Treasury, one of which is its role as the Treasury's fiscal agent in both the domestic and international spheres. As such, it serves as the Treasury's banker, making payments against checks and on security coupons, issuing currency, and performing similar activities. It also operates for the Treasury in the foreign exchange market as agent for foreign loans, stores and ships gold, and performs other international operations.

Almost constant interchanges take place between the Federal Reserve and the Treasury on these matters. Operations must be carefully coordinated, but few policy problems arise in this sphere. I doubt if the Federal Reserve Board has to take up more than one or two questions in this entire area each month.

A second area of general interchange is in the sphere of debt management, just discussed. The Federal Reserve advises the Treasury (which not infrequently rejects the advice) as to what form of debt issue will have the best effect for the economy. Because the Fed is constantly operating in the government security markets, it develops a good deal of day-to-day information. Other recommendations flow from the general economic analysis of the Federal Reserve staff.

Finally, discussions are held on the formulation of economic policy. The secretary of the Treasury is a key economic adviser to the President and has primary responsibility for international monetary matters. Since these areas are also of interest to the Federal Reserve, interchange of ideas occurs. The degree and extent of these discussions have varied greatly, depending on how the President seeks his economic advice and how influential his secretary of the Treasury is in comparison with other economic advisers.

Relationships with the Congress

Congressional presence is felt at each meeting on monetary policy. The Federal Reserve Board believes that its flexibility, its ability to hire good staff and to generate new ideas are important. It recognizes that to continue to operate as it does, it must satisfy a majority of Congress. Thus, what concerns individual congressmen in the monetary field automatically concerns the Federal Reserve. On particular issues, the question may arise of how much weight to give to the position of a few of the most outspoken congressmen. This becomes a political judgment: What policies suggested by congressional leaders represent the views of Congress as a whole? Are they strongly enough held to lead to some change in the *status quo* if the Federal Reserve is not responsive?

In some meetings Congress exerts pressure in a different way. Many economic policies depend on a positive action by Congress. This is frequently true in the fiscal area, but also applies to international monetary arrangements, price-wage policies, and specific credit votes. This situation, of course, affects the vote taken by the Board or the Federal Open Market Committee. The monetary policy adopted is selected with a view to obtaining the best combination of statutory and Board action.

Congress has the constitutional authority to employ any means appropriate for carrying out its credit and monetary powers, its powers "to coin money" and "regulate the value thereof," "to borrow money on the credit of the United States." Under these powers, Congress established the Federal Reserve to exercise the governmental functions of reserve banking, to regulate in the public interest the volume, availability, and cost of money and credit. Congress indicated its intent that the Federal Reserve, with a view to the public interest, act according to its own best judgment and discretion within the mandates or guiding principles established by Congress.

The System has always recognized its responsibility to Congress. Policy actions are reported, formerly with a lag of a year, but now within ninety days—a recognition, as we noted earlier, that less secrecy is better. The System stands ready to testify or to answer specific questions submitted by congressional committees or individual congressmen.

Congressional surveillance is exercised primarily through investigations and questions. Congressional advice as to current monetary policy is received from public speeches by congressmen and occasionally by letters. On the whole, congressmen act in an exemplary manner with respect to the Board's functions, particularly those in the regulatory sphere. Congressmen's contacts with me as an individual Board member were almost entirely requests for information.

To the best of my knowledge, the Board has rarely if ever been subjected to congressional pressure in any specific regulatory case. While the staff and the Chairman are contacted occasionally, they make it clear that any congressional letters or calls with respect to a particular case will appear in the public information file on that case, available to all. On the other hand, congressmen have been more active in opposing general regulatory changes, such as those under the Bank Holding Company Act dealing with the rights of banks to be active in general fields, and have sometimes succeeded in delaying such actions.

As part of its nonpartisan structure, the Board attempts to maintain good relations with all congressmen. While this is primarily the responsibility of the Chairman and two legislative representatives, all members cooperate in this endeavor. On the whole, lobbying is low-keyed and purely factual, aimed at demonstrating the logic of the Federal Reserve's position. Only occasionally have the regional resources of the Federal Reserve System been called into action, and have current and former Federal Reserve Bank directors been urged to use their political influence in situations that are considered crucial.

Relationships with Financial Groups

It is often alleged that the Federal Reserve is unduly influenced in its actions by financial interests. Chart 2 shows that, in my estimate, the power of these interests is far less than many fear. There are many reasons for this misconception, however. For instance,

—Commercial banks own the stock of the Federal Reserve Banks and elect six of the directors of each.

—By law the Federal Reserve Board must meet and seek advice at least four times a year from the Federal Advisory Council, usually composed of twelve of the nation's major bankers.

—Through even-keeling and its rules for maintaining orderly markets, the System has given special consideration to the operations of government security dealers.

—Financial institutions and individuals are the source of a great deal of the information used in making monetary policy.

—There is a well-recognized tendency for regulatory agencies to be strongly influenced by those they regulate. Those regulated are far more interested in what the agency does than are ordinary citizens. They pay particular attention to its actions, appear at all hearings, write letters, call and make their presence felt as strongly as possible. They arrange informal and social occasions to meet with individual Board members. More requests for speeches come from financial groups than from any other segments of the public.

While there may have been times in Federal Reserve history when financial groups did exert an undue influence, I believe that in recent years the weight of bankers and other financial forces has probably been felt less on Federal Reserve policy than elsewhere in Washington or the nation.

All members of the Board, including those who have come from the financial community, are aware of the danger of giving undue weight to information from those who have an axe to grind. As a result, messages from the financial community are carefully examined with their inherent biases in mind. In fact, any statements from interested parties receive less attention than do identical ideas from more neutral sources.

Furthermore, the Board wants to protect its reputation to insure confidence in its monetary decisions; it does not want its regulatory decisions to open a flank to attack for failing to represent the public interest. The laws concerning regulation, as drawn by Congress, however, do lead to what has been called a competition in laxity. Increasing reserve requirements as a tool of monetary policy illustrates this conflict. Commercial banks oppose increases in reserve requirements because any diversion of assets from income-yielding loans and investments to nonearning reserves in deposits at the Federal Reserve directly decreases their profits. As deposits expand, the effect of increasing reserves is to raise the amount banks must pay to the federal government for the franchise and privilege of being able to create part of the money supply.

In considering an increase, the Federal Reserve Board faces a dilemma. The System invests the added required reserves and pays the yield to the U.S. Treasury. The added reserves improve monetary policy and raise federal income. But the banks receive no added income, only the extra costs of demand deposits. Any bank may decide not to pay its fair share to the federal government and opt out of the Federal Reserve System by becoming a state nonmember bank. It can then use its reserves to purchase earning assets. The bank's profits increase; the Treasury's income goes down. Each time the Federal Reserve Board considers changing reserve requirements as a monetary tool, the immediate advantages must be weighed against the long-term losses which result when banks leave the System, losses which include both reduced income for the federal government and a reduced control over money.

This regulatory dilemma exists because the banks can get out of the Federal Reserve System. Under pressure from the banks, Congress has maintained a dual banking system. It is specifically to preserve such dilemmas that the commercial banks have fought so vehemently to maintain competing regulatory agencies—the Fed, the Comptroller of the Currency, and the FDIC. Competition in laxity gives banks considerably greater room to maneuver; it is thought of as a guarantee against regulatory intransigence and a means for them of reducing costs and payments to the government.

The Structure of the Federal Reserve System

The relationships both within the Federal Reserve and with other groups are somewhat complicated by the fact that the act establishing the System attempted to retain a good deal of monetary power in regional and private banking hands because of the congressional fear of creating an effective central bank. In the 1920s and 1930s, the conflict between the Board in Washington and the District Banks reduced the effectiveness of the Federal Reserve. However, since 1933, one of the strongest trends has been the erosion of the power of the regional Federal Reserve Banks. This is reflected by their status in Chart 2.

Formally, the System is a mixture of public and private control and of centralized and regional monetary power. The President appoints the Board of Governors with the consent of the Senate. On the other hand, the presidents of the Reserve Banks, who have five votes on the Open Market Committee, are not strictly government officials. The Regional Bank presidents are selected by the boards of directors of their Banks with the approval of the Board of Governors.

The twelve Federal Reserve Banks are nominally owned by their member commercial banks, but they operate as public service institutions. Sometimes they claim the rights of governmental bodies, at others those of private banks. The fact that their sole purpose is to increase the national welfare, not the profits of their member banks, is obscured at times because the member banks elect six of their nine directors. The Board of Governors appoints the remaining three, including the chairman and vice-chairman. Although the directors have a good deal of responsibility for seeing that the Reserve Banks are well operated, many policy decisions are made uniformly for the twelve Banks, either by the Conference of Federal Reserve Bank Presidents or by the Board of Governors.

Recommendations to Reform the System

A complete study of the monetary and financial system of the United States was published by the Commission on Money and Credit in 1961. Among many other recommendations, it suggested a major restructuring of the Federal Reserve System. Ten years later, G. L. Bach, an expert on the Fed, repeated the Commission's basic recommendations, which followed those he had made to the Hoover Commission in the late 1940s. In his words, "The central issues appear to have changed little over the last two decades."

In order of importance, Bach's recommendations were;

—The Federal Open Market Committee should be abolished. Responsibility for monetary policy (open market operations, reserve requirements, and discount rates) should be centered in the Federal Reserve Board.

—The Federal Reserve Board should be reduced in size from seven to five members with staggered tenure terms.

—The Board Chairman's term should be made roughly coterminous with the President's.

—Special geographical and occupational qualifications for Board members should be eliminated.

—Technical ownership of the Federal Reserve Banks by member banks should be eliminated through retirement of the present capital stock.

The major thrust of these recommendations would be to centralize the authority over monetary policy in a unit, the Board of Governors, that is clearly part of the government and to streamline the decision-making process. The effect would be to reduce still more, by altering the legal structure, the minimal influence still retained by private bankers in the System. The merits of these proposals depend upon both the assessment of the actual strengths and weaknesses of the Federal Reserve under the current structure and the potential effect of the proposed changes on the performance of the System's functions.

On one point there is no debate. Virtually all agree that the Chairman's term should roughly coincide with that of the President. Since the Chairman must work closely with the Administration, representing the Board to the Administration and vice versa, it makes sense to acknowledge this relationship. An incoming President should have a vacancy on the Board which he can fill, if he so desires, with a Chairman with whom he believes his Administration can work closely.

The suggestion that all the policy-making functions of the Federal Reserve System be centralized in the Board is more controversial. This proposal was defeated in the 1935 reorganization. The major loss from centralizing would be the weakening of the regional structure. The potential gains are, I believe, far greater. Centralization would increase efficiency and would improve decisions by making them less subject to bargaining and to compromise at the lowest common denominator.

Although the existing procedures function quite well, the advantages of abolishing the Federal Open Market Committee seem substantial. The current arbitrary division between open market questions, the discount rate, and the other instruments could be removed. Monetary policy could be handled as the continuous, coherent process that it is. At present, decisions on all tools, including those controlled by the Board alone, tend to be delayed until the FOMC meets so that they can be coordinated with open market policy. More significant, however, would be a reduction in the number who debate policy. Currently the FOMC is too large, its decision-making process is awkward, and it is overly subject to the pressures of time and the need or desire of some of its members to return promptly to their district headquarters. At one time it was thought preferable to have a weak Federal Reserve, on the assumption that fragmented policies would be better than strong ones. That has proven to be untrue. The Fed's poorest decisions have come when it was weakest and most divided.

Continued ownership of the Federal Reserve Banks by their members makes no sense. It is a source of public confusion and frequent attack upon the Federal Reserve System. It is a vestigial and sentimental remnant of the System's beginnings and can easily be changed.

The pros and cons of reducing the size of the Board to five and cutting each member's term to ten years seem to me balanced. There is no sacred number so long as the Board is large enough to insure that issues are carefully considered. There have been many times when seven different backgrounds and specific inputs were useful and few instances where the extra numbers caused problems; but the same statement could probably be made if there were only five members. At times some members have not carried their weight; a larger number allows more dead weight to be carried without adversely affecting the Board's functioning. The main value of the long term is probably its uniqueness compared to other governmental agencies, and therefore the strength it gives the Board as a whole.

I strongly favor the suggestion that the Board cease to be thought of as representative of regions or special interests such as finance, industry, commerce, and agriculture. It should be recognized as composed largely of technicians and spokesmen for the public interest at large. The idea of representation assumes that policy making is based primarily on value judgment rather than knowledge, an interpretation I think wrong. In any case, a small working Board is not likely to represent adequately all of the myriad interests in the country. Thus it seems much better to have a Board which is intended to represent the nation as a whole rather than the present system in which a few major groups are theoretically, but not in fact, specifically represented.

The Federal Reserve Act assumed a need for familiarity with local conditions at the bank level. It was assumed that monetary conditions and policy would vary with the credit conditions and needs of business, industry, and agriculture in the local districts. Time has made this concept obsolete. The Federal Reserve now deals with national monetary policy. There cannot be, and are not, regional variations in monetary policy. The contributions to debate made by the presidents of the Regional Banks range from excellent to poor. They do not depend on where they are from, but upon their own abilities and those of their staffs.

In sum, I see no especial value in either the regional concept or the idea that bankers, whose special knowledge is more than outweighed by a conflict of interest, ought to be directly represented in the monetary decision-making process. There is no evidence that the required regional or special interest representation on the Board and the FOMC has any particular impact.

The present structure of the FOMC means that national policy is influenced by a group of officials chosen in a basically undemocratic manner. The District Bank presidents are approved by the Federal Reserve Board, but selected by private directors. As a result they are twice removed from the democratic process. There is some support for the present process, however, primarily because it is undemocratic. This follows from the belief that monetary policy should be removed as far as possible from the political process. I do not believe that this is a good idea for either the country or the Federal Reserve. While the range of value judgments of the presidents is as wide, its center position is considerably more restrictive than that of the Board. There are many possible reasons for this tilt. The selection process for the presidents emphasizes more conventional and conservative characteristics. Perhaps the Board is too close to the politicians in Washington or perhaps the presidents are too close to commercial bankers in the field.

The function of determining discount rates, now shared by the Reserve Banks and the Board, would be improved by centralizing it in the Board. The present split control over discount rates has many drawbacks and I know of no advantages that it offers. For the most part, the directors of the Reserve Banks gather together for only a few hours each month and yet are expected, in setting discount rates, to make critical decisions on the timing or direction of monetary policy. Because most directors recognize their lack of expertise in the intricacies of the problems involved, they follow the suggestions of their local president. In the few cases where either they or their executive officer wanted to move independently to create monetary policy, their actions have been vetoed by the Board in Washington.

In recent years, on several occasions sharp discount rate increases were suggested by individual bank boards as a result of exasperation over events in foreign exchanges or concern over inflationary expectations. In each instance, the discount rate change was motivated by a desire for a dramatic move. In many, if not all, of these cases the District board was willing, whether unknowingly or not, to accept a sharp recession. To me these decisions either reflected a bias toward less concern over lost jobs in the employment-price trade-off sector or else revealed outdated views of the monetary system. In several cases, the requests came in the midst of delicate foreign or domestic negotiations and, if adopted, would have been extremely harmful.

While the Board in Washington can and did stop these particular proposals, and while it can force discount rates to be changed, the problem of coordination remains awkward and difficult, leading to frustration for all. On the one hand, the District Banks may put pressure on Washington. Leaks as to proposed changes in the discount rate at times appear in the press for this purpose. On the other, the need for action by boards in twelve places makes it difficult for Washington to design a better relationship between discount rates and financial markets.

There are, of course, also some cogent arguments for preserving the regional input. The proposed changes would mean that the regional Federal Reserve Banks would lose their residual responsibility for monetary policy and would be left only with operating functions, making it more difficult to attract the caliber of men who have so far occupied the presidencies of the Banks and served on their boards of directors. At a time when the decentralization of federal power has become a matter of considerable interest, the Federal Reserve is recognized as one of the few regional bodies in the United States with any status. Its personnel and publications are regionally oriented. Its role in local communities is greater than that of most other federal agencies. The Banks appear to run both more efficiently and with a higher output of service than do more centralized federal departments. There is the danger that, if monetary policy functions were removed, the Banks would carry out less well their remaining functions, namely their handling of discounts, holding of member bank reserves, operation of the payments mechanism, fiscal operations for the Treasury, and regional research activities.

The directors' role of collecting and disseminating economic information seems potentially important; but use of the data has been difficult. In most cases it duplicates information gathered from other sources and, in the few cases where it has differed, its degree of reliability has been erratic. While no studies have been made specifically, my feeling is that there have been a few examples where the information was extremely good and a few where it was extremely bad. The record appears to be similar to a random variable in the decision process, making its overall value close to zero. Many members of the Federal Reserve System , however, would put far more weight than I do on the value of the Regional Banks in disseminating good information on monetary policy. In any case, while this may be a useful function, I do not believe it is a critical one.

In sum, the problem is that of maintaining both a high-level management and a regional presence if the proposed changes are enacted. They have been valuable. The Fed's efficiency is good. Its regional input has been worthwhile and, at times, excellent. And it is certainly questionable whether these values could be retained if monetary powers were removed from the Regional Banks. When any changes are made in the Federal Reserve's structure, there should also be a major effort to insure that the positive values of the System are retained.

The Position of the Federal Reserve

The most significant issue in how the Federal Reserve influences and is influenced by others boils down to the question of potential bias in its views as to correct national economic policy. The goals and, to a considerable extent, the monetary policy targets that the Federal Reserve adopts at any time are a function of the value judgments of the members of the FOMC.

As I indicated, its peculiar structure does mean that the Federal Reserve Banks exert some pressure, though not a great deal, in the direction of higher interest rates and less money. And there are certainly those who believe that these judgments ought to be biased toward the restrictive side in monetary and economic policy. This is clearly the point of view of those who favor the present private and regional framework for the Fed's decision-making process.

The more basic question, however, is how the actual policies followed by the Federal Reserve compare with those of other groups which influence the economy. My feeling is that, while they may have been a good deal more conservative than the rest of Washington in prior periods and while they retained that reputation thereafter, since 1961 they have not departed much from the central position of the administration in power.

President Kennedy's personal views differed less from the Fed's goals than from those of his own economic advisers. During the first years of the Johnson Administration, the System's goals were more restrictive than the President's, as the Federal Reserve put more weight on price movements than on full employment or increased output. However, the effect on monetary operations of the divergent goals was slight. And, after January 1966, when all agreed that the problem was one of too rapid an increase in demand and fears of inflation, the views converged. Until the end of the Johnson Administration, no difference in goals existed between the Federal Reserve and other parts of the government.

Again, under President Nixon differences in goals were slight (see Chapters 10 and 11). All accepted a policy of gradualism in 1969 and 1970. In 1971 the Fed did not attempt to force the economy to the inflated growth rate projected in the Economic Report that year because it realized that the projection was purely political, with little or no basis in economic analysis. Money was simply made available to accommodate most spending desires. After a month or two, the Administration, too, was willing to see the Report forgotten, as its own goals reverted to the logical ones which most economists had maintained.

In the Nixon Administration the general agreement did not at first extend to Federal Reserve operations. The Administration contained a large number of monetarists who, in the view of the Fed, had an inadequate understanding of what monetary policy did and could do. At the same time, the Administration economists believed the Federal Reserve was wrong in its ideas of price determination, particularly as to the existence of cost-push inflation and the need for an incomes policy. After the Administration adopted wage-price controls in 1971, much of the conflict disappeared. Although the Treasury and White House still believed that the Federal Reserve could improve its operations, they were not clear as to how.

I believe that, since the Federal Reserve's goals have not differed much from those of the Administration in power, it follows that they may be close to the mainstream of American political thought. How and whether the mainstream differs from more specialized groups is, of course, more a matter of opinion. From my many discussions with banking and financial representatives, I would judge that these groups believe the Federal Reserve ought to be more aggressively restrictive. They are disappointed that the Fed failed to guarantee the value of gold, stable prices, and other such objectives. They fear that the Board's espousal of the goals of high output and low unemployment as proper for a central bank are an ill omen for the future. On the other hand, labor groups and many debtor groups believe the Federal Reserve is too restrictive. They insist that the Fed could insure low interest rates and an adequate availability of credit if these were included in the System's goals. They fail to see the trade-off costs involved.

While I think a good deal of the System's bias has been removed, there is always a danger that it can creep back in undetected. By its nature the Fed interacts far less frequently with debtor groups or the less wealthy than with the Establishment, which prefers a more restrictive monetary policy. The System must constantly reexamine its goals and objectives with the danger of inherent bias in mind. The Fed has always, rightfully, prided itself on putting the public interest first; it must be ever vigilant to maintain this ideal.

CHAPTER EIGHT

Economic Forecasting:
The Foundation for Policy

A FREQUENT WASHINGTON SIGHT in the past twenty years has been an indignant member of Congress, seated at the tribunal of the Joint Economic Committee or the Banking or Finance Committees, probing at the Chairman of the Federal Reserve Board in a struggle to find out what was happening to monetary policy, or even how the Federal Reserve went about formulating policy. Senators Paul Douglas and William Proxmire, Representatives Wright Patman and Henry Reuss, and many others have turned away in complete frustration, convinced that the Fed either did not know what it was doing or feared to tell its congressional overseers how monetary policy was formulated.

Critics of a suspicious nature claimed that the Federal Reserve refused to articulate its methods of operation and theoretical concepts so that it could pursue its own goals rather than those of Congress and the Administration. A small kernel of truth can be found in these charges, for the Federal Reserve did picture itself as a body always under political pressure to allow more inflation. One method of lessening those pressures was to claim that the critics simply could not understand the complexity and intricacies of monetary policy.

On the whole, however, Congress was being told as much as the Federal Reserve knew. One cause of the debates of 1966 was that

167

there was no articulated, logical theory of how monetary policy worked. A majority of the FOMC believed that policy was too complex and too variable to spell out in any detail. The 1966 conflict over how to measure and control monetary policy was only one in a long series. Similar controversy occurred each time monetary policy had a significant role to play. Confrontations were particularly sharp in 1969, 1970, and 1972.

In fact, the problem had been explored in 1964, although in a more relaxed atmosphere. At that time, there was widespread fear that lack of a system of measurement would cause the Federal Reserve to tighten prematurely and too much. As evidence of this concern, the House Committee on Banking and Currency asked Professors Karl Brunner and Allan Meltzer to conduct a study of how the Federal Reserve arrived at decisions and conducted monetary policy. Like other students of monetary policy, they could find no logical theory or model in use at the Fed. They saw no indication of any desire to explain or measure what was happening. Their report concluded by calling attention to "the generally inchoate nature of the Federal Reserve's conception of the monetary processes. . . . The evident disregard of rational methods of policy making was partially explained in terms of the Federal Reserve's inherited procedures."

As outside pressures began to build up on the Fed, changes were also occurring inside the System, brought about in part by the gradual and normal changes in the composition of the FOMC. President Kennedy appointed George Mitchell to the Board of Governors, the first practicing professional economist to be a member in many years. Several of the newer bank presidents were also economists trained in current theory.

In the face of dissatisfaction both outside and within, the FOMC did reexamine its policy against using measurement and analysis. In 1964 a subcommittee consisting of three economists—Mitchell of the Board, Eliot Swan and George Ellis, presidents of the San Francisco and Boston Banks respectively—reported to the full Committee. They concluded that the directive was incomplete, sometimes internally inconsistent, often too vague, and that it failed to show what policy was intended in explicit enough terms for the manager to follow the Committee's wishes. They recommended that the directive become more comprehensive and explicit. They raised numerous questions which outsiders had also been asking: How should monetary policy be analyzed? How should it be measured? How specific should the FOMC be both in its policy formulation and in its public statements? They were not able, however, to convince their colleagues that a problem really existed. Only three of the twelve members of the FOMC supported their point of view. The rest were satisfied that the questions they asked could not or need not be answered. But even though they were defeated this time, the issues of measurement and removing ambiguity from the System's operations remained alive.

The Resistance to Change

In the debate surrounding the events of 1966, I joined those who felt strongly that poor measurement and the lack of an analytical framework prevented the System from determining the proper amount of reserves. It was my opinion that the Fed could not fight inflation effectively and select proper targets for monetary policy without knowing what was happening to the demand for money. And, once the target was selected, there had to be more control over operations. To formulate policy on the intangible basis of the tone and feel of either the economy or the financial markets was to invite serious mistakes. I fought hard for change. At first a majority opposed any modification of policy, but eventually a grudging compromise was worked out.

The issues seemed so clear to me that I found the delays very frustrating. I asked others in the System who agreed with me why we could not make faster progress. Perhaps out of greater cynicism, perhaps out of longer experience, they attributed most of the delays to inertia or to psychological difficulties. The inertia was evident. It is difficult at best to move any large group which has long-standing traditions; even a small minority, if they feel strongly, can slow developments. When a split does occur, the influence of the Chairman becomes strategic. On this issue, Chairman Martin led the group who felt that Federal Reserve policy had to remain an art rather than a science. However, while he opposed the introduction of any specific analytical framework, he did believe in research and knowledge. He allowed and even encouraged the staff to explore new techniques, but at the same time he adhered to his belief that real quantification was impossible, that it would downgrade judgment and intuition, and therefore would lead to greater errors on the part of the Federal Reserve.

As an economist, Arthur F. Burns took exactly the opposite view when he became Chairman. He was concerned over the lack of exactness and various other shortcomings in past Federal Reserve operations. In consequence, from his first day in office he put the weight of his position behind greater quantification. Even so, the inertia and internal opposition were great enough to slow progress considerably.

The psychological resistance of the Federal Reserve has been well described by Jack Guttentag of the Wharton School, one of the most acute observers of the System, who had previously spent eight years as an economist at the Federal Reserve Bank of New York. He concluded,

> The real barrier to the adoption of a complete strategy is largely psychological. The Federal Reserve would have to relinquish the illusion that it "takes account of everything," while exposing its real objectives nakedly to public scrutiny. This could be risky. There is much unreasonable hostility to monetary policy to begin with, and it is likely that in some cases further exposure would merely invite more vigorous attack.°

Naturally, those who have opposed an analytical framework and measurement have not agreed with this analysis, but have based their position on three other propositions, each of which has some intellectual appeal:

—Knowledge is too slight and uncertainty too great to permit the selection of any particular goals, form of analysis, or measurement of monetary targets.

—Given the lack of knowledge, attempts to quantify monetary de-

---

° J. M. Guttentag, "The Strategy of Open Market Operations," *The Quarterly Journal of Economics* 80, no. 1 (February 1966).

cision making will diminish the intuitive skills and judgment necessary for the best decisions.

—Precise statement of Federal Reserve goals and policies would decrease the possibilities of achieving them, while increasing the benefits to certain private individuals or groups.

The Lack of Knowledge

There is general agreement that in the application of economic theory to the problems of government, knowledge is not adequate for highly accurate decision making. This problem exists at many levels: For instance, the economy's goals are not immutable, the weight to attach to sectoral or similar problems varies greatly, and the public's views on a proper trade-off may shift.

Data on the current state of the economy and where it is headed are often sketchy. The Federal Reserve has an excellent information system; yet at decision times there is always a need for more. As a major source of its own data, the Fed is only too aware of how poor statistical information may be: Data contain collection errors, they are subject to major revisions, they tend to be biased and have large random components. Any tendency to accept them uncritically can lead to horrible mistakes; they must be analyzed and the validity attached to them must depend on prior experience and judgment.

One of the main arguments against the use of too specific a target has always been that it is like following a will-o'-the-wisp: once one succeeds in tracking a path accurately, the figures are revised and one finds that he has really tracked much too large or too small a target. One can set a goal at a 4 percent growth in money, congratulate oneself on hitting it, and then find six months later that, according to revised figures, money had actually grown at 6 percent and 50 percent more money than was wanted had been created. This is a valid, but not unanswerable, attack on the use of specific targets.

There is an even greater problem than the data gap. We have noted that some of our major models differ by as much as 300 percent in their estimates of the power exerted on spending from the creation of new money. Thus, while we can predict the direction in which a policy action will move the economy, there are many differing theories and empirical estimates of how important the impacts will be, when they will occur, and what indirect or secondary effects they may have. There is no agreement as to which measure of monetary policy will be the most accurate and useful. Milton Friedman, one of the leading students of the monetary system, concludes that, while most economists can agree on a general theoretical framework for monetary analysis (such as that described in Chapters 2 and 3), vast areas of disagreement exist as to how to fill in the framework.

In my speeches as a governor of the Federal Reserve, one of my hardest tasks was to convince people of the fact that we do not know as much about money as people think. At any given time experts are always far apart in their advice as to the best monetary policy. Periodically I have asked economists a question which the Fed must answer daily, "From December 1965 through 1972 member bank reserves grew at a rate of roughly 6 percent a year. Spending on the GNP grew about 40 percent faster, or 8.4 percent a year. If the FOMC at its next meeting were to cut by 20 percent the rate at which the Federal Reserve furnished reserves, how would you expect this to affect spending, and when?" Typically, the answers would vary from "Spending will drop by at least 20 percent" to "It would barely change the rate of spending in the coming year." A sampling of good analysts will frequently show estimates of monetary impacts varying by 100 percent or more.

Within the Federal Reserve there have been major differences about which monetary instruments are most effective and over what period they will be felt. So-called experts speak of the ease with which the Fed can control the money supply. However, those within the System believe there are lags of six months or more before an action to change the money supply will be fully effective. The failure of outside critics to consider actual operating problems has been one of the reasons the Fed has reacted to them so negatively. Too often they appear uninformed or pressing for an unsuitable goal. Often they concentrate on a single aspect. Those within the System are aware of the oversimplification. They know that additional information exists which the critics have ignored. The attitude of the Fed, however, can sometimes be too rigid, causing it to reject ideas and suggestions which have merit.

Intuition

Some members of the FOMC object that quantification and measurement in the monetary field would lead to concentrating too much time and effort on those elements which can be expressed in numbers at the expense of important variables which cannot be quantified. Some situations can be expressed only in terms of "more" or "less." Through intuition, an experienced observer can often spot movements and dangers before they appear in the statistics. Furthermore, a model which deals in magnitudes and timing of policy changes is likely to be accepted as valid because its statistics look impressive, even though it may have a high probability of error.

Members with this opinion add that operations are too complex for formal quantitative directives. To them, making monetary policy is an art. Unexpected events occur; instructions cannot cover all eventualities. The manager of the Open Market Desk must be given freedom to carry out policy flexibly. The Federal Reserve Bank of New York deals minute by minute with the money market, shaping its action to the events and needs expressed in the market. The money market consists of the banks, traders, dealers, and brokers who buy and sell daily billions of dollars worth of short-term securities. Although not organized into a formal or informal exchange, this market handles a volume of transactions amounting to over $10 billion a day, a figure far surpassing that of the organized exchanges. Since all pressures funnel through this market, it measures immediately what is happening. It is like a "real-time" computer. Information from this market makes it possible to keep abreast of the latest, up-to-the-minute developments.

The Drawbacks of Greater Public Knowledge

To most people, the Federal Reserve is mysterious. It is not the Delphic oracle, but it may not be far removed. It fights inflation with unseen, but powerful tools. It may make mistakes, but they are hard to document. As long as its policy statements remain cryptic, no one can keep score or record its errors. There is no batting average published for the Fed.

A strong, self-protective society exists within the Federal Reserve System. When under attack, its officials tend to stick together. In any discussion of improving quantification and making operations more open, someone will always ask why the enemies of the System should be given more information—that is to say, more weapons—to attack it. It cannot be denied that, with more specific policies, the opposition might become fiercer and more successful. Changes in money affect different groups in very different ways. Bankers may make more money with higher interest rates, while builders may lose. Consumers are generally more concerned with interest they pay than with interest they earn. The relationships between monetary policy and fewer jobs or inflation are hard to explain. The result is that clearly expressed and announced policies may engender more opposition and make it more difficult to act for the general welfare. Interest groups strongly affected are the most likely to have strong lobbies.

Fixed public positions may also be harder to change. One of the theoretical values of monetary policy is its flexibility. If the Fed is pinned down by a public statement of what it is trying to do, it may be less willing to move. No one likes to admit error. From experience, I would agree that shifts in positions and compromises are easier if not on the public record.

It is also said that, if the Federal Reserve regularly announced its policy decisions each month, the market would falter as the announcement time approached. Those wanting to minimize risks might avoid holding security inventories. If, however, dealers have to discover by observation that there has been a shift in policy, they adjust gradually and over a longer period, thus causing less abrupt changes in market prices. On the other hand, discount rate and reserve changes currently are announced immediately and the market handles them without difficulty.

Another argument put forth against announcement of policy changes is that if the Fed is too specific it may enable individuals and firms to profit at the expense of the general public. Vast sums of money move through security markets. Federal Reserve policies, when announced explicitly, would not mean much to the average citizen. Only specialists could interpret them, thus increasing their profits inordinately. Most experts on markets, however, would take the opposite position. They believe that the better the information, the better the market. Under the present system, market experts can profit from the delay in releasing information. Hidden information is valuable to people in the market, and they can afford to spend a lot to obtain it. Their information systems, based on a continuous study of Federal Reserve operations and statements, are good. They can afford to search out special insights (a careless phrase in conversation can be valuable). After those inside the market have profited from their knowledge, they make it available to customers and eventually to the public. Of course, they may make mistakes in their reading of the Federal Reserve, but, on the whole, many do make considerable profit at the expense of those less intimately involved in day-to-day government security operations.

The Need for Quantification

I never found the arguments against quantification and against public explanations of monetary policy very convincing. Rather, I deplored the lack of clear statements of doctrine. With most of the other economists on the FOMC, I fought constantly for greater quantification. It is not possible to make sound policy without agreeing on basic operating principles and procedures. The failure to be specific has been harmful.

Although the uncertainties, complexities, and lack of knowledge are admittedly great in the field of monetary policy, I feel that a factual definition of the problems should be fused with intuition in decision making. It is not generally true that organized facts impair judgment; on the contrary, the better the understanding of an issue, the easier it is to reach a decision, even if it remains primarily a judgmental one. Research into decision making under uncertainty shows that ways can be devised to combine judgment, facts, and lack of information rationally so as to give improved results.

The failure of the Federal Reserve to be more specific has probably limited increases in its knowledge. Academic economists and people in the banking field, as well as the Fed's own staff, have been less productive because of it.

Further, it is impossible to measure degree of success or failure without a clear picture of the objective sought. Without a specific goal and target, there can be no accountability either within the System or to the public and Congress.

The Fed is responsible only for monetary policy, yet economic events have many causes. This means that it is necessary to distinguish the impact of monetary events from that of other forces. Since money must be managed, decisions must be made. The failure to define problems in concrete and specific terms does not mean that they can be avoided. It means either that decisions are less well made or that they are delegated to operating people. The FOMC should use its own best judgment. The path of monetary variables and their impact on the economy should not be determined primarily by operating decisions.

The Introduction of Formal Forecasts

The first, and probably most significant, move toward a more comprehensive approach to policy making was the inauguration of a formal forecasting system. This improvement came rather easily. The first memorandum I wrote after being appointed to the Board suggested the vital need for such a system. Projections of the GNP, credit, or the money supply were totally lacking at the time. The FOMC met every two or three weeks and, in the light of current economic events, determined policy. At the next meeting, in less than a month, policy could be altered if conditions had changed. It was felt that the frequency of meetings made longer range forecasts unnecessary. I pointed out that this was a wasteful and inefficient procedure. Vast amounts of data were supplied by the staff before and during each meeting, but without analysis or interpretation. It was as though the material were divided into three piles:

one pile of data pushing the economy upward, a second of data showing no change, and the third indicating a drop in demand. Each Committee member could then mentally weigh the size of the three piles and make up his mind whether or not the economy was in danger of excess expansion. There was no way of measuring whether an expansion was desirable or dangerous. It was impossible to ascertain the magnitude of a push or how long it would last. It was also impossible to relate the projected changes in monetary policy to the expected course of the economy.

The staff was eager to make the change. They were chafing at being restricted primarily to evaluations of the current state of the economy, feeling their expertise was underutilized. They had already been preparing bootleg forecasts and now were free to use them. Their first discussion of the outlook for the future came in October 1965 and their first forecast for the year was in 1966.

It is true that the Federal Reserve operated for over forty years without a formal projection of spending, output, prices, and employment and that, on the whole—especially since World War II —its record in recognizing changing economic conditions and altering policy has been good. But there have been several instances when the failure to understand the long time lags between changes in monetary instruments and their impact on output, employment, and prices has negated the stabilizing effect on prices that was intended. In fact, destabilization can result if the increase in spending brought about through changes in monetary policy takes effect at a time when other forces in the economy have already expanded spending to a point where demand is too large. Acceptance of the formal forecast stemmed from the Fed's desire to improve on its past performance and the increasing recognition of the existence of long lags between a policy action and its effect on the economy.

Since they were introduced, the Fed's annual forecasts have steadily improved. This is less true, however, of projections of operating factors and of monetary variables. Although they are better, I do not believe that anyone can yet project with creditable accuracy how changes in reserves will alter money, credit, and interest rates, and how these in turn will affect the economy. Monetary decision makers still do not know whether most policy actions have helped or hindered; we only know that we are improving.

We have succeeded in avoiding for over forty years the type of financial crisis that used to occur every nine or ten years.

The degree of uncertainty still evident means that existing concepts and models must be constantly tested to develop better theories, data, and judgments for the future. The Federal Reserve has put more emphasis along these lines in recent years:

—A large expenditure of effort is made to maintain and improve the flow of information. The knowledge sought includes both qualitative and quantitative data of past and current situations as well as forecasts of the future.

—Many different models are used. All are under continuous study, with elements being constantly revised so that each will encompass the latest developments in both theory and actual events. The models are used to simulate various policy options and changes in nonpolicy spheres so that the sensitivity of the economy may be estimated.

—Policy is not usually altered in response to week-to-week or short-run movements in the data. Longer time spans are used to avoid the pitfall of overinterpretation of short-run developments. Insofar as possible, attempts are made to give proper weight to the past reliability of the data.

—Policy is not based on a literal acceptance of any specific model. Rather, it develops from discussion and debate which allow for the inclusion of judgments about the economy and the model and value judgments as to goals, all of which tend to be excluded (or deeply buried) in the more formal models.

—A variety of policy tools and several monetary variables are encompassed in the analysis and decision-making process. It is recognized that each tool may have a differing impact on each monetary variable, depending on circumstances. Further, in particular periods, both tools and monetary variables may reach limits beyond which any movement may endanger some of the desired goals. Flexibility is maintained in both plans and operations to allow switching policy variables as indicators move outside their normal range.

The Method Used in Forecasting

Chart 3 shows an abbreviated list of the series which the staff projected for the Federal Reserve each week or each month. The monetary series were forecast for each week in the succeeding quarter and for each of the next four quarters. Some of the other series were also forecast on a weekly or monthly basis, but they were usually presented to the Board showing forecasts for each of the next four quarters.

When we examine the titles in the list, we find that they include most of the factors required to operate monetary policy, to measure what is happening in financial markets, and to assess the general economy:

—The five series for the monetary instruments (section 1) are the variables which are completely or almost completely controlled by the Federal Reserve through its own operations.

—The six measures of the monetary variables (section 2) are the variables whose movements may be measured as the targets for monetary actions. Their levels result from interaction between the forces controlled by the Federal Reserve and the market.

—The five fiscal variables (section 3) are summary measures of fiscal and debt policy.

—Most series cover spending and income in current dollars (section 4). There are twenty basic series in this group.

—The division of spending into physical output (section 5), employment (section 6), and prices (section 7) depends on spending (section 4), potential output (section 8), and past reactions in these spheres. There are fifteen series in these sectors.

—Finally, there is a separate and very complete balance of payments sector which can be summarized in eight or ten series (section 9).

The series are forecast in many separate ways. Some forecasts depend primarily on trends, some on past cyclical movements, some on surveys, some purely on a judgmental feel of the current situation. Other series are derived primarily from econometric

equations and computer models of past relationships. Forecasts are
based on a blend of judgmental and econometric models. The
overall structure follows the GNP and flow of funds accounts. Use
of an accounting framework guarantees that the parts add up to a
logical whole. A computer is also used to insure consistency of the
parts and the total projection. In addition, the final judgmental
forecast is checked against a similar projection from a large-scale
computer model. Such a comparison allows certain assumptions to
be reexamined. To test alternative policies, staff judgment sets the
basic assumptions. How the economy is expected to develop under
these assumptions is projected primarily by simulations made with
a large-scale econometric model.

Chart 3. *Forecast Items*

1. Federal Reserve monetary instruments

    Total reserves
    Reserves available to support private nonbank deposits
    Borrowings of reserves by member banks
    Net free reserves
    The Federal funds rate

2. The monetary variables—targets or indicators of monetary policy

    The money supply (M_1)
    The money supply (M_2)
    The bank credit proxy
    Funds raised, nonfinancial sector
    The 3-month Treasury bill rate
    The rate on new issues of Aaa corporate bonds

3. Fiscal variables

    Federal government receipts and expenditures (NIA basis)
        Receipts
        Expenditures
        Surplus or deficit
        High employment surplus or deficit
        Net Treasury borrowing

4. Spending—GNP—and income

    Personal consumption expenditures (3 series)
    Gross private domestic investment (6 series)

Net exports of goods and services (2 series)
Government purchases of goods and services (3 series)
Income estimates (6 series)

5. Physical output
    GNP in constant dollars
    Industrial production
    Housing starts, private
    Sales, new autos
        Domestic models
        Foreign models

6. Employment and unemployment
    Civilian labor force
    Unemployment rate (percent)
    Nonfarm payroll employment
    Nonfarm payroll employment, manufacturing
    Average work week, production workers, manufacturing

7. Prices
    GNP implicit deflator

8. Potential output
    Gap between potential and actual GNP
    Total labor force
    Capacity utilization, manufacturing

9. Balance of payments
    Exports of goods and services, by category
    Imports of goods and services, by category
    Balance of goods and services, by category
    Remittances and pensions, net
    U.S. Government, grants and capital
    U.S. private capital
    Foreign private capital
    Balance on current account and long-term capital
    Balance financed by official Reserve transactions

The intermixture of judgment with mathematical models is common in most economic decision making. There is general agreement that for short-run policy, econometric models of the economy by themselves have serious disadvantages. They must be adjusted to take into account the fact that a current situation may deviate from the normal assumptions upon which the models are based. They work better when the current judgment and knowledge of experts augment mechanical rules.

The degree to which the underlying series derive from formal forecasts varies greatly, as does the extent of supporting series maintained by the staff. The projection of housing starts, for example, may require up to twenty separate forecasts and one hundred different series. Some of these will be based on computer models, some on eyeball projections derived from past trends, knowledge of the current market, and the basic assumptions as to the strength of the economy.

Because of offsetting errors and because economic trends are important, the projections of major totals are usually quite good. Trouble is encountered, however, when attempts are made to relate the forecasts to changes in monetary policy. Problems occur in two spheres:

—The margins of error in the monetary variables are large. Furthermore, the errors are not closely correlated to changes in the economy.

—The impact of past and expected monetary changes on a forecast made by judgment is difficult to quantify.

Unfortunately, in a judgmental model few valves exist through which a new assumption can be inserted. The staff may agree that excess slack will exist next year and attempt to measure how much the slack can be reduced if the money supply is increased by an additional 2 percent, or if interest rates are reduced 100 basis points (1 percent) below projected levels. The problem of coordinating the expansion which may be created in individual sectors and, at the same time, insuring the proper degree of interaction is almost insurmountable. The assumptions underlying the projected developments in each sector must be reexamined. For example, as a result of much work and past experience, it might be possible to estimate how the housing sector will be directly affected by the monetary change. The same is true of plant and equipment. However, what we do not know about the impact of interest rates on consumption far surpasses what we do know. We have rough multipliers relating different sectors, but they are not suitable for simultaneous movements. For this reason, alternative policies in the judgmental model must be measured more informally. Or an econometric model may be used in place of the basic judgmental system. When we use econometric models, however, we find vast differences in their projections of monetary impacts. Consequently, the actual decisions as to what is likely to occur depend upon judgment and the maximum utilization of the numerical and analytical framework in conjunction with the information furnished by different econometric models.

To some this may seem to be very little advance over the intuitive approach. What was actually accomplished by the fight over measurement? The answer is, a great deal. It is much easier to decide to increase the money supply by 5 percent and not 7 percent if one can examine in detail a reasonable judgmental model based on a 5 percent assumption. It will show the expected degree of slack, how fast the economy is expected to close the gap between output and potential, and also where strains may be expected. If the estimated outcome is unsatisfactory, other alternatives can be examined. But, since knowledge about them will be a good deal less exact than the initial model, arguments and errors are far more likely to occur.

As a result, decisions will not be self-evident. They will depend on individual judgments and on what risks the decision makers are willing to take. Some may fear to push expansion unless there is a 95 percent probability that unemployment will not go below 4.5 percent. Others may not worry unless the probability is at least 50 percent of its dropping below 4 percent. In any case, while projections will not be exact, they may still be good enough to allow each one to take a position.

Results of the Projections

An examination of past forecasts is helpful to see how they work. Table 1 summarizes the results of eight projections made at the Federal Reserve during the typical period 1967–72. These economic forecasts did not differ greatly from those made elsewhere in this same period. Each of the projections was made four to six weeks prior to the start of a new calendar or fiscal year. The top half of the table shows the results of the projected change from the level for the current year to the level for the next year. The bottom half of the table shows the forecasts of where the economy will be in four quarters. Since they average recent past changes with the future, full year forecasts are usually better than four quarter forecasts, which are completely in the future. Four quarter forecasts are actually for a fifteen-month period, since available information does not cover the current quarter in which the projection is made.

The table shows that the Fed does very well in projecting the level of future spending. The errors in the top half of the table for the next year's GNP average less than .6 percent; and, even four quarters out, the error was only slightly over 1 percent. Furthermore, the errors for the components were not much greater. Real output and prices had about the same error as the totals. Unemployment showed a slightly larger percentage error, but that is because the base figure is comparatively small. Even the maximum error was not very great. The worst error for an annual forecast was 1.3 percent, made for the fiscal year 1969. Going out four quarters, there were two errors of slightly over $20 billion, or 2 percent of the GNP.

When we look at the percentage of error made in forecasting the changes (column 7) between two years in contrast to the actual level (column 6), we find larger errors, as would be expected. The error of $5.4 billion is a higher percentage of the forecast change in the GNP of $56.7 billion than of the new level of $932.1 billion. But, still, they are not large. For spending, as an example, 92 percent of the year-to-year changes were properly forecast; the error was only 8 percent. Other errors are greater. The year to year movements in price and output are off by about 20 percent, for instance.

While it is not evident in the table, errors were not random. They tended to be biased. This probably says something about the period, and perhaps about the forecasters. Most projections (seven out of eight for the current dollar GNP) were too low. Price increases were underprojected in every period. Errors in the next year's level of prices ranged from under .1 percent to just over 1 percent. On the average, price increases were underestimated by .75

TABLE 1. *Average GNP Projections, 1967–72* °

FORECAST FOR YEAR-TO-YEAR MOVEMENT	LEVEL		CHANGE		ACTUAL	ERROR AS % OF †	
	PROJECTED (1)	ACTUAL (2)	PROJECTED (3)	ACTUAL (4)	ERROR (5)	LEVEL (6)	CHANGE IN PERIOD (7)
GNP (in billions of $)	$932.1	$937.0	$56.7	$61.6	$ 5.4	0.6%	8.1%
GNP in 58$ (in billions of $)	$721.3	$720.5	$18.3	$17.5	$ 3.9	0.5%	21.1%
GNP Implicit Price Deflator (in %)	103.8%	104.6%	3.8%	4.6%	0.75%	0.7%	16.3%
Unemployment (in %)	4.5%	4.4%	0.6%	0.5%	0.3%	5.7%	46.5%
FORECAST FROM 4TH QUARTER TO 4TH QUARTER							
GNP (in billions of $)	$951.2	$960.8	$55.8	$65.4	$10.1	1.1%	15.7%
GNP in 58$ (in billions of $)	$726.9	$727.7	$18.7	$19.5	$ 6.7	0.9%	31.4%
GNP Implicit Price Deflator (in %)	103.5%	104.5%	3.5%	4.5%	1.0%	1.0%	22.0%
Unemployment (in %)	4.8%	4.7%	0.7%	0.6%	0.6%	11.7%	88.0%

° The average was computed from eight projections. It may not add to total because of rounding.
† Actual minus projected. Based on absolute individual errors and not on errors of mean. Absolute differences may exceed those obtained by subtracting column 3 from column 4.

percent. Since the average price increase was 4.6 percent, this
meant that year-to-year increases were missed by about one-sixth.

In contrast, the projections of real output or of the GNP in 1958
constant dollars were evenly divided between too high and too
low. The error was almost zero, if we simply add all of the projections. But, if we take a more meaningful form, the mean of the absolute errors so that the minuses do not offset the pluses, they
worked out at .6 percent.

Unemployment projections depend upon changes in real output,
in productivity, and upon the numbers in the labor force. The average miss for unemployment was .3 percent per year. Since the
average change in levels was less than 1 percent in each year, this
is a rather large miss for the year-to-year movements.

It is not clear how much improvement in the overall projections
made by the Federal Reserve can be expected. The forecast errors
are not large compared to the known errors in the indexes being
projected. The revisions in the GNP estimates have frequently
been as large or larger than the differences between the best and
the poorest forecasts.

A serious question for monetary theory and monetary policy is
the fact that the projections of the GNP are far better than the
projections of the monetary variables. The errors for the projected
monetary variables were about three times as large as errors in the
GNP, and frequently blanketed the area in which most of the controversy over monetary policy takes place. For example, many of
the debates over whether money should be tighter or easier deal in
terms of 1 or 2 percent changes in the annual rate of increase in
money. Yet these were about the size of the errors made in the
monetary projections. Most monetary discussions deal with rates of
growth of the money supply and changes in those rates of growth,
which is a considerably more difficult number to forecast than is
the change in the total stock of money. On the average, the errors
in projecting the changes in the money supply were close to 25
percent per year. The errors in projecting the year-to-year changes
in the rate of growth of the money supply were close to 50 percent.

At times the errors were exactly opposite in direction to that
which would have been expected. In 1968, compared to the forecast of November 1967, the money supply increased by 2.4 percent-

age points, or 50 percent more than expected. On the other hand, the growth in the GNP was actually under that forecast, which means that one of the largest misses in a positive direction on money accompanied the only negative miss on current dollar spending. Obviously one would have expected the contrary: that more money should have caused more spending. As an opposite example, in fiscal 1970 the money supply grew by 20 percent less than projected, but spending grew by more than the forecast. If we examine other monetary variables, we find errors as great as or greater than those in the money supply.

All of the forecasts raise another question. They were made at the beginning of the year with certain assumptions as to monetary and fiscal policy. Quite often the policy assumptions were wrong because policy was changed, either inadvertently or as a matter of decision. Yet the forecasts worked out quite well, showing how little we know about the effect of policies. Had their assumptions as to the effect of policies been correct, the Fed could not have made as good forecasts as it did; errors in the monetary sphere had less effect than expected. Such a situation is most unsatisfactory for forecasts used to evaluate policies.

The forecast results do mean, nevertheless, that the Fed has, a year in advance, a fairly good picture of the type of movements which can be expected in the economy. But still there are times when the difference between excessive or normal growth, or between prosperity and recession may be only 1 percent of spending. In such years, policy planners will have a great deal of trouble and they must worry over possible errors in their projections. However, often a clear projection that growth will speed up or slow down is sufficient information for planning.

Errors in the estimates of the relationships among the monetary variables may cause greater difficulties than the overall errors in the spending forecast. All such problems are compounded by the uncertainty as to when the monetary movements have their major impact. Also, to the extent that the projections, which tend to span only the year ahead, do not encompass the time span over which monetary changes have an impact, they are less useful. Longer-run projections are possible only with some type of econometric model, but the attendant errors are far greater.

Although occasionally decisions seem clearly logical and debate is perfunctory, such is not the normal situation. In more typical cases, the uncertainties in the situation make decisions extremely difficult. They require an analysis of the underlying situation, educated guesses as to how accurate the pattern projected for each of the proposed policies may be, and finally judgment as to which developments appear most probable and therefore which policy is most likely to achieve the desired goals.

An Application of Forecasting

The period of June to October 1968 was a humbling experience for economic forecasters and policy makers. It remains etched on the minds of all participants as a major defeat in the battle against inflation, proving how delicate was the balance between too little and too much spending.

All policy makers were aware that the economy was in a precarious state in the spring of 1968. Although their growth had slowed, war expenditures were still an inflationary force. Meanwhile, most other sectors had recovered from the 1967 slowdown. The economy was rocketing ahead. The GNP in the first half of 1968 rose at an annual rate of over 10.5 percent. Unemployment fell to 3.5 percent.

The Federal Reserve braced itself for a replay of 1966. Between November and April, the Fed had raised its discount rate by 1.5 percent, to a 5.5 percent postwar record. By June, Treasury bill rates had risen over 1.5 percent, of which .75 percent had occurred in the past six months. Bank borrowing was back to its 1966 high. For two months total reserves and the bank credit proxy (member bank deposits) had been falling. Only the money supply (M_1), as is not uncommon, was moving contrary to other measures; it was growing at a 6 percent rate.

This spurt in the economy had been correctly forecast. To forestall the inflationary pressures, President Johnson, in the summer of 1967, urgently requested Congress to enact an income tax surcharge of 10 percent. (Everyone would compute his tax in the normal way and then pay 10 percent more.) Along with most policy makers, I spent a good deal of time trying to convince Congress and the public that the surcharge was urgently needed. We failed. The public did not see the danger; or if they did they were not eager to pay more taxes to combat it. Congress was not willing to act merely on a projection of faster growth; and they too may have doubted the forecasters' accuracy. They would not fire against inflation until they saw the whites of the enemy's eyes.

As spending accelerated, business began to urge that their taxes be raised. Pressure started in the banking and housing industries, which saw the monetary handwriting on the wall, and soon spread to most others. Congress was impressed when corporate executives descended on Washington to demand not the usual cut, but an increase in taxes. Foreign exchanges were undergoing one of their recurrent crises; if the United States failed to act in a fiscally responsible manner, foreign governments would accelerate the run on our international reserves. Congress finally acted when it became convinced that the surcharge was necessary to save the dollar. President Johnson signed the Revenue and Expenditure Control Act of 1968 on June 25. It imposed a 10 percent income tax surcharge, retroactive on individuals to April 1 and on corporations to January 1.

In anticipation of the possible passage of the act, the Federal Reserve, like most federal economic agencies, prepared a forecast of how it would affect the economy and the financial markets. Almost all of these forecasts were very wide of the mark. Because the forecasts formed the basis for a number of far-reaching policy moves, the errors had serious consequences and many economists —myself included—wore sackcloth and ashes for a long time thereafter.

The forecasts all overestimated the amount by which the new surcharge would depress spending. The Fed's forecast predicted a slowing of GNP growth from 10.5 percent in the first half of 1968 to 6 percent in the second. The GNP did, in fact, slow, but only to an 8 percent rate; the forecast was off by $9.8 billion. The principal sectors that the forecast underestimated were inventory accumulation and housing. In the fourth quarter, the economy was 1 percent higher than expected, but this amount was critical to an economy balanced on the knife edge of inflation. Instead of the predicted 3.9 percent unemployment rate, unemployment fell to 3.4 percent, which was enough to send the economy into an inflationary spiral.

While the forecast was certainly one of the factors that influenced monetary policy in the wrong way for the next four months, I doubt that it played as important a role as many believe. Even without it, monetary policy would have relaxed some, partly because there was an implicit agreement with the Administration, Congress, and the concerned public that this time fiscal policy would carry the ball. The financial markets recognized both this and the fact that the demand for credit would fall as the new tax paid for more of the war. As government borrowing decreased, interest rates would fall. Investors and speculators reacted to the bill's passage by running up their inventories of securities in anticipation of the fall in interest rates. Their purchases moved prices up somewhat and interest rates down.

With hindsight, it is evident that measurement problems again plagued the Fed during this period. Most of our discussion was still centered on money market conditions. The Federal funds rate fell about a quarter of a point, and net borrowed reserves went from $385 to $150 million. The fall in the funds rate seemed insignificant; they hovered near 6 percent, whereas they had been 4 percent only a year before. On the other hand, the decrease in bank borrowing through the discount window did remove pressure from the individual banks. It was this relaxation that worried those FOMC members who were Reserve Bank presidents.

The monetary aggregates also presented a mixed bag. The growth in the money supply (M_1) slowed sharply from 8.5 percent in the quarter prior to the surcharge to 5.5 percent in the following critical four months. On the other hand, the annual growth rate of total reserves moved from negative to plus 11 percent, while bank credit went from negative to a 14 percent growth rate. The meaning of these figures was clouded because banks were purchasing for future distribution to other buyers new issues of the federal debt, and the sharp increase was thought to be temporary. Since this underwriting caused difficulties in making seasonal adjustments, there was some feeling that the estimated growth was overstated.

My views during this period were expressed in my statement at the July 16 FOMC meeting, the first after the surcharge was voted:

> For the past six months the Committee properly and gradually established a very restrictive monetary policy on the assumption that there would be little or no fiscal restraint. The largest fiscal restraint program in history has just been passed. It would not be sensible to vote for the same monetary policy now that the package has passed that was voted before. . . . The Committee should move from a monetary policy that remained restrictive even after recent market changes to a neutral one, that is, a policy where the Federal Reserve attempts to achieve a normal growth in deposits and the market determines rates based upon demand. . . . We should adopt a trend rate of growth in bank credit or total deposits as a longer run guide to operations. Specifically I believe that an annual rate of growth of 8 to 9 per cent in both the credit proxy and total deposits in the coming six months would make monetary policy neutral and should be adopted as a goal.

I maintained this position until events forced a tighter money policy in December. Even though bank credit grew considerably faster than my target, I failed to fight to curtail it because I mistakenly ascribed its growth to data that were erratic and which I thought would reverse.

This episode contained three ingredients that remain of utmost significance in the problem of managing the dollar and which have become still more obvious as time has produced subsequent examples. First, although forecasts were generally good and have become better, they probably contain an irreducible level of uncertainty. The Council of Economic Advisers and many others use a range of plus and minus 1 percent as a measure of this uncertainty. Unfortunately this range may encompass points that require very different policy decisions. Given this degree of uncertainty, the development of a decision-making process remains in an embryonic stage. As the experience of 1968 demonstrates, failure to develop the necessary policy flexibility and response to forecasting variance can lead to unfortunate results.

Secondly, the events showed that, even though the need for a better system of measuring monetary policy had seemed clear as early as 1966, little progress had been made. There was still only slight agreement on a proper set of targets or measures. The bank credit proxy was being used in the proviso, but not in a satisfactory form. The action which triggered the proviso was month-to-month credit movements, which were recognized as erratic, rather than longer-term growth rates, which accumulated to larger numbers. If the targeted increase for a longer period had been used, policy would have reacted more rapidly. Furthermore, even on the few occasions when the limits to the proviso were exceeded, the manager acted only hesitantly to tighten. He felt constrained in his moves because the Committee and the markets still concentrated most of their attention on money market conditions.

Finally, it is clear now that, even had the targets been properly chosen, there was a failure to develop operating procedures and guides that would have made it possible to reach the selected targets. The information received daily and weekly by the Desk and the System is voluminous, erratic, and frequently contradictory. It must be processed and screened in order to make it useful for operations. Failure to develop good control and data systems leaves monetary policy to follow a meandering and costly path, even when it is aimed at the proper target.

It must be noted that policy choices are based not only on the forecast of the domestic economy, but on what is happening and is expected to happen in the international sphere as well. Since the outlook for both the domestic and the international situations is considered in detail before a target is selected, we need next to look at why and how foreign events influence the managing of the dollar.

CHAPTER NINE

International Monetary Relations

TELEVISION CAMERAS came to the Federal Reserve Building on Friday, March 15, 1968. They were accompanied by banner headlines, "London Shuts Markets in Gold Crisis." Front-page stories reported that a day of wild speculation in the London gold market had led the United States to request the British authorities to close the market. The British cabinet had declared a legal bank holiday. At the same time, the United States invited its six partners in the gold pool to meet the following day in the Federal Reserve Building in Washington.

The gold pool was a device whereby the major countries pooled their purchases and sales of gold to industrial, speculative, and other nongovernmental producers or buyers. Initially the British government had held the price of gold in London at roughly $35 an ounce by supplying gold from its reserves if the demand of private buyers was raising the price above $35 and by buying gold as the price fell. However, using its reserves to perform what was in reality a responsibility for all the major countries turned out to be awkward. As a result, the eight major holders of gold (France dropped out just before this period) had agreed to have the Bank of England act as their joint agent. Losses or gains of gold resulting from the pool's operation were distributed in accordance with a fixed formula. At the same time, gold transactions continued to take place directly among central banks. Central banks which lost gold to the pool could request that the United States make up their losses.

In the three and one-half months prior to the closing of the pool, central banks had lost about $2.7 billion of gold to private buyers. Almost half of this sum had hemorrhaged out in the days immediately preceding the closing of the London market. Of the losses of all central banks, over 80 percent had come from the gold reserves of the United States which, at that point, held roughly one-quarter of world monetary gold.

Along with their headlines and stories about the Washington meeting, newspapers reported that, by a two-vote margin, the Senate had approved Public Law 90-269. This act removed the requirement in the Federal Reserve Act that a reserve of 25 percent in gold certificates be maintained behind all Federal Reserve notes in circulation. On this day the total amount of gold held by the United States just about equaled the required reserve. It would consequently have been impossible for the U.S. to have furnished gold to anyone if the Federal Reserve Board had not had the authority to suspend the requirement. Furthermore, it had taken the necessary action to do so in case the Act had not passed that day. Still, the uncertainty as to whether the United States would continue to sell gold was one of the factors leading to the run on gold. The display of partisan politics that had already delayed passage of the act could have been expensive to the United States and the world economy.

The crisis was resolved by an agreement at the meeting to reduce the importance of gold to world monetary authorities. At the conference the governments involved set up a two-tier gold market. While central banks would continue to buy and sell gold to each other at $35 an ounce, they would not buy or sell gold in the commercial markets. In these markets, prices would be free, fluctuating with the supply and demand of producers and speculators. Thus one part of the world's gold, contained in central banks, continued to serve as a monetary asset (there was facetious talk of dyeing all such gold a distinctive color) and all the remaining gold was to be treated as a commodity similar to any other metal, although surrounded, in many minds, with a special mystique. To the surprise of most pessimists, who believed the world could not function without the existence of an international monetary system based on gold, this agreement reduced the crisis and prevented any serious recurrence for the next three years.

Maintaining the *Status Quo*

The events of this March weekend confirmed a conviction which had been forming in my mind over the previous three years and which I called Maisel's Law: "In most monetary situations, particularly in the international sphere, necessary action and reform will take place only as the result of a crisis." In other words, few statesmen are willing to take decisive actions that may entail potential risks unless forced to act by a crisis.

I had begun to suspect this was true in consequence of my first year in office. Along with most outside observers of the Federal Reserve, I had the impression that the balance of payments (the deficit or surplus in the flows in international reserves) was one of the Fed's most critical concerns. The rapidity with which I had been appointed was due to events in the international sphere: the balance of payments crisis, the imposition of voluntary foreign lending controls, and so forth. About one-fifth of the time in FOMC meetings was spent discussing the balance of payments and other international events. For this reason, as soon as I joined the Board, I started an intensive review of the international situation. The conclusions that I came to, after a great deal of hard work, I still think were proper ones. The underlying approach to the balance of payments problem seemed all askew. We were not attacking the main issues. Furthermore, the actions being taken seemed extremely *ad hoc* and expensive; they treated symptoms and not the underlying disease. A new approach to the international monetary mechanism was required.

In my view the balance of payments (or international monetary) problem consisted of three distinct but related issues: liquidity, confidence, and adjustment. The first two had to be treated together. International problems of liquidity and confidence resembled those which had led to the establishment of the Federal Reserve System. World trade and the need for international reserves were growing at a rapid rate. The supply of gold, the ultimate international monetary reserve, was barely expanding. As a result, more and more dollars were being accumulated as reserves, and the ratio of gold held by the United States against its international liabilities was constantly decreasing. As the ratio fell, countries began to worry about what might occur if there were a run on the dollar. Would they get in line fast enough, or would the gold window be slammed shut in their face before they collected? Had they better withdraw gold now to be certain of obtaining it before it fell into the hands of hoarders—i.e., all other countries? Similar questions of liquidity and confidence had led to the perennial crises of the national banking system that preceded the formation of the Federal Reserve. Monetary systems are based on credit and faith; if these are lacking, a liquidity crisis occurs.

It seemed to me quite clear that action on an international scale similar to that which established the Federal Reserve ought to be taken. New international reserves unrelated to gold should be created. While the new reserves were being negotiated, we could instill confidence by guaranteeing the gold value of other countries' reserves by issuing special certificates denominated in gold. These would carry an interest rate somewhere between that now paid on the United States Treasury bills which most countries were holding as reserves and the zero interest rate they would receive on gold. The difference between the rates paid would go into a guarantee fund to make up the losses on the gold certificates in case we decided to change the price of gold. (As a matter of record, such a certificate and fund would have been very profitable to the United States; countries which held their reserves in interest-bearing Treasury bills rather than gold earned far more than they lost as a result of the eventual devaluation.)

Even more drastic action was required in the international monetary system to establish an adjustment mechanism where none existed. Exchange rates ought to change in the course of time, but the Bretton Woods system was based on fixed exchange rates. There was great opposition to any change in the price of the dollar. While it was not certain that the dollar was overvalued, it ap-

peared probable. Our current reserves were less than the amount
of capital that wanted to leave the country at existing exchange
rates. This was what lay behind the establishment of the extremely
awkward, so-called voluntary foreign credit restraint program. I
felt that the need for an adjustment mechanism ought to be publicly recognized and a new international agreement urged. In the
interim, partial adjustment might be made possible by widening
the buying and selling prices of gold, and therefore of other currencies. At the same time, capital controls ought to be replaced by
a flexible overseas investment tax which could vary in rate depending upon the amount of adjustment pressure required.

When I tried to interest other Washington policy makers in
these ideas, I made no headway. It was clear that there was an
overwhelming desire to maintain the *status quo;* some believed in
the existing system and that any tampering with it was wrong.
After my first speech expressing the view that the world might be
better off if the role of gold were reduced, I was approached by
one of the country's most distinguished bankers who headed a
large, international bank. He patted my shoulder and sighed, "You
know, young man, you may be right. But I consider it very un-
seemly for a Governor of the Federal Reserve to talk that way
about gold."

A more likely reason for the lack of interest in such changes was
that action of the type I proposed could only come about if a crisis
developed. The lack of unanimity on what moves to make and the
difficulty of negotiating sensitive multinational agreements made
change unlikely so long as operations continued. And, in fact, the
very act of negotiation might force such a crisis. Furthermore, it
was best not to tempt the fates. No one was certain how important
the mystique of gold and the fixed exchange value of the dollar
were politically. Everyone was afraid to rock the boat. Clearly this
was the reason that, in his speech announcing the end of convertibility and therefore a fall in the price of the dollar in August 1971,
President Nixon first assured the nation that the value of the dollar
would not be reduced. Five years earlier, the fear of a popular reaction if the price of the dollar was changed had been even
greater.

As I attempted to get reaction to my views, I discovered I had almost no leverage to obtain serious consideration of my proposals. Contrary to general belief, the Federal Reserve plays only a minor role in the formulation of international monetary policy, and even that is not a function of any specific rights that it has in this sphere.

The International Exchange System

The international functions of the Federal Reserve are the most complex, the least understood, and the hardest to describe. I believe that a majority of the FOMC does not have a clear understanding of the basic situation in the international field. I admit that I hesitate to trust my own analysis in this area. Perhaps because the Federal Reserve has virtually no statutory functions in the international sphere, the procedures for determining the System's own views are poor. In my experience, few if any international policy matters were weighed carefully by either the Board or the FOMC.

The responsibility for the balance of payments; for the setting and maintaining of exchange rates; for the negotiation, determination, purchasing, and spending of international reserves belongs entirely to the Administration, primarily centered in the President and the secretary of the Treasury. This is as it should be. International monetary relationships cannot be separated from foreign policy. Our balance of payments is determined primarily by our policy with respect to trade, international investments, military expenditures abroad, Agency for International Development (AID) allocations, and agreements on exchange rates and the handling of reserves. Fiscal action with respect to some of these factors may also be significant.

The most critical decisions in the international monetary sphere are concerned with determining the rates of exchange among currencies. The exchange rate is simply the price of one currency in terms of another, the rate at which currencies exchange for each other. As an example, if a Mexican has to offer 12.5 pesos to obtain a United States dollar, or a tourist wanting to buy pesos can purchase 12.5 pesos for a dollar, the exchange rate is 12.5 pesos per dollar, or $.08 per peso.

The prices of currencies, or their rates of exchange, are determined by forces of supply and demand similar to those operating in any other market. While in theory the price of a country's currency could be allowed to find its own level, as in any other market, this rarely occurs. Because the currency price affects all export and import prices, as well as prices and income for all other international transactions, it is always treated as a unique problem. Major efforts are made to influence the exchange rate, both through domestic and international policies and through the use of international monetary reserves.

To see how this works, let us take a simplified example. An American who wants to travel in Japan or to buy a Japanese camera will need yen. He obtains these yen by selling dollars to a bank which offers him yen at the going rate of exchange. The bank, in turn, offers dollars to Japanese tourists or importers. All of the dollar-yen transactions occur in the foreign exchange market. As in any market, the price or rate of exchange will depend on the number of dollars compared to the number of yen being offered. If the supply of dollars grows and the number of dollars demanded does not grow, the price of the dollar will fall and the price of the yen will rise.

Under the International Monetary Fund agreements in effect during most of my service at the Fed, if the price of yen in dollars began to rise, the Bank of Japan was obligated to increase the available supply of yen by purchasing sufficient dollars to stop the yen exchange rate from rising to more than 1 percent above par. If the price of yen fell because of an increased demand for dollars, the Japanese central bank would hold the rate up by furnishing enough dollars to buy up the excess yen. The dollars held by the Japanese government and central bank plus gold, special drawing rights, and other currencies made up the Japanese reserves. If the Japanese felt they had too many dollars, they could ask the United States government to purchase the dollars with gold.

During much of the period, the Canadian exchange system worked somewhat differently. The Canadian government did not agree to support the Canadian dollar within fixed exchange rates.

Instead, it allowed the rate to be largely determined by the exchange market. If more U.S. dollars were offered, the price of the Canadian dollar would float higher. In fact, however, the Bank of Canada controlled the amount of change or float by entering into the market on one side or the other (if a government controls the float to any extent, the term *dirty float* is used), but it allowed for wider swings over time than could have occurred under the fixed-rate system.

The ability of a country to maintain a fixed exchange rate depends on its having sufficient reserves to buy up excess supplies of its own currency offered in the exchange market. In the case of the United States, excess dollars are initially purchased by the foreign central bank. Under the fixed exchange system, the foreign central bank could then ask the U.S. government to repurchase with gold any dollars it considered excess. However, as the 1960s progressed, foreign governments were faced with a dilemma. They knew that if they asked the United States for gold they were likely to be refused. The dollar would become inconvertible. They could then continue to support the price of the dollar in terms of their own currencies by continuing to accumulate dollars, or they could allow the price of the dollar to float downward by staying out of the exchange market. Since August 1971 this decision as to whether to accumulate more dollars or to allow the price of their currencies to float higher faced foreign governments every time the demand for their money in terms of dollars rose. It created a dilemma because it was hard to decide whether the change in rates was necessary to correct a basic disequilibrium or whether rates were being driven higher by speculation. If the movement was primarily speculative, could it be halted by the accumulation of enough dollars by the foreign country? Or would the country finally lose the battle to the speculators, who would profit on their sales of dollars while the foreign central bank would take a loss on its accumulation.

Because they are concerned over the impact of movements in the price of their currencies on their domestic economy and on international trade, all countries develop policies designed to affect their exchange rates by controlling the amount of their currencies offered in the exchange markets. They do this by influencing the amount of their foreign trade and financing. All of these international transactions are summarized in the balance of payments accounts.

Desirable or necessary policies differ depending upon whether a country is attempting to maintain a fixed or relatively fixed exchange rate or is allowing its currency rate to float. They also depend upon whether it is gaining reserves or has adequate reserves to pay for the excess amounts of its currency offered in the exchange markets.

When a country gains reserves it can, unless forced to act otherwise by other countries, simply continue to amass the foreign currencies. On the other hand, a country which is losing reserves must take prompt action itself. Unless other countries are willing to hold its currency and thus, in effect, lend it foreign exchange (which others have been willing to do with the dollar) it must take action to bring its international accounts into balance. The whole purpose of holding reserves is to give their owners flexibility. To the extent that a nation holds and is willing to spend reserve assets acceptable to others, it can finance imbalances in its foreign accounts. When it runs out of reserves it must take other action.

Possible actions should be examined in the light of the basic theory of why nations cooperate in the international monetary sphere. This primary aim of international economic policy has been stated in the Articles of Agreement of the International Monetary Fund as including, "The expansion and balanced growth of international trade . . . and the contribution this makes . . . to the promotion and maintenance of high employment and real income and to the development of the productive resources." The 1930s demonstrated the dangers of economic nationalism, while teaching the advantages of economic interdependence. The prosperity of every nation depends somewhat upon the prosperity of its neighbors, a fact leading to the generalization that nations can prosper only if they prosper together; they must act together to create an economic environment conducive to their mutual welfare.

Each country must decide what maximum contribution to its welfare it expects from international trade and investment. It must then weigh this expected gain against the potential disturbances to its internal economy which may result from the discipline required by international monetary relationships, a discipline imposed either directly from creditors or indirectly from movements in exchange rates and shortages or surpluses of international goods.

Factors Influencing the Balance of Payments

International monetary problems develop when a country loses or gains international reserves too rapidly. When the losses or gains become excessive, the conditions causing the reserve movements must be changed. We call the mechanism by which international accounts are evened when they are out of balance (or in disequilibrium) the adjustment process. It is the central issue for any country running too large a deficit, or too large a surplus, in its payments accounts.

To understand this problem and why it is of fundamental importance, it helps to sort out the main reasons why a country may run a balance of payments surplus or deficit.

The Balance on Goods, Services, and Remittances

The largest sector of our international accounts includes a wide variety of current transactions, such as exports and imports of goods and services, military expenditures and sales, travel and transportation, income and payments on investments, and a variety of other miscellaneous factors. Until 1971 this sector showed a large net balance in favor of the United States. In early periods, the net total was large enough to offset fully deficits in other accounts. For most of the past decade, while this account continued to show a surplus, it could not cover payments in other sectors. As a result, U.S. international reserves dropped steadily while U.S. debts to foreign governments rose. The rapid deterioration of this account in 1971 signaled the disintegration of our entire reserve situation.

The current account balance is influenced by cyclical forces, by shifting prices, by movements in tariffs and government aids and restrictions on trade, as well as by the longer-run factors of tastes and productivity. Large changes in a country's exports and imports can result from movements in domestic production and income. Foreign goods and sales to foreigners are competitive with domestic ones. The greater the pressure on a country's own resources, the more demand will be filled from overseas and the less goods will be sold abroad. If a country's production and income decline, its trade balance usually becomes more favorable. Fewer goods (including goods from abroad) will be purchased and more effort will be devoted to export sales. The trade balance will improve.

Price and wage movements within a country and among countries vary over time. In recent periods of inflation, these forces have been particularly important in influencing the balance of payments. Accounts may be knocked out of kilter because countries' economies change at differing rates. The balances of trade reflect relative movements in the productivity of individual national economies. They can also be altered when new resources (for example, gas or oil) are discovered or old ones are used up.

As the United States economy has become richer and more service-oriented, there has been an increased demand for foreign goods and travel. Some changes in this pattern are probably explained by rising income, but some may also reflect a real change in tastes. Policy considerations—domestic as well as foreign policy decisions—also alter trade relationships and, hence, affect international reserves. The Common Market and the Kennedy Round have had significant influences on trade. Agricultural prices and subsidies react to local domestic pressures and to foreign ones. Trade negotiations seem constantly under way.

Shifts in Capital Flows

By far the largest movements in reserves, however, are caused by capital shifts. For example, between 1969 and 1970, the outflow, or deficit, from reported long- and short-term capital flows out of the United States increased by about $16 billion. From 1970 to 1971 it again went up by $6.5 billion. There were also nearly $10 billion more in losses shown in the "errors and omission" column, which almost certainly reflected capital movements. Thus we see that a deterioration of over $32 billion in the United States' international reserves occurred in two years, almost entirely as a consequence of private capital movements. As a matter of interest, total U.S. reserve assets were less than $17 billion at the end of 1969, an amount obviously insufficient to meet such massive shifts. During the currency crises of 1973, movements through exchanges were so rapid that foreign central banks accumulated over $9 billion in only a few days. Clearly, attempts to maintain semirigid rates were leading to an ever-increasing amount of speculation and shifts of short-term capital balances. All other countries face a similar international reserve problem, since potential capital movements are large enough, given our current system, to overwhelm completely the amount of reserves any nation can hold on hand.

In normal periods, capital movements may alter their pattern because of basic economic factors. Relative interest rates among countries shift. Expected profits change. Taxes may make foreign investments more attractive, or vice versa. As such influences affect the desirability of investment within a country, foreign capital or investment is attracted or repelled.

More dangerous, however, are shifts in expectations and speculation about movements in exchange rates. When the expected changes in rates are large, they cause violent and sudden capital movements. The fear of losses or hope of gains from changes in currency exchange rates may inspire rapid shifts of so-called hot money. Political crises, fear of war, or fear of capital controls can also lead to large and abnormal flows of funds.

Official Expenditures

The final major factor in the balance of payments accounts is government expenditures, grants, and loans. In the last decade, these items have run in the vicinity of $9 billion a year, with somewhat more than half consisting of military expenditures. At times offsets arise from loan repayments and military sales. Shifts in these accounts due to the Vietnam War and also to changes in the funding of the AID and NATO programs have been significant.

Movements in these accounts may be completely unrelated to the exchange rate or other market forces. Governments use their international financial positions to fulfill national objectives. The decision to spend a country's resources for war or for national security is not made, or modified, out of any consideration of prices or profitability. The resulting movements of monetary reserves, whether in the form of currencies or gold, are tied to political, military, and diplomatic judgments not economic ones.

International Events and Federal Reserve Decisions

Events in the international sphere not only make news; they influence Federal Reserve decisions. I have estimated that as much as 20 percent of the time of the Federal Open Market Committee was taken up with international data. Because of its more diverse responsibilities, time spent by the Board was relatively less.

The Government

Most of the actions to offset or correct monetary crises must be taken by the Administration and are managed by Treasury or cabinet committees. The Treasury, through the secret United States Stabilization Fund, with the Federal Reserve as agent, buys and sells the country's international reserves—gold, special drawing rights, and foreign currencies. It also may borrow foreign currencies and lend dollars through operations with the International Monetary Fund, or directly with foreign governments through a swap network.

The government can also influence the balance of payments through trade policy. Tariffs, tariff surcharges, taxes, quotas, subsidies on international purchases, sales, and services of any kind have all been and are being used by most countries to change their balance of payments. The United States has also utilized direct and indirect controls and the investment equalization tax to influence international capital movements. The Administration delegated to the Federal Reserve the operation of such controls over financial institutions through the Voluntary Foreign Credit Restraint Program. Government expenditures and loans abroad, particularly through military and AID programs, have also had massive effects upon the need for international payments. Finally, and most important, the government can determine or influence the exchange rate between the dollar and other currencies and the dollar and gold.

The Federal Reserve

The FOMC also makes decisions which have some influence on flows of international reserves. A review of international monetary developments, including movements in exchange rates and reserves, accompanies each review of the state of the domestic economy. Prospective international developments influence the monetary targets selected. In addition, the FOMC authorizes purchases, sales, and loans of foreign currencies. International considerations enter into the selection of the monetary target because open market operations have some effect on the balance of payments. The level of domestic spending affects the balance of trade. Perhaps more significantly, international capital flows respond to relative interest rates at home and abroad. If interest rates fall in the United States while they rise in Europe, some capital will be held abroad to take advantage of rate differentials.

Purchases, sales, and borrowing of foreign currencies or lending of dollars to other central banks and governments are specialized open market operations designed especially to alter, for a time, official foreign reserve movements. Loans of foreign currencies are primarily "swaps." The swap programs were designed to aid during speculations against a country's currency, to cover temporary imbalances, or to allow intervention to steady a country's exchange rate. They are used to guarantee exchange values. The Fed's joint lines of credit with other central banks and governments in 1973 totaled over $11 billion.

Let us see how the swap operates. Assume that in a period of convertibility a foreign government received dollars, but was afraid that the dollar might be devalued. It would want to hold international reserves whose price was fixed in its own currency rather than dollars. Instead of demanding gold, the country could ask the Federal Reserve to buy the excess dollars by borrowing its currency from the country's central bank. As a result, the United

States would owe the country marks or francs or pounds or whatever else was borrowed, instead of dollars. If, with such a debt, the United States devalued, it would have to repay the debt at a later date by buying the foreign currencies in the market at a higher rate. Under a system of floating rates, the country borrowing on swaps is responsible for buying back the currencies borrowed at whatever rates exist in the market. At the time of the August 1971 suspension of convertibility, the Fed was in debt for $3 billion. Losses on these borrowings were subsequently close to $400 million. The countries which had protected part of their reserves by swaps received, in effect, more dollars.

The swaps were initiated as a way for the Federal Reserve to make dollars available to foreign countries needing them to buy their own currencies in the market in order to maintain their value. Important loans of this type succeeded in avoiding devaluation for Italy, Canada, and other countries in periods when their currencies were under attack. It was only when the dollar became clearly overvalued that borrowing, instead of lending, by the Fed became the general rule.

The Role of International Monetary Policies

The decision as to what role international trade and investment is to play in national goals is clearly a critical one for the government. I felt throughout my service in Washington that it was never really faced up to properly. Partly this was because of Maisel's Law, that reform will be undertaken only after a crisis has occured. Partly, I believe, it was because the State Department failed to recognize how important economics is in the foreign policy picture. Furthermore, there was a failure to present the President with a clear picture of the relevant costs of different options.

The Federal Reserve did not do much better. While it was in a peripheral position where the ultimate policy decisions were the President's, I still felt we were being asked to use our policy instruments to support unsound policies and were failing to perform our function of flagging these issues properly for the President and the nation. It was a case in which both the Treasury and the President were willing to overuse the monetary instruments because they seemed politically less expensive to the Administration than if it used its own tools. The costs of Fed action, however, were significant to the country. The situation was analogous to the Treasury's asking the Fed to peg the domestic bond market during and after World War II, to save costs on the public debt: We were being asked to peg international reserves. I believed it was the duty of the Fed to point out the costs as cogently as possible; only in this way could we be certain that they were properly included in all Administration reviews and analyses of the costs and benefits of existing policy.

On national economic policies, the Fed emphasized the importance of its independent position, which enabled it to safeguard its policies from domination by the Treasury and to take (as it does) an independent stand. In the international field, however, the Board and the FOMC were failing to perform this critical function. Unfortunately, the occasions on which it was possible to take such a stand officially were limited. Most Fed decisions had no clear-cut international input. Foreign considerations tended to be limited to routine approvals of swaps, or were simply among the many factors which an individual member of the FOMC assessed when he voted for a particular target.

One of the few occasions when this was not true, however, was at the time of the March 1968 gold crisis. My opinion as to what I felt the nation and the Fed should have done with respect to gold and the international monetary system between 1965 and 1971 is set forth in a memorandum (see pages 210–12) that I sent to the Board and to various members of the President's cabinet and subcabinet who were deliberating on what position the United States should take at the Washington gold conference.

The memorandum grew out of a special meeting of the FOMC on Thursday, March 14, 1968. The Committee, with Governors Mitchell and Robertson and myself dissenting, authorized an increase in the Fed's swap lines by $2 billion and, in effect, approved the plan of the special manager for foreign operations to borrow up to $8.5 billion additional in foreign currencies in an attempt to save the *status quo* in the gold negotiations. I felt that, in this case, the Fed had the duty to point out to the President, the Treasury, and other members of the cabinet why we thought borrowing billions in foreign currencies would be unwise, that we would be throwing good money after bad. While I was willing to vote the funds if the President determined that such a policy was necessary to the national interest, it seemed clear to me that the Fed was failing in its responsibility to Congress and the public if it did not make its views known to the President before he made his decision.

Since the vote was passed over our dissent, it was clear that a majority of the FOMC did not agree with this point of view. Chairman Martin was agreeable, however, to my sending the memo to the governmental decision-making group on a personal basis.

The Adjustment of Imbalances

Each time the dollar appeared to be in trouble again, in addition to authorizing swaps to paper over losses in reserves, the Federal Reserve had to decide whether the international situation ought to cause a change in its monetary targets. If the Fed did not act or if its policies failed, the Administration would have to use some of its tools.

The Income-Price Effects

A country losing international reserves or sustaining a drop in the price of its currency comes under pressure to tighten money in order to slow the growth of domestic income. This may, but need not, be related to internal price pressures. Tightening is expected to lower GNP, and therefore imports, while making exports more profitable. However, such a policy is both more necessary and more logical for countries in which exports and imports make up a large share of the GNP than for the United States, where international activities are relatively insignificant. In the first place, countries in which the international sector is large have little choice. Their deficits can grow large and reserves inadequate. Another important reason for their greater willingness to act is that in these

BOARD OF GOVERNORS
OF THE
FEDERAL RESERVE SYSTEM

Office Correspondence

Date March 15, 1968

To   Chairman Martin

Subject: Gold and Swaps Policy

From   S. J. Maisel *SJM.*

(STRICTLY CONFIDENTIAL FR)

This memorandum explains somewhat more fully the background of my vote yesterday <u>against</u> expanding the Federal Reserve swap network and <u>against</u> employing it actively until we reach new agreements with our swap partners. These agreements should specify how over the intermediate period we are to share possible losses of gold to speculators as well as how to cover reserve gains by foreign banks as a result of the current over-valuation of the dollar. They should also cover longer term agreements looking toward the demonetization of gold and toward ways in which new methods of exchange and trade adjustments can be activated.

I am not optimistic that such agreements are possible. In effect, then, I am arguing that the present system cannot be maintained. Our bargaining power will be greater if we immediately refuse to fund through swaps, or gold sales, speculative attacks on the dollar. This weekend's negotiations should seek temporary standstill agreements on reserve movements while more basic changes are negotiated. These agreements should include methods of dealing with speculative reserve losses that would not require the United States to give exchange value guarantees on foreign reserve gains.

I. The United States faces three somewhat separate problems:

   1. Gold speculation and the price of gold.
   2. Speculation against the dollar in terms of other currencies.
   3. The methods of adjustment of the price of the dollar relative to gold and other currencies.
       (a) In the short run (defined as: "end of Vietnam War plus three years").
       (b) In the long run.

The United States is in a true state of foreign exchange disequilibrium which will not be corrected under existing policies. As a result we cannot meet the immediate problems of speculation or the long-run adjustment problem without basic policy changes.

The required policies include new international agreements covering each of the above problems, i.e.,

   1. Exchange rate adjustments.
   2. Meeting currency speculation.
   3. Gold policy.

To: Chairman Martin   -2-   March 15, 1968

Unless new policies are agreed to and actively implemented by eight or nine of the Group of Ten countries, the present international monetary system will not be stabilized. We will only be throwing good money after bad. Until new policies are agreed to, the United States should embargo sales of gold and should give minimum support (simply enough to avoid extreme day-to-day fluctuations) to existing exchange rates.

II. There are three basic causes of the current situation:

1. The relative price of the dollar is too high in terms of our existing and potential international commitments.
2. The Bretton Woods international monetary system lacks a real method of adjustment for key currencies.
3. The reserve base lacks both a method of normal growth and is inherently unstable because of potential movements among its components.

The magnitude of the problems would be somewhat smaller if our international commitments were reduced or partially assumed by others. A relative decrease in the price of the dollar (an increase in the dollar price of foreign currencies but not necessarily gold) is also necessary. While such a relative shift could come about as a result of a less inflationary or more deflationary monetary-fiscal policy in the United States compared to our trading partners, I feel confident such relative shifts cannot solve the short-run problems and are extremely unlikely to solve the long-run problem.

III. To solve the short-run problem at existing exchange rates, we would need

1. More controls over foreign expenditures, both public and private.
2. More taxes on foreign expenditures.
3. A highly deflationary monetary-fiscal policy.
4. A method of insuring long-run adjustments.
5. The clear understanding on the part of our foreign partners of what the real problem is plus a firm commitment to cover almost the entire expected foreign exchange needs of a violent period of private speculation plus a considerable share of the needs brought about by our current disequilibrium.

Since I am pessimistic about the possibilities and effectiveness of cutting our short-term exchange needs much if at all by either monetary-fiscal policies (because short-run elasticities are too small) or by tax and control policies, this means we must have new adjustment policies. The adjustment policies will have to include methods of gradually changing the exchange rates among key currencies. In addition, they probably should include more flexible trade adjustment procedures than now seem possible under GATT. Finally, a better procedure for handling different types and growth rates of reserves may be necessary.

To: Chairman Martin   -3-   March 15, 1968

In the intermediate period while these are being negotiated and made effective, we will need firm commitments by others as to the amount of their dollar gains they will fund over an intermediate period. Unless these commitments cover both their total possible reserve gains due to speculation plus some of the considerable gains that they will receive due to the fundamental disequilibrium in the current system, the existing system will collapse.

IV. The problem of gold speculation is separable to some extent from that of exchange requirements. It could probably be met by a massive infusion into the private markets from existing monetary gold stocks plus an embargo of three to five years by the major central banks of gold purchases. This would mean an immediate partial demonetization of gold with adjustments in reserves made through certificates, SDR's, or Fund drawings. It would look forward to a total demonetization when better systems of exchange rate and reserve adjustments come into effect.

Unless the other major countries agree to a partial demonetization of gold, we should probably embargo all gold sales. This would look forward to moving toward a new system of two or a few monetary blocs with special agreements on settling of accounts among and between them.

Obviously no solution is good. Since all are difficult, on the surface there may appear to be some major advantages of sticking with current policies and hoping for the best. This policy, however, has already been tried for too long. The British experience plus the failure of the Gold Pool operation since November lead me to believe that we cannot be optimistic. We should retain only minor hopes that we can reach equilibrium without a major change in the system. We risk great losses with only a small chance of gain if we continue to put off basic decisions on how policies should be changed.

cc: Other Members of the Board

countries the cost of tighter income may be felt more abroad than at home. As imports fall, jobs are lost among foreign, not domestic workers. In the United States most of the unemployment occurs at home. Slicing back growth of domestic income is an acceptable technique only if a deflationary policy is desired for internal reasons, when excessive demand is leading to both domestic inflation and foreign payments imbalances. On the other hand, if the domestic economy is performing properly, attempting to achieve balance through lowering incomes may be an intolerable policy. Seeking external balance primarily at the expense of domestic programs, income, and employment is both bad economics and probably poor politics.

Unfortunately the present state of the economic art is still inadequate when it comes to reliable estimates of the costs versus the benefits derived from cutting domestic demand to reduce a balance of payments deficit. While estimates of the magnitudes involved are unreliable, they do indicate that the process is expensive. Some studies suggest that for each decrease of $10 billion annually in the GNP (assuming for the moment no price side-effects), U.S. imports of goods and services should drop by $550 to $650 million. Even though American producers with less domestic demand would try to sell more abroad, exports would be expected to drop also because countries whose incomes decrease as a result of selling less to us would buy less from us. Depending on foreign reactions, on the time period, and on the amount by which the other countries can offset the decline in their income, the net gain in the entire balance of trade has been estimated in the range of $150 to $350 million for each $10 billion drop in U.S. GNP. In other words, if domestic monetary policy were used to tighten money, and it only lowered income without influencing relative foreign prices or capital movements, a GNP decline of from $85 to $200 billion per year (or from 10 to 20 percent of total output) would be needed to offset a balance of payments deficit of $3 billion.

Tighter money and lower income produce another indirect effect. With higher unemployment, prices rise less rapidly. Whether, or how much, prices will fall is not as clear. Relative prices do appear to have a considerable impact on international payments balances. Some estimates suggest that a 1 percent drop in wholesale prices relative to those of the rest of the world would be expected to improve the trade balance by anywhere from $400 to $600 million per year. If these estimates are roughly correct, to adjust the balance of payments by $3 billion, U.S. wholesale prices would have to improve by somewhere between 5 and 8 percent compared with those for the rest of the world.

Interest Rate Effects

Changing open market targets can have another effect on the balance of payments. Creating less money can cause domestic interest rates to rise. If people are convinced of the continued rigidity of exchange rates, short-term capital flows primarily reflect differences in interest rates among nations. For instance, a company expecting no change in exchange rates will prefer to receive 6 percent by investing in Montreal to 5 percent from holding money in New York. Longer-term capital flows are less affected by short-term changes in domestic rates; they depend upon the expectations of individuals and corporations as to the relevant rates of profits and risks in different countries.

The Federal Reserve has come under periodic pressure from foreign governments and central banks to "harmonize interest rate policies," by which is meant in most cases to raise rates in the United States to the level charged abroad. I opposed such suggestions in the FOMC because I know of no reason to expect that similar interest rates should prevail and be the proper ones for the major nations of the world. Differences should be expected because financial institutions and fiscal policies differ greatly in each country; their incomes expand and contract in distinct phases. There is little or no relationship among the tax rates and savings habits of various countries. Prices move at different rates. To change U.S. monetary policy in an attempt to equalize domestic interest rates with those abroad may be either excessively inflationary or deflationary depending upon domestic aggregate demand and on desires to save or invest in real capital goods. There have been times when the domestic situation called for a shift in monetary policy which was useful in influencing international capital flows. Clearly, in these cases interest rates could be and were harmonized. The argument to raise rates or lower them for international purposes seemed invalid to me, however, when to do so was incompatible with domestic policy.

Government Instruments

The discussion of capital movements points to the use of other instruments to bring the exchanges into balance. During most of my Washington service, I felt that each time the Fed was asked to conduct monetary policy for foreign reasons at the expense of the domestic economy, a waste was incurred that could have been avoided if the government had used its instruments properly.

We have seen that, in the short run, massive movements in capital are the major causes of shifts in the balance of payments. The largest of these flows are due to speculation—or more politely, the attempt by multinational firms to insure that they profit rather than lose if exchange rates move. When exchange rates are fixed, the costs of transferring money, in the hope that the current exchange system may break down with a consequent major adjustment of rates, are small compared to the possible gains. If exchange rates moved more freely, the risks and costs of these speculative movements would be far higher.

Capital movements have always been recognized as a distinct problem in the international monetary field. They can frequently cause disequilibrium in and be harmful to the country losing funds. As a result, the postwar monetary agreements place them in a special category. A country can use controls to regulate capital movements, even though controls are improper to maintain exchange rates when the current account is in fundamental disequilibrium. Nevertheless, procedures for controlling excess capital movements remain a source of major controversy. For instance, the United States was under pressure for most of the past decade to impose controls over capital flowing abroad. Although administrative problems are considerable, I believed that controls might make sense in specific instances, namely, to dampen speculative movements. But it seemed to me wrong to impose such controls in an attempt to hold the exchange rate at an artificial level. Therefore, I did not favor the capital controls in the form in which they existed.

They were, however, the responsibility of the Administration; and, as long as basic policy required a rigid exchange rate, they had to be used and administered by the Federal Reserve.

It seemed to me that capital controls could be improved and made more suitable to control speculative movements, which they did poorly, and I attempted to convince others that changes should be made. But, while a majority of the Federal Reserve Board agreed, little action was possible. So long as we retain a hybrid system with semirigid exchange rates or a controlled (dirty) float, pressures will continue on the Federal Reserve to use monetary policy to influence capital movements as well as on the Administrations to use direct controls over capital. I, therefore, urged that exchange rates be made less rigid and that, as an initial step, wider margins be introduced. Either of these changes can increase the risk involved in speculation and thus can cut the volume of large-scale capital flows. Wider, but not wide enough, margins were finally adopted.

Other methods of adjustment combine trade and fiscal action. Purchases abroad can be restrained by tariffs, quotas, or other controls. Systems of special taxes on foreign investment or trade have been devised and used by the United States and others, theoretically to permit a temporary separation of some parts of the domestic economy from foreign ones. Many countries offer subsidies, cheap credit, or other aid to exports.

Policy in this entire sphere has grown in a haphazard, *ad hoc* manner. When we examine the statements of the government officials involved, they often make little sense. They contain a mixture of protectionism, fear of exchange movements, and beliefs left over from the days when we were trying to save gold. There is a failure to differentiate between instruments needed in periods of temporary imbalances and ones concerned with the long-run development of the international payment, investment, and trade systems.

Adjustments through Exchange Rates

Recognizing the difficulty of adjusting flows of international funds through changes in income, interest rates, or controls, most economists after the mid-1960s argued that the balance of payments problem could be solved only by a system which allowed exchange rates to adjust. In contrast to the minor, and often undesired, results which occur when monetary policy is used to attempt to correct international imbalances, changes in exchange rates have an immediate effect on relative prices and a greater and more immediate effect on international equilibrium. If the exchange rate of the dollar falls, i.e., if it costs more dollars to buy a German mark, the effect is to raise the price of German goods sold in the United States. For example, if the dollar is devalued by 10 percent, the cost of a Volkswagen in the United States, assuming that its price in marks does not change, will rise approximately 10 percent or, say, from $2,000 to $2,200. Fewer Volkswagens will then be sold in the United States. At the same time, U.S. machine tools can compete better in Brazil because their costs fall relative to German ones, and exports from the United States will rise.

I was one of those who felt equilibrium could be reached only through changes in exchange rates. From 1966 on, I argued the case for a new adjustment mechanism. (The arguments were basically extensions of those found in my memorandum, pages 210–12.) The question is why this policy, which seemed so obvious to many analysts then and to most of them now, failed so completely to influence five secretaries of the Treasury and two Presidents. Why did those who made the decisions insist for so long on maintaining an overvalued dollar rather than allowing the exchange rate to move, even after it became very obvious that the imbalance was creating major difficulties in our internal economy?

Both before and after August 1971, when I was asked this question, I simply quoted my law of no action except in crises. Obviously, however, both Administrations justified their policies by citing other reasons. It is worthwhile to consider some of them because each one is bound to reappear in the future during the course of adjusting to a new international monetary system. While not quite as applicable in a system of floating rates, they still apply because countries remain concerned over the magnitude and volatility of their exchange rate movements.

First, and probably most important, is national pride. Changing an exchange rate is looked upon as a defeat in a major international contest whose importance falls somewhere between the

Olympics and a war. As an example, on several occasions the United Kingdom made major sacrifices in order to maintain a fixed price for the pound sterling, even though the relative value of the pound had been set almost arbitrarily and was improper. Similarly, many people in the United States felt that altering the exchange rate for the dollar was an admission that our economy's competitive performance must have been poor and indicated some basic weakness in our character. However, if we look at a major competitive index, the unit labor costs in manufacturing, we find that at the time of the devaluation in August 1971 the United States had been ahead for most of the prior decade. In fact, relative to our competitors, unit labor costs in the United States rose above their 1961 base only in 1969; in all other years they showed a relative improvement.

A second factor is that a fixed exchange rate serves as an outside pressure for better internal economic policy. Protection of the dollar can be invoked as necessary to protect the national honor. Thus people who fear a bias toward inflation and, in particular, believe that most Administrations err on the side of too much spending, feel that international constraints on what a government can do are extremely valuable. The restrictive functions of a central bank are made easier and it operates better to the extent that it is subject to foreign pressures toward tighter money.

This argument used to strike me as basically illogical. I felt the American people were far more concerned with inflation than they were with exchange rates. But my Washington experience taught me differently. A group of congressmen who held the swing votes on many fiscal issues could be appealed to by a call to save the dollar when they could not be convinced of the advantages of fiscal responsibility merely to fight inflation.

Third, it was claimed that fixed exchange rates were necessary to maximize the advantages of international trade and investment. This assumption cannot be derived from theory, but was said to be the lesson learned from experience by men in the field. Canada, however, had floating exchange rates for much of the postwar period. Most studies of this experience have found it worked well and, further, that flexible exchange rates gave the Canadian economy a decided advantage. As experience with floating by major countries grows, this claim will be thoroughly tested.

A fourth argument holds that having New York as the financial center of the world is profitable for the United States. Since those knowledgeable about exchange rates are primarily those who profit by this fact, I have always been somewhat suspicious of this view. It seemed possible that the national welfare was being confused with the personal welfare of those trading in the international exchanges. Furthermore, on casual observation, it appears that London is a more profitable financial center since the devaluation of the pound than when great efforts were being made to hold the value of sterling fixed.

A fifth argument merely pointed out that international trade was expanding rapidly and successfully under the regime of fixed rates. Why take a chance by changing a winning combination?

A final point is the one I believe has the greatest validity and which I have cited frequently in pointing out the potential costs and dangers of exchange rates freely fluctuating with no limits or intervention. In many countries the exchange rate, or the price of the country's currency, is the most important of all prices. A change in the exchange rate alters the relationship between export and import prices and between jobs in the export and import industries. There is a shift in real income from one group in the country to another. Since the impact on exporters in many countries is concentrated and obvious, whereas the favorable effects on prices of lowering the cost of imports when the exchange rate is rising are diffused, the political outcry is immediate. Countries, particularly those dependent on export expansion to give an impetus to the domestic economy, hesitate to raise their exchange rates for fear of losing their competitive position. On the opposite side, a country that devalues finds that its import prices rise; if these play a significant role in the economy, inflationary pressures may be increased. The net effect of these factors is strong enough to make the exchange rate an extremely important price, both economically and politically. No country wants to give up control completely over such a vital price, whether the control be relinquished to other countries or to the most perfect, impersonal market. This reluctance is even stronger if it is believed that freely fluctuating market prices can be dominated by speculative swings in capital movements.

These arguments appear much weaker now than they did when used to justify the adamant stand for no adjustment through exchange rates. Perhaps other forces were at work. Supporters of fixed rates may have believed that adjusting rates in some way downplayed the importance of international trade and commerce. And a good internationalist had to support the secretaries of the Treasury and State in their positions or be thought of as an isolationist who did not recognize the importance of foreign relations. In addition, I believe that there was poor analysis and a failure to recognize the dangers of attempting to prop up an overvalued dollar. It is significant that economists of all persuasions supported the need for greater flexibility. Those who supported the fixed rates seemed unconcerned over the costs of their policies.

These costs were brought out more clearly following August 15, 1971, when the dollar was made nonconvertible. At the Smithsonian negotiations in December 1971, the U.S. government estimated the size of the fundamental disequilibrium in the value of the dollar. These estimates indicated that the policy of maintaining the dollar's price rigid in the face of fundamental changes in the world's production and trading patterns and of shifts in the value of other currencies had caused an estimated shortfall of $13 billion in the basic balance of payments. In the course of these negotiations, the other major industrial countries agreed that, if the U.S. devalued against gold by 8.57 percent by changing its purchasing price from $35 to $38 an ounce, they, on the average, would revalue their currencies upward against gold. The net result was that the value of the dollar in terms of other currencies would fall by 10 percent or so. It was estimated that, after a considerable adjustment period, this devaluation would improve the United States' basic balance of payments by $8 to $9 billion. In effect, all agreed that the United States dollar had been overvalued by at least 10 percent. Similarly, it was agreed that U.S. exports of goods and services were at least $8 billion below a desired equilibrium level. The new crisis and adjustments of 1973 made it appear that even the U.S. estimates in 1971 of the costs of an overvalued dollar were too low. The agreement to change the price of gold to $42.22 per ounce was believed a sufficient devaluation, but speculative capital flows continued.

Because the problems in this area are understood by very few, the unfortunate effects on the domestic economy of the overvaluation of the dollar had rarely been brought out in public discussions prior to this time. I had estimated that overvaluation was responsible for a loss in jobs and output in the United States of over 1 percent. In effect, these jobs had been exported by our unwillingness to change the exchange rate of the dollar. It seemed to me that a great deal of the rise in protectionism, the demand for import quotas and marketing agreements, was a direct result of the overvaluation. Jobs were not lost across the board. Unemployment hit only in specific industries in which foreign competitive pressures were greatly increased as a result of the incorrect exchange rate. These industries, properly, demanded protection. At the same time, this situation threatened the long-run welfare of the nation. The industries were correct in their analysis that they temporarily needed aid, at least until the dollar was properly valued. However, if we changed our entire approach to international trade in deference to purely short-run conditions in certain industries, we would be less well off in the long run.

The Federal Reserve's International Record

The impact of international questions on actual decisions made by the Federal Reserve was much smaller than the amount of time devoted to them. The dollar is managed primarily to achieve domestic, not international, objectives; few conflicts arise between policy determined entirely on domestic grounds and that which would be adopted for the purpose of affecting the international monetary situation. I estimate that international considerations caused a change in the actual target of the FOMC, during the period I served on the Fed, from what it would have been on purely domestic grounds in only eight out of more than one hundred directives. In some additional cases, the directive was shaded, but not drastically, because of international reserve flows. The percentage of Board policy decisions affected was probably about the same. In addition, the System engaged in swaps, administered controls for the Administration, and carried out other routine functions.

I was more dissatisfied with the actions of the Federal Reserve in the international sphere than in any other. This was true partly because I believed the Administration was asking us to support an illogical policy, partly because I felt some of my colleagues were overweighting international considerations in their votes on targets in the directive, and partly because the organization of the Board and FOMC for international decisions was poor.

The Position of the FOMC

Three distinct viewpoints on the weight to attach to the balance of payments existed (and I believe still do) in the Open Market Committee. The number of supporters for each view is fluid.

One group recognizes that the authority and responsibility for the balance of payments rests with the Treasury and not the Federal Reserve; but they believe that international monetary problems are so important, both because of their domestic impacts and for the well-being of the world, that the Federal Reserve must assume major responsibilities in this sphere. They are strongly influenced by the fact that central banks have traditionally assumed such a responsibility. As we know, under the gold standard, and still today in many countries, the protection of international reserves is the major function of central banks.

This group gives great weight to international flows as a determinant of monetary action. When the balance of payments shows a large deficit, more restrictive monetary policy is called for. Tighter money means that the Federal Reserve is fulfilling its international responsibility. Over the past ten years the balance of payments has served as an important argument for restrictive policies, since the overvalued dollar led to constant balance of payments deficits. In their view, continuous stress on the balance of payments was advantageous to the Federal Reserve, as the external pressures justified a tighter, and therefore better, overall economic policy. There is considerable overlap between those in this group and those who believe the System's policies ought to be biased toward the restrictive side in domestic policies.

A second, middle group holds that international monetary problems are important, but does not accord them the priority of the first group. At times, the United States balance of payments situation may be improved through Federal Reserve action without any great sacrifice of other goals. Furthermore, some costs engendered to aid international stability are acceptable because they, in turn, create benefits for the domestic economy. Consequently, when they feel that international conditions are critical enough, they are willing to modify policy from that which would be chosen on purely domestic grounds.

A final group, of whom I was one, also was willing to support occasional decisions of this latter type. We agreed that benefits are gained from a properly functioning international monetary system. However, only in rare cases is monetary policy efficient in remedying balance of payments problems. International reserve movements do not respond readily to domestic income, price, and interest shifts, especially not in comparison to the large potential and actual reserve movements which result from speculation, shifting expectations, or other forces. Consequently, only rarely should monetary policy be altered for international monetary considerations; it is far better if the United States government uses instruments other than open market operations to achieve the desired international results.

This last group was generally supportive of the need to alter exchange rates, believing that struggles to maintain a rigid exchange rate for the dollar, given its basic overvaluation, were futile and wrong. Movements in exchange rates may be necessary, both because they lead to a better international monetary system and because they reduce the pressure on domestic monetary policy.

At any given time, probably two members of the Board and three members of the FOMC (not always the same people) gave international events a good deal of weight in their judgment on monetary policy and decisions. When major international considerations pointed clearly in a given policy direction, these members would change their goals for monetary policy somewhat from those which they otherwise would have supported. Contrary to the gen-

eral impression, however, throughout my tenure, a majority of the
Board was unwilling to change domestic policy much, if at all, for
international reasons. The result was that only a small number of
decisions taken by the Committee were significantly influenced by
the balance of payments.

In the eight out of somewhat over one hundred directives which
were dominated by international considerations, the influence was
not always in the same direction. In five cases a tighter policy resulted. Because of the loss of international reserves, the Committee
voted to tighten sooner than they might otherwise have done. Conversely, in three of the eight cases international events delayed
tightening. In these situations the Committee would have agreed
on a somewhat more restrictive policy had it not feared that, if interest rates rose in the United States, the pound, the franc, the lira,
or some other foreign currency would come under increased pressure and would have to devalue. That, in turn, would lead to an
attack upon all fixed exchange rates; and the dollar, as the linchpin
of the international monetary system, would be the next to suffer a
speculative attack.

In four cases the international situation appeared to play a significant role in determining at least the timing for changes in the
discount rate. The only really controversial case occurred in December 1965. As I have noted, while the balance of payments may
have influenced one or two votes, it was not the primary factor in
the actual decision to raise the discount rate. In November 1967
the discount rate went up after the devaluation of the pound sterling; in this case it would have been raised earlier except for the
sterling problem. In March of 1968, during the gold crisis, an increase in the discount rate was logical on domestic grounds. However its timing was determined by the hope of decreasing the pressure on gold. Finally, in April 1971 the discount rate might have
been lowered for technical market reasons, but the move was delayed because of large-scale Euro-dollar flows out of United States
banks back to European markets. To lower the discount rate in the
midst of such movements would make it appear that the Federal
Reserve had no interest in international problems. It would be
adding insult to injury.

The Federal Reserve Banks

The careful weighing of the needs of the domestic economy against those of the balance of payments by the Board contrasted markedly with the actions of Federal Reserve Banks. I felt that they often responded automatically to impulses to tighten as a result of instincts remaining from the pre-1933 period when the Banks had major responsibilities to maintain the gold reserve behind Federal Reserve deposits and notes.

In several international crises, one or more of the boards of directors of the Regional Banks recommended that the discount rate be raised, sometimes by as much as 30 percent or more to show the concern of the Federal Reserve over international events and to indicate that the System was taking firm action to fight the crises. Each of these suggested changes was rejected by the Federal Reserve Board in Washington, in some cases because it was concluded that the policy would be harmful for international reasons. The type of increase and the alarm it revealed were more likely to trigger the event it was meant to halt than to save the pound, the franc, or the dollar when they were in trouble. The discount moves that were not rejected for international reasons were rejected because of the basic belief of the majority of the Board that monetary policy was primarily to be used for domestic purposes. If increasing interest rates was not wise for domestic reasons, then the balance of payments problem had to be met in some other way.

The Federal Reserve Board

It is difficult to say what views a majority of the Board held with respect to international questions while I was in Washington, because international questions rarely came before the Board. I believe a majority were in favor of more flexible exchange rates, but I am not certain, since there was no procedure for either the Board or the Open Market Committee to consider fundamental questions of international monetary relations.

The Chairmen of the Board, acting as advisers to the secretary of the Treasury, met often with the Treasury, the White House, and foreign central banks. But the policies they advocated in their meetings with other groups were those determined by the Administration, not by the Federal Reserve. I felt that, during this period, both Chairman Martin and Chairman Burns were personally more in accord with the basic Administration policies than was the Board as a whole, and they may even have gone beyond the Administration in the importance they attached to gold and a fixed exchange rate. As a result, and because the Federal Reserve had no "need to know," they avoided any discussions of basic policy except when the Fed was asked to use a specific instrument which it controlled. These requests usually came in emergencies and, as a consequence, they did not receive careful consideration and there was a failure to work out detailed plans and theories.

A typical situation was of the type which occurred during the 1968 gold crisis. The FOMC would be asked on an emergency basis to vote billions of dollars for support of the Treasury's international reserve position. In several such cases, a majority or minority of the Board indicated a disagreement with the basic policy on the grounds that greater flexibility in exchange rates or the two-tier gold system were objectives to be sought, not feared. In each case, however, the answer was that the President or the secretary of the Treasury had determined that such actions were necessary as a matter of national policy. In some cases, efforts were made to limit the actions to a short term so as to avoid lengthy support of the Treasury by a theoretically independent Federal Reserve; but on the whole these were not successful.

In a similar manner, the Board administered the voluntary foreign restraint program for the President. It has been credited with doing a good job, but on several occasions a majority of the Board requested that the Administration either remove the controls completely, ease them, or make them more logical. Again, however, the responsible party, the President, on the basis of advice from the Treasury and others, refused to act, so the Board continued to administer the controls as well as it could under existing policies.

The Board on its own issued regulations dealing with Euro-dollars. These were considered by the Board to be of concern to domestic policy, through their influence on bank lending, as well as to international reserves. A Euro-dollar borrowed abroad and lent in the United States has a favorable effect on the balance of payments, reducing the pressure on international reserves. In its Euro-dollar regulations, the Board acted on its own responsibility for domestic credit, recognizing, however, the interest of the Treasury in this matter. The regulations were drawn with the hope of increasing international reserves.

In summary, I believe the Federal Reserve record in the international sphere is at best mixed. Some excellent work was done in laying the foundation for "paper gold," i.e., special drawing rights, and also for recent negotiations on an improved international monetary system. In various crisis negotiations, such as those over the two-tier gold system or over particular devaluations or revaluations or floating of currencies, the Fed's input has been significant. In these negotiations with other governments and central banks, the Chairman, one or two Board members, and members of the staff have made valuable contributions.

On the other hand, I feel that the Federal Reserve must share in the general responsibility for a government policy which attempted to maintain the *status quo* for far too long. Fixed exchange rates became a drag on the economy, yet the Federal Reserve did little to bring the situation closer to a necessary decision. It took a crisis to bring action.

The question of how to maintain properly functioning international exchanges remains critical. The list of unresolved problems has changed little since 1965. Policy makers continue to worry about the relationship of gold to other international reserves, the lack of confidence in currencies, the degree of rigidity or flexibility in exchange rates, the control of speculative capital movements, and the way in which internal policies should be altered in response to international imbalances. Each time the Federal Reserve reconsiders monetary policy, it must estimate both the domestic and international effects. Of equal importance, it must continue to weigh and make clear to the government and to the public the relative costs of using monetary policy, as opposed to other types of government action, in attempts to overcome unwanted movements in the international sphere.

CHAPTER TEN

The Search for a Monetary Target

Richard Nixon was probably the first President to take office vowing that he would slow down the U.S. economy. The nation's No. 1 football fan had a "game plan" that his advisers said would stop inflation without much pain to the public or danger to the politicians. No need to tackle wages and prices directly. No need to get involved in messy strikes or stop end runs by steel prices. There would be no mandatory controls, no nasty squabbles between the White House and business or labor leaders, no interference at all with the free market. Instead, Government would simply balance its budget and pump less money into the banking system. As funds became scarcer in the private economy, business would simmer down and so, too, would prices. For a few "awkward months," predicted Nixon's economists, the nation would suffer mild "slowing pains" of high interest rates, little growth in production, some drop in profits and a moderate rise in unemployment. Eventually, inflationary pressure would be wrung out of the economy and normal expansion of output and hiring could resume.°

THE NEW ADVISERS of President Nixon were basically monetarists. During the election campaign of 1968 and after, they had attacked the Federal Reserve for overreaction. They claimed the money supply had been cut too much in 1966 and expanded too much

° *Time*, June 1, 1970, p. 39.

thereafter. The monetarists offered an appealing policy for the new Administration. Their doctrines were libertarian; a minimum of government action would be best. If the money supply grew at a constant rate, so would spending, output, and prices. Because past money supply movements had been erratic, some minor disturbances might occur before the new stable path was reached. The best policy would be one of "gradualism." The existence of excess demand and rising prices could be ignored. If the Federal Reserve created money in the proper amount, inflationary pressures would disappear and growth would return to a normal path. With money expanding properly, the economy would be stable. The composition of spending would not be troublesome either; with a controlled money supply excess demand from one sector, such as the war, would simply force curtailment in other sectors, such as consumption or housing.

It was apparently on the basis of this type of analysis that President Nixon, in his first presidential press conference, summarized his views, "We can control inflation without an increase in unemployment." Most members of the Administration seemed convinced that all that was required to accomplish this task was a steady growth in the money supply.

Almost immediately the endemic debate over proper economic goals for the economy and the role of monetary policy erupted. Within the Federal Reserve, discussions centered around the choice of a monetary target. There was a searching challenge to the continued use of money market conditions as a measure of policy.

The Committee on the Directive

A channel for reexamining the problem of selecting a target had already been opened. In the fall of 1968 I had suggested to Chairman Martin that he appoint a new subcommittee of the FOMC to examine its operations, pointing out that such a committee could serve two important functions. First, a reexamination of FOMC operations, particularly with regard to how it chose its monetary targets and operating guides, would be timely, since Martin's term had only one year to run and it appeared, on the basis of past statements, that he would offer his resignation to the incoming President. A change of Chairmen would inevitably occasion a review of many procedures. Secondly, and equally important in my mind, it was necessary to codify the unwritten theory of operations in current use so that the new Chairman would understand how the System worked. No Chairman could afford the long learning time required to master techniques handed down through a purely oral tradition.

Chairman Martin agreed, and in October 1968 appointed me to be chairman of a Committee on the Directive, with Presidents Frank Morris of Boston and Eliot Swan of San Francisco as the other two members. As a committee, we drew up a set of topics for our staff, which was composed of a dozen of the better monetary economists in the System, assigned part-time to the task. At the same time, I began to circulate and publish a series of papers I had been working on which described the procedures then in use and their drawbacks as I saw them.

The Failure of the Proviso

Despite the experience of 1966 and the introduction of monetary aggregates into the proviso clause of the directive, no significant change had occurred in the FOMC's functioning. The directives of the Open Market Committee continued to speak of firmer or easier money market conditions or additional monetary restraint. While the adoption of the proviso (see pages 85–86) had been thought of as a significant step forward, it failed to function usefully, and what seemed a great victory for quantification turned out to be illusory. In an examination of operations at the start of 1970, the staff concluded that, although the proviso clause had constrained the degree of accommodation to some extent, its effect in practice had been rather minor. The proviso clause never led to any substantial change in money market conditions.

The FOMC had been willing to tolerate wide swings in the monetary aggregates. The proviso clause was not accepted as a strong element in the target. The manager was not directed to alter money market conditions sufficiently to attain the specified growth in the monetary aggregates, but only to move them slightly in the right direction. The acceptance of money market conditions was so complete that, even when the Committee itself met, the tendency was always to shade them only a little for fear of major market reactions.

As a result of this failure to use the proviso to shift money market conditions more rapidly, in several important periods, movements in money and credit occurred at a much faster or much slower rate than they should have. With hindsight it is easy to see how unnecessary the movements were. But, more importantly, the movements were not sensible in terms of the policies the Federal Reserve said and thought it was following. The failure to track targets was particularly evident in 1969.

Monetary Goals and Targets

Whether or not 1969 was a good year for monetary policy is a matter of opinion. Some believed that the squeeze was not tight enough. At least two members of the FOMC, George Mitchell and I, and most monetarists (of whom Milton Friedman and George Shultz, then the secretary of Labor, were the most outspoken) felt that after midyear, policy tightened too rapidly and too much. In any case, as the year unfolded, there were several major disputes over what monetary policy should be. Some of the quarrels concerned the goals. More contentious, however, was the problem of the targets used. Both issues came to a head as the year ended.

I joined with a majority of the Board of Governors in supporting the Administration's concept of gradualism. Demand was growing more slowly than potential output. The gap should be allowed to widen in order to help slow the rate of price increases. In the Administration's view, the market would bring down prices without the need to resort to other policy measures. Some assumed that a less rapid growth of money would directly halt the rise in prices. Others put their faith in market pricing. Excess supply meant lower prices.

While agreeing with the Administration's goals, I doubted their analysis. Since excess demand in the economy still persisted, growth in spending should be curtailed. As supply caught up, some diminution in price rises would occur; but not as much as hoped for by the Administration because, contrary to their views, the Federal Reserve's monetary actions would have little effect on the trade-off of the added spending between prices and output. I felt that, if price developments during the course of the year were as unsatisfactory as I expected, the Administration would have to deal with prices directly, probably by adopting some form of incomes policy.

A minority of the Board, but, I felt, a majority of the Federal Open Market Committee, disagreed with the policy of gradualism. They felt that spending was expanding because of inflationary expectations. Spending would fall only if expectations declined. To change expectations would require a shock, not a gradual tightening. A sharp decrease in money and credit might be a sufficient shock, but a more serious recession might be needed to halt the growth in spending and prices.

In addition to being split two ways on goals, the FOMC was divided three ways in its choice of a monetary target. Many on the Committee wanted the lowering of inflationary expectations to be the target. They believed the System had to operate in such a way as to shift the expectations of businessmen, borrowers, and lenders. Every action had to be weighed by its impact on expectations, not on other traditional measures such as interest rates, money market conditions, the money supply, or credit. A second group, including many of those accepting the Administration's goals, wanted to retain money market conditions as the intermediate target. That was the way the System had operated in the past. They believed money market conditions gave the best results and saw no reason to change their prior views.

Mitchell and I wanted the Committee to use monetary aggregates, including bank credit, the money supply, and reserves, as the target. We based our choice both on our belief in the aggregates and on our dissatisfaction with the other targets. We proposed that the Federal Reserve set as a target cutting the growth rate in the aggregates roughly in half compared to the end of 1968.

We should stick with this target for the entire year. We considered ourselves gradualists. We wanted to pick the monetary target which would give the best chance of reaching the newly elected administration's set of goals.

Our prescription was not very different from that of the monetarists, but it was arrived at by a completely different analysis. We did not follow a fixed rule. We picked a money growth rate which appeared likely to coincide with the desired slowdown in spending. We were willing to adjust the rate of supplying reserves depending upon how the various definitions of money and components of the monetary aggregates moved. Furthermore, we recognized that the impact of slower monetary expansion would spread over a considerable and unknown period into the future. Too large a decline in the rate of money growth now would force too rapid an acceleration later on. This we wanted to avoid.

Differences in Targets and Measures

In Chapter 3 (pages 51–58), I noted that economists and the members of the FOMC used at least four distinct intermediate monetary variables as measures of what was happening to monetary policy. Each might give a different view of whether money was sufficiently tight or restrictive. Such differences in their comparative verdicts were particularly evident in the first three months of 1969.

Misunderstood Concepts

But, before pointing out some characteristics of the targets, let me attempt to clarify a couple of major misunderstandings. A great deal of confusion exists between the concepts of money market conditions and interest rates as monetary targets. Minutes of the Open Market Committee reveal as much confusion among policy makers as among their vocal critics.

The problem arises because the Federal funds rate is an interest rate. But the two targets can, and should, be differentiated. Each is pursued with a different purpose in mind. Money market conditions are picked as a target primarily to stabilize the money markets. The Federal funds rate and net borrowed reserves measure events in these markets. Money market conditions are less affected by and have less impact on total spending than other rates.

The interest rates of primary concern as a monetary target are those believed to affect spending, such as long-term rates, mortgage rates, and relative yields and costs of capital goods. Target levels are picked in order to shift the desires of consumers and investors to spend. At times, also, the Fed concentrates its purchases in longer-term securities simply to add its demand in this sphere, on the assumption that it may have a minor beneficial effect on these long-term rates.

It should be clear that, when either interest rates or money market conditions are used as monetary targets, except for concern over the disruptive effect of sudden, sharp movements, the object is not to prevent interest rates from moving. Except under special circumstances and for short periods, no one in the Federal Reserve believes that interest rates can or should be pegged. The Fed does not control the demand for money or credit; it only influences the supply. It can cause rates to rise rapidly by refusing to add reserves. On the other hand, if demand is increasing strongly, an attempt to hold interest rates level would require large inflationary injections of reserves which would eventually lead to higher rates or runaway inflation.

There is also a confusion about the use of money and interest rates as targets. They are sometimes thought of as competitive; but that is not the case. A relationship exists between the amount of money demanded, the amount supplied, and interest movements; and between interest movements, shortfalls, and overages of money and spending. If we know enough about any market, we can use either quantities (money) or prices (interest rates) to make policy. For instance, a manufacturer has the choice of setting a price and producing the quantity demanded, or of producing a given supply and allowing the market to set the price. If the price is the same, the quantity produced should be the same in either case.

When we lack information, however, we must ask ourselves which measure will be better. Are we more likely to reach our goal by watching interest rates or growth rates for money? If we know a great deal about the relationship between money and income and believe no other effects are important, we should use money as a target. If we believe the relationship is uncertain and variable, or that financial objectives should be considered, then we should use as much other information, such as interest rate movements, as possible to pick the proper target and to adjust it from period to period.

The heart of monetary policy is setting bank reserves to help achieve the desired mix of objectives. If nonmonetary forces lead to too little spending, reserves should expand money at a rate faster than normal. If the real money supply rises faster than the nonincome demand for money, people will spend more. Similarly, if the interest rate falls below the profitability of investment, people will invest more.

Choosing the proper growth of money is complicated by the fact that reactions extend so far into the future. Reserves added today may change the availability of money, interest rates, and spending over the next two to four years. While we do not know exactly when these movements will occur, we know that when they do we do not want them to alter spending counter to the economy's goals. Adjusting reserve movements to avoid adverse reactions in the future may require frequent changes.

Control by watching only movements in money will succeed best if inflationary expansions in income are the only significant source of increased demand for money. When income is expanding too fast, holding to a targeted growth rate for money will raise interest rates and will place the weight of money in opposition to the increased spending. Spending and income will be restrained closer to their desirable path. On the other hand, if the demand for money has increased for nonincome reasons, a failure of the Federal Reserve to expand reserves and money will be harmful. Interest rates will rise; spending and income will fall below their optimal course; output will fall; men will be idled. The unfortunate financial effects of rising interest rates will have been introduced and the economy will be worse off, with no offsetting advantages.

But there are also other reasons for accommodating demands for money that appear in the market place, rather than rigidly constraining supply. The day-to-day and month-to-month demand for money is extremely erratic. In one month even the seasonally adjusted money supply may grow at a 10 percent annual rate, only to be followed by a similar fall. The unadjusted, or actual, amount of money fluctuates even more. These movements reflect short-term changes in demand. For example, tax and dividend payments cause sharp shifts in people's money balances. Part, but only part, of these movements is allowed for by seasonal adjustments. The remainder appears as large increases or decreases in the money supply. Other and equally important rapid shifts in demand result from speculative operations in the foreign exchanges, stock market events, major bond issues, or sudden movements in liquidity. If the Federal Reserve failed to meet these sharp changes in demand, a tremendous burden of adjustment would fall on the financial system.

Money Market Conditions

On the whole, at the beginning of April 1969, those measuring monetary policy by money market conditions were satisfied. In this period, as opposed to 1966, the Federal funds rate and net borrowed reserves had been moved up more rapidly. The Fed had refused to add to reserves of its own volition and total reserves had not increased, even though there was a sharp increase in bank borrowings at the discount window. This higher level of borrowings, in turn, was expected to lead to a slower expansion of credit and spending.

Those who believe in money market conditions as a monetary target feel strongly that, in addition to the advantages we have just noted for allowing some increases in money to match certain movements in demand, its accommodative features have the major virtue of minimizing interest rate fluctuations. This policy is good because:

—The danger of a liquidity crisis is less than if an attempt is made to control growth in money without attention to rates. Unsettling and unwanted swings in rates in the capital markets are avoided. We have noted how liquidity needs expanded at the time of the Penn Central failure. Only a few critics believe that the Federal Reserve should have refused to meet these demands. These were not funds to be spent, but to be hoarded. Similar but less spectacular changes in the demand for money may occur often.

—Perhaps more importantly, sharp interest rate changes may disrupt economic decisions. Swings in the money supply or bank credit can destabilize the behavior of borrowers and lenders. Decision units rely to a great extent on the interest rate structure as a source of information about what is happening in credit markets and to the economy.

Moreover, since money market conditions have served as the keynote of Federal Reserve policy, changes are likely to be followed by speedy market reactions. The level of net borrowed reserves and of Federal funds is obvious to the market. Any movements in money market conditions cause banks and dealers to reexamine their strategies. If they decide the Fed is going to loosen monetary conditions, lenders lose no time in reshaping their policies. It is not uncommon to see government bond dealers and banks, the most volatile purchasers, increase their demand for securities by $3 to $5 billion in a very short time. Interest rates on short-term securities may fall by 100 basis points (100 basis points =1 percent) in less than a month. Consequently significant effects may be felt in the economy well before levels of reserves or of the money supply have reacted to the new policy.

As 1969 progressed it became clear that this tendency of the market to follow money market conditions closely also entailed severe disadvantages. It tended to lock the Federal Reserve into a fixed position. The Fed lost flexibility because it feared the market would receive incorrect signals.

Interest Rates

Those who held interest rates to be the proper monetary target found that between the December 1968 discount rate change and the beginning of April, the three-month Treasury bill had risen from 5.75 percent to not quite 6 percent. In a rather unusual situa-

tion, long-term rates had moved up somewhat more than short-
term ones: The rate on newly issued Aaa corporate bonds went
from 6.9 to 7.3 percent, while the yield on outstanding long-term,
tax-exempt state and municipal bonds rose from 4.5 to 5 percent.

Higher interest rates ought to cut down on inflationary spending.
They would make it less profitable to invest in plant and equipment; monthly payments on houses would rise, and when the returns on earning assets were capitalized, their value also would be
less. But whether these movements would cut investment would
depend upon how much of the change in rates was due to expected
future price increases. It was possible that investors felt that prices
would rise so fast that the real (corrected for price movements)
rate of interest had actually fallen. If so, it would be more profitable to expand purchases in order to buy goods that continued to
produce profits at the same or a higher real rate than before.

Those who believed in the interest target had to decide how
much of the movement in rates was due to real forces and how
much merely to changes in price expectations. Some adjustment
had to be made for nominal rates rising faster than real rates, but
how much was not certain. The fact that there is no good measure
of real rates greatly complicates the use of interest rates as a target. For example, prices had been rising steadily over the past several years. If one believed that these price changes would have a
rapid effect on price expectations, the change since December in
nominal rates was small enough compared to price movements so
that real rates might actually have fallen, even though nominal
rates had risen. On the other hand, if one believed that price
changes took twenty years or so to influence price expectations in
interest rates, then most of the movement recorded in the nominal
rates would reflect a change in real rates.

This problem, too, was to become more important during the
course of the year. Interest rates on new issues of high-grade corporate bonds at 9 percent seem extremely high by historical standards. But were everyone expecting prices to rise by an average of
6 percent a year during the life of the bond, they then were estimating the real rate at only 3 percent. Since people's ideas as to future prices are unknown and also fluctuate widely, we are never
certain what level they expect for real interest rates. Yet real rates

are the critical ones for most real investment and spending decisions and they, therefore, are what must be evaluated in setting a monetary target.

It was not peculiar to this period that there was a divergence between movements in the Federal funds rate and those of other interest rates, particularly those which theory credits with exerting the largest impact on spending. The Federal funds rate can move away from other interest rates for many reasons. A small change in the Fed funds rate, as we have noted, may trigger a major shift in expectations of future interest rates and in security inventories, causing the other rates to react sharply. Movements in the Federal funds rate, which are controlled by the manager, are less volatile. Furthermore, as tightness in the reserve situation accumulates, more and more pressure is put on bank liquidity. Banks adjust their liquidity through selling securities. Thus movements in interest rates become cumulatively greater the longer the banks have been in debt. Finally, and perhaps more importantly, longer-term interest rates fluctuate in accordance with movements in the basic demand of the economy. In contrast, the Federal funds rate is primarily dominated by the net reserve situation of the banks.

Money

Since December 1968, the narrowly defined money supply (M_1) had been increasing at a rate of about 2.5 percent. In contrast, the more broadly defined money supply (M_2) had been decreasing at the same rate. The same was true of the bank credit proxy, another name for total deposits in member banks. Total reserves had not changed at all. On the other hand, the measure of high-powered money (the monetary base—currency and member bank reserves) had grown at an annual rate of 4.5 percent. All of these elements are included in the monetary aggregates. The weight assigned each one in the monetary aggregates is not fixed. It can vary, and has, over time and among individuals.

These conflicting movements brought out one of the major advantages of using the monetary aggregates as a target rather than a single definition of money. The contradictory movements make it possible to get a better feel for what is happening to the demand for and supply of money. Special factors acting upon one definition of money and not another can either be given greater weight or disregarded.

Starting in 1966, I urged that the Federal Reserve use the monetary aggregates as its primary monetary target, that it determine how many reserves to create on the basis of an examination of movements in total reserves, the money supply, and bank credit. It ought not to follow a simple rule, but should take into account changes in the demand for money needed for hoarding or for non-income transactions. A monetary aggregate target is consistent with a wide variety of economic theories. No particular judgment is implied as to the importance of monetary flows compared to interest rates, expectations, credit market conditions, fiscal policy, or any other form of policy.

Although knowledge of the demand for money is inaccurate, we can, as a first approximation, assume it is related to the amount of spending. While short-run swings in velocity are normal, money and the GNP tend to expand together. As a result, from a desired growth rate in the GNP, a range can be estimated within which movements in the monetary aggregates are supportive of the hoped for expansion.

In watching the target, however, we should not neglect movements in interest rates. They both affect and reflect movements in the demand for money. They also influence directly investments, wealth, and financial institutions. Since we know that velocity of money does change and therefore no fixed relationship exists between money and income, we cannot afford to waste the information on what may be happening to both income and the demand for money given us by interest rates, by current market information, as well as by other observations of the economy.

We saw that the proviso made use of the bank credit proxy as a measure of monetary change. The use of bank credit as a target shows how confusing monetary terminology can be. To some supporters of money as a target, bank credit is a closely related concept with major administrative advantages. The bank credit proxy, while closely related, is less erratic than other measures of money. Good estimates of the credit proxy are available more quickly than are estimates of other monetary aggregates. The fact that currency is not included may be an advantage, since there are major difficulties in measuring currency in the hands of the public, as well as the demand for it. All types of substitutes for currency have been developed. The credit card is an obvious example. At the opposite end, currency disappears overseas and into safety deposit boxes, without any relationship to the income demand for money.

The credit proxy appeared to have many of the theoretical and empirical advantages of a wider group of monetary aggregates. Disadvantages were offset by the greater stability and reliability of its estimates. However, to good monetarists, using the term *bank credit proxy* was like waving a red cape in front of a bull. When the Federal Reserve talked about the money market and interest rates, it used the term *credit conditions*. Monetarists feared that *bank credit* was simply another term for money market credit conditions. Furthermore, credit implied concern over bank lending rather than bank deposits, the main component of money. The necessary equality of a bank's assets and liabilities and the close alignment of their movements with the broad definitions of money were of no importance.

Expectations

In recent years, economists and the popular press have put more emphasis on the importance of inflationary expectations. Some spending, some price increases, some portion of interest rates may originate in fear of future inflation.

It seemed to me that by the spring of 1969 about half of the members of the FOMC were sufficiently impressed by this concept to consider it as a new target for monetary policy. They were dissatisfied with the apparent tightening based on the measures of money market conditions, interest rates, and the monetary aggregates, and felt that expectations per se should be the direct target of policy. These members argued that the average lender, businessman, and consumer had become convinced that there would never be another recession. Anticipating that prices would keep rising, households and corporations kept spending more and lending less. In the face of this inflationary mentality, the best course for the Fed was to pursue an anti-inflationary policy so clear that no one could mistake its intentions. Therefore monetary aggregates or interest rates should not be used as a target. Any move to prevent the money stock from falling or to counteract rising interest rates due to contracting credit would be taken as a sign that the Fed was not serious, and expectations of future inflation would be reinforced. Businesses and families would spend even more; interest rates would shoot up.

This line of reasoning boiled down to the idea that what the Fed actually did mattered less than what people thought it was trying to do. Even if interest rates or movements in the money supply gave warning that policy needed adjusting, the Fed should make no change for fear of being misunderstood. To engage in open market operations might have perverse effects; instead of lowering rates, purchases of securities could drive prices down and interest rates up.

Problems arise when believers in this intangible target attempt to translate it into terms on which operations can be based. Expectations cannot be measured. We see what is happening in markets, but actions are the result of both expectations and concrete economic events. Since it is impossible to separate their influences, we do not know how important each factor may be. Furthermore, if we agree that perverse results are possible and if we disagree in our concepts of what is perverse, then the same observed event can lead people to diametrically opposite conclusions as to what is happening to expectations or how they are being influenced by Federal Reserve action.

As a result of these measurement problems, increased emphasis was put on such concepts as feelings of tightness, which the proponents of the expectations target felt were more important than how much spending would rise or fall, or what was happening to interest rates or the money supply. Thus, in April 1969, they tended to ignore the data measuring movements in the more traditional targets. Instead, they favored basing policy on their estimates of how the public felt and would feel about the future.

The Effectiveness of Policy

In late March 1969, there was increased concern about the rate of growth in the economy. GNP rose somewhat faster than expected. So did prices. The unemployment rate, instead of rising, fell to 3.3 percent, the lowest rate reached throughout the 1960s. The tighter monetary policy did not seem to be affecting the economy. Businesses reported no planned cutback in investment. Large corporations in particular seemed to be accelerating the inflation by raising prices, hoarding labor, and continuing to build plant and equipment at excessive rates.

The strong economy led the Federal Reserve to reexamine its policy. It was unanimously agreed that the discount rate was out of line and it was raised by .5 percent to a new 6 percent level. But disagreement existed about other policies. A number of the policy makers felt that monetary policy had to be tightened more rapidly. Only the immediate onset of a recession could break inflationary expectations. They advocated an increase in required reserves and a further tightening of money market conditions. The others continued to support the Administration's goals of gradualism. The monetary screw had been tightened. Now it should remain in this new position and the ups and downs of previous policies should be avoided.

The majority of the Board was satisfied with the developments in the three basic targets of money market conditions, interest rates, and the monetary aggregates. They did not want a more restrictive policy. They were willing, however, to attempt to influence expectations. They, therefore, voted in April to increase reserve requirements in order to give the market a shock. The increase in required reserves need not change policy because it could be offset by furnishing the necessary additional bank reserves by open market purchases of securities. It was thus possible to get an announcement effect and to try to affect expectations without changing the actual monetary variables.

All Board members except me seemed happy to accept inflationary expectations as a secondary target, at least for the time being. I voted for the discount rate increase, but dissented from the increased reserve requirements because I felt that the System ought to maintain monetary aggregates as a target and follow the game plan of the Administration. In attempting to influence expectations directly, the System would be tracking an incorrect target and would have no real measure of what it was doing.

The April action was just the start of the skirmish, however. A strong minority wanted further tightening, a greater shock to the economy, with an increased likelihood of recession. During May, June, and July, four Federal Reserve Banks voted to jump their discount rates from 6 to 7 percent. It was clear, and in fact they so stated, that their proposed discount rate increases were not based on what was happening in the money and credit markets; they wanted a shock effect in order to make a direct attack upon expectations. (In cases such as this, it is never clear how much of the action of a District Bank's board of directors reflects strong feeling among the directors and how much reflects the desires of the president of the Bank. In most cases, it is understood that the Bank president can greatly influence, if not completely dominate, the votes of the directors on the discount rate.)

The Federal Reserve Board, however, disapproved the actions of these Districts, with the effect of leaving the discount rate unchanged. The Board was not willing to shift policy further. It believed that the System had the basic duty to watch money and credit, not attempt to deal with expectations alone.

By August, the split in the FOMC, as well as among economists around the country, had widened. Money market conditions had tightened rapidly. Interest rates were again at record levels. Among the monetary aggregates, total reserves, and especially bank credit, were declining. Only the narrowly defined money supply (M_1), primarily because currency was still growing rapidly, showed an annual rate of growth of 2.5 percent.

It seemed clear now that the economy was slowing down. Even if money expanded in the 3 to 4 percent range, there would be a recession. Unemployment would rise; housing would decrease sharply. These projections proved to be accurate. Throughout 1969 and 1970, policy was made with the help of good forecasts of spending. Both the direction and the magnitudes of movements were projected well.

At the August meeting of the FOMC, some of the members wanted a still tighter monetary policy. They focused on price increases and inflationary expectations. Because prices were still rising, I felt they would welcome a more severe recession than that projected. But the majority of the FOMC remained gradualist. The Administration, too, still had a goal under which real output would continue to expand, to avoid the stigma of a recession, but not as rapidly as potential output. Jobs would not keep pace with the growth of the labor force. Unemployment would rise to 4.5 percent by mid-1971. Prices would rise less rapidly, either because of excess supply or the slower growth in money.

The gradualists, however, were split in two factions. The larger group was concerned about possible signals that might be misread from market operations. A second group wanted a midcourse correction. The larger faction feared that any easing of money market conditions would be taken as a signal that the Federal Reserve was changing direction. This would induce ease and raise inflationary expectations. This group was even further divided. Some were pleased that existing money market conditions were leading to less credit and higher interest rates. Some were concerned that monetary policy was too tight. They would welcome a slippage toward greater ease as long as it did not follow obviously from the operations of the Desk or a change in the directive.

The experiences of this period bring out one of the weaknesses of money market conditions as a target. The directive remained virtually unchanged for nine months, calling for "maintaining the prevailing firm conditions." Yet these words had no operational meaning. "Conditions," as measured by the Federal funds rates and net reserves, rose sharply for the first four months under the unchanged directive and then eased off slightly.

In August George Mitchell and I came out strongly for what we called a midcourse correction. It seemed obvious to us that maintaining money market conditions as a target would lead to a tighter and then still tighter monetary policy. The economic expansion was ending. The firmer monetary policy would coincide with a recession. Its impact would spread far into the future. Monetary policy would be stunting expenditures during the recession and there would be danger of a depression and a financial crunch. If the System failed to pick a proper target now, it would be likely to flip-flop too far again when ease became necessary. As in the past, money market conditions as a target were leading to too tight a policy. Soon it could become too accommodative. The System should shift to a monetary aggregates target to avoid whiplashing the economy.

There was another reason for urging a shift in the target. Even if market conditions were not changed, monetary policy would increase its pressures on the economy. Banks were running out of liquidity. They were using up their right to borrow from the Federal Reserve, and they would have to adjust loans or securities. Under these conditions, the effect of maintaining the Federal funds rate and net borrowing at a given level was to create an ever-tighter monetary impact on spending. But the majority of the FOMC feared that, when the market saw the Federal funds rate and net borrowing declining, it would assume that the Fed wanted to ease and would attempt to beat the move to lower interest rates by rushing out to buy securities and increase loans, thereby increasing money and lowering rates more than desirable.

Mitchell and I argued that, by announcing what it was doing, the Board could avoid this problem. The decreases in the Federal funds rate necessary if policy were to be held constant instead of tightening still further could be accomplished. If the Federal Open Market Committee stated that it was now using the monetary aggregates as its target instead of money market conditions, its action would not be misunderstood.

We believed that the System, by refusing in this and similar cases to clarify its policy and its actions in the market, was forcing itself to accept a poorer policy than was necessary. We saw no reason for the Fed to paralyze itself and penalize the economy. The System had the right to make clear to the market what our target and policy were. We should do this clearly in a public announcement. If we did, we would not have to fear that the market would draw incorrect assumptions.

I voted against the directive in the FOMC meeting of August 12, 1969. According to the published record,

> In dissenting from this action Messrs. Maisel and Mitchell indicated that they did not advocate loosening monetary and credit restraint. However, they did not want monetary policy to become more and more restrictive. It appeared to them that trends in monetary aggregates and the availability of credit were indicative of increased tightening that would be heightened if money market conditions were maintained at the levels called for in the directive favored by the majority. In order to guard against an undesirable further tightening, they favored a directive calling for operations to moderate such contractive tendencies, if prospective declines in monetary aggregates should in fact occur, while maintaining the position of over-all monetary and credit restraint.

By mid-October 1969, I was convinced that we were entering a recession in which a mistaken monetary policy would be extremely harmful. Inflationary expectations were not a logical goal or target because we did not know how to measure or to influence them, and the attempt could lead to a disastrous monetary policy. After a group of speeches in which I tried to point out what goals were possible and how targets related to goals, I sensed general confusion over the drift of monetary policy.

My dissents, released after ninety days, had not been reported properly in the press. The questions of a logical target and policy were being obscured by the debates over monetarism and inflationary expectations. The matter seemed to me so critical that for the first and only time while I was on the Federal Reserve Board I called a special press conference on December 8 to explain to the public the issues as I saw them.

The fight was not, as monetary fights had traditionally and often incorrectly been reported, one between advocates of greater tightness or greater ease. The question at issue was whether the Federal Reserve could adopt a monetary target that would enable the System to control monetary policy instead of merely influencing the money market. I argued that money and credit were becoming tighter and tighter even though the money market conditions used as an operating guide had not changed. While the Federal funds rate had decreased slightly, all other interest rates reached new highs almost daily. The major monetary aggregates of reserves and bank credit had fallen sharply over the past six months, and the narrowly defined money supply was virtually unchanged. If the System failed to change its target, there would be another sharp zig-zag. Restraint was overshooting a desirable level. When this was recognized, the FOMC would overcorrect in the opposite direction. If it failed to zag, the impact of the growing restraint would deepen the coming recession. A major depression would become more probable. Unemployment would be higher and growth far less than called for under the accepted goals for the economy.

The press reports on my interview were excellent. They explained the problem of targets and goals as I saw it. There were mildly favorable editorials in the *Wall Street Journal* and *Journal of Commerce*. I felt that I was expressing an idea whose time had come. All that was necessary was to find a way for the FOMC to change its target without too much trauma.

The Shift in the Monetary Target

The period (December–January) following my press interview was an extremely complex one for monetary policy. The thrift institutions and the housing market came under the same type of intense pressure as they had in 1966. Short-term interest rates in money markets were so far above the maximum interest rate ceilings (Regulation Q) that many thrift institutions were losing deposits rapidly. Their solvency was endangered. While vacillating daily, the Home Loan Bank Board seemed to want higher ceilings. The Administration was divided, but most economists felt that the loss of funds was dangerous. A bare majority of the Federal Reserve Board agreed that Regulation Q ceilings would have to be raised.

The Board was split down the middle as to whether monetary policy was too tight at this time. Chairman Martin shifted his position and came out in favor of an expansion rather than a continued contraction of money and credit. Having made up his mind, he was willing to take the responsibility for the move, even though he had less than two months left in office and could have delayed, forcing the decision on his successor. At his confirmation hearing, Arthur Burns, who would become the new Chairman on February 1, 1970, also spoke in favor of an expansion in money. Other Board members made it clear that they would not support any specific downward movement in money market conditions, which was the change in open market operations necessary if growth in money and credit were to take place through action of the FOMC. On the other hand, if time and savings deposits expanded as a result of higher Regulation Q ceilings, they would not want to force money market conditions still tighter in order to hold total deposits constant. Thus a change in Regulation Q could lead to a more moderate policy.

In December the Administration was fighting for a tighter fiscal policy. It wanted the tax surcharge extended at 5 percent for six months. The President preferred that the Federal Reserve not change monetary policy until fiscal policy had jelled. This meant that, to coordinate with the Administration, no easing action could be taken at the December meeting of the FOMC. Meanwhile, as chairman of the Committee on the Directive, I was preparing a new proposal for selecting monetary targets and guides. I met with Burns at the White House early in December to explain the work of the committee and to brief him on my understanding of Federal Reserve operations. In early January, the New York *Times* outlined in considerable detail the report I had submitted to my fellow FOMC members calling for a change in the target to be used in the directive.

Matters came to a head at the January 1970 meeting of the Open Market Committee. Before the meeting I had asked the staff to draft an alternative directive based on a monetary aggregates target. This would give the FOMC a chance prior to the meeting to see all of the implications of the target that Mitchell and I had been pushing. The staff also drafted a directive calling for no change in policy together with one which would have moved to less firmness, but which retained money market conditions as the target.

I guessed that the FOMC would remain split. Because of their fear of expectational reactions, the majority of the Committee would again vote against the staff proposal to move to slightly less firm money market conditions. On the other hand, one or two of this majority would probably support some relaxation in policy so long as it was not obvious; they would prefer a drop in the Federal funds rate, if it could be obtained without an expectational impact.

My reasoning was correct. A majority opposed a change in money market conditions. However, the FOMC adopted a directive of the type Mitchell and I had been advocating. The directive had three separate provisions: It expressed the desire "to see a modest growth in money and bank credit." This was the first time that the FOMC had specifically adopted the monetary aggregates as a target. In the next sentence, the directive retained the previous wording calling for the maintenance of firm conditions in the money market. This was to placate those who feared reactions to an eased policy. Finally, the manager was directed to modify conditions if it took greater ease to obtain the desired growth in money.

The following meeting, in February, was the first chaired by Burns. By this time, it seemed to more observers that the economy was in a recession. Still, a majority of the Committee, made up of those who wanted a more serious recession and those who feared the effect on expectations of changing money market conditions, wanted to stay with the existing directive. But a minority advocated a further change in the directive to encompass a moderate growth rate in the monetary aggregates and easier money market conditions.

When Chairman Burns spoke, it was clear that he agreed with the minority. We were probably entering a recession. A depression was possible. Money and credit should grow at moderate rates, even if easier money market conditions were required to insure the growth. After the most bitter debate I experienced in my entire service on the FOMC, several views shifted and a changed directive was adopted. (The shift in key votes is a measure of the inherent powers of the Chairman, who can always sway the votes of one or two members of the FOMC if he makes a determined effort.)

This debate, spanning two meetings, was a critical one for the Federal Reserve. The FOMC by a bare majority had changed its goal from an ever-tighter monetary policy to one in which money and bank credit would expand. Since demand for money was barely expanding, interest rates would decline. The change in objectives was possible because a majority of the Committee had agreed to measure monetary policy in some way other than money market conditions. A new target, money and bank credit, had been adopted. No longer would monetary policy be characterized as tight or easy on the basis of relative movements in the Federal funds rate and net borrowed reserves. It was recognized that what is necessary is a measure of the influence monetary conditions are having on spending. This must be estimated initially from changes in the amount of money relative to the demand for it, or in the resulting changes in prices (interest rates) seen in the market.

The Report of the Committee on the Directive

The report of the Committee on the Directive was made available to those members of the FOMC who had not yet seen it at the beginning of March. It was discussed at length in April. The report and its supporting staff papers succeeded in meeting my principal objective. It gathered into a logical series a codification of the framework within which monetary policy was being made. New decision makers, when they joined the FOMC, could be initiated more rapidly into the mysteries of monetary policy. Because the staff papers were published, interested outside observers could also improve their understanding.

More importantly, the report documented some of the facts and concepts supporting the case for shifting from a target based on money market conditions to one based on the monetary aggregates. It was clear, at least to the directive committee, that money market conditions was a poor target because it had only a slight relationship to desired goals. Furthermore, we reported our view that monetary policy was still being made with too short a horizon. While important changes had taken place in the System's forecasts, there was still too little consideration given to monetary movements and their expected impact on the goals for the economy. The

FOMC ought to pick its monetary target further in the future; it needed better projections and models of the relationship between money and the economy.

The need for a target that could be quantified was also emphasized. When monetary policy was couched only in terms of firmness or ease, it was too indefinite to measure. The same is true of attempts to use nonmonetary targets, such as prices or inflationary expectations. They cannot be related to any specific change in Federal Reserve operations.

While a majority of the FOMC supported our general views, agreement was far from unanimous. Counterarguments were based primarily on the acknowledged uncertainty of estimating the relationship between monetary targets and spending. Given the lack of knowledge, why not stick with traditional targets? Money market conditions did reflect the market's reactions to Federal Reserve policy. Banks and the government bond traders are important institutions. Foreign currency movements and opinions of other central banks are influenced by short-term interest rates. Why change?

Part of our difficulty in convincing the rest of the FOMC that a change was necessary was due to the prejudice against anything that smacked of a monetarist position (see Chapter 11). The shrillness of the monetarists' attack and certain obvious flaws in their reasoning had alienated Committee members, evoking an almost automatic negative reaction. The principal focus of the opposition to the use of a money supply type target was the linkage in monetarist theory of the need for a good target with the idea that money ought to be created in accordance with an automatic rule. This prevented many within the Fed from paying as much attention as was merited to the monetarists' valid arguments for a good measure. Our directive committee attempted to offset these negative views.

The two strongest arguments we used in convincing the FOMC to adopt monetary aggregates as a target were:

—The past record, which showed too much expansion of money at the wrong times. It was hoped that using a monetary aggregate target would correct such mistakes in the future.

—A demonstration that which target is best depends on what information is available to work with. Given the present state of knowledge, the relationship between money and spending can be estimated more correctly than that between interest rates and spending.

The choice of a target is influenced by the uncertainty in interpreting the week-to-week readings of the monetary variables and in the lack of specific knowledge of the relationship between money, spending, and prices. A target or guide that is best in theory might be worst in practice because of this uncertainty.

Many observers believe it makes sense to have provisos requiring shifts between alternate targets when certain conditions are met. Such provisos permit the use of information gained when the variables such as interest rates, expectations, market data, and the individual components of the monetary aggregates move in separate and unexpected directions.

As an example, targets for the monetary aggregates should be set at logical levels and should be tracked on a monthly or quarterly basis. Because demand is erratic and there is noise in the statistics, and because short-run variations in the supply of money are useful to meet short-run movements in demand, the tracking should not require day-to-day or even week-to-week conformity.

However, if interest rates move beyond a previously determined range, the target should be reexamined. If the cause of the movements remains unclear, the rate at which money is being furnished should be changed temporarily in order to halt too large a swing in interest rates. Interest rate movements beyond certain limits may be more harmful than allowing the monetary targets to expand somewhat beyond the initial target path.

Both theory and a few simulations with large-scale models seem to agree that a mixed strategy or a switching rule, calling for use of a secondary target such as interest rates when certain conditions arise, will work better than putting all one's faith in a single target.

No one should stick with a switched target too long, however. The further either target moves from its normal range, the greater are the probabilities that the assumed relationship may have changed, in which case the entire strategy needs to be reexamined.

In 1970 the FOMC remained too divided to go beyond a very general agreement. In the debate a strong minority still wanted to use money market conditions both as a guide to operations and as a target. I felt that some were worried by any attempt to use specific quantitative targets and believed that a fuzzy directive was a better one. Others feared what would happen to the public's opinion of the System if it became evident from the directive how much uncertainty existed in the formulation and operation of monetary policy. Their view seemed to me to be that the Federal Reserve had to maintain a front of wisdom and omniscience at all costs.

It was finally settled that the basic target was to be the monetary aggregates of money and bank credit over the next three months. However, no attempt would be made to weight different aggregates or to designate one as more important than the others (although in fact M_1 has been given greater prominence in decisions).

Moreover, between meetings the manager was to continue to operate in terms of money market conditions. Thus the FOMC changed its target, but not its operating guide. The FOMC would continue to issue instructions or operating guides to him, through money market conditions. He would be given a desired range of the Federal funds rate and net borrowed reserves. These conditions would be discussed in the meeting, in the light of staff estimates of which money market conditions were compatible with the desired target path for the monetary aggregates. If the aggregates were not on the targeted path between meetings, the manager would change conditions slightly in the direction needed to return the aggregates toward the selected course. At the next meeting of the FOMC, a new set of money market conditions would be debated. The most critical change was the agreement, which the market would understand, that a movement in money market conditions would not mean that monetary policy had changed. Policy was to be measured by movements in the monetary aggregates.

CHAPTER ELEVEN

The Challenge of the Monetarists

IT IS DOUBTLESS EVIDENT that I believe the Federal Reserve should have placed more emphasis in its procedures and operations on changes in the quantity of money. I agreed with the critics who charged that money market conditions were an illogical measure of monetary policy. Furthermore, the failure by the Fed to clarify, even to itself, its goals and objectives impeded its operations. Throughout my service on the Board, I sought to increase the role of money as a useful measure and target.

At the same time, I carefully avoided characterizing myself as a monetarist and, in fact, remained critical of those whom this term describes. The debate over monetarism has been so vigorous and plays so large a part in any discussion of monetary policy that it is worth explaining my position, as well as the obvious animosity toward the monetarists of a large number of those in the Federal Reserve System who believe that the monetarists are extremists, characterized by all the excesses of true radicals.

Monetarist Theory

I have used the term *monetarists* without defining it because it is virtually impossible to find a definition that would encompass all those who fall into this category. At the academic level, monetarists are only partially in agreement over the content of monetary theory. While the monetarist doctrine has been given its greatest impetus by Milton Friedman, professor at the University of Chicago, the monetarists are far from a monolithic group.° There are at least four separable propositions lumped into monetarism:

—The stock of money rather than interest rates is the best target and guide for monetary policy.
—Changes in the amount of money are the main cause of changes in monetary income.
—The Fed should increase money according to a fixed rule at a constant rate.
—Changes in money change expectations and, consequently, spending.

I shall not attempt here the complex task of distinguishing the different academic viewpoints, but shall treat monetarism as it has been dealt with in the press and other media coverage, where it has had its greatest influence on the Federal Reserve.

However they may differ on details, all monetarists emphasize the need for the Fed to use the money supply as a target or measure of monetary policy. Monetarists are believers in the quantity theory, based on the famous equation $MV = PT$ (the amount of money $[M]$ times its velocity $[V]$ equals prices $[P]$ times transactions $[T]$.) Because PT is also total expenditures, we know that velocity is simply the amount of spending divided by the amount of money ($V = \frac{PT}{M}$). This equation is formally true.

The debate over monetary policy concerns the content of each variable: What is money and how does it influence spending and velocity? Monetarists believe that, because the velocity of money is stable or because it changes in a predictable manner, the money supply is directly and reliably linked with the overall level of

---

° For an attempt to construct a general approach to the monetarists' position, see Milton Friedman, *A Theoretical Framework for Monetary Analysis*. Occasional Paper 112 (New York: National Bureau of Economic Research, 1971). For the difficulties encountered, see the various papers in the *Journal of Political Economy* 80, no. 5 (September–October 1972).

money spending. Monetarists want the Federal Reserve to use the money supply as a target because, in their view, changes in the money supply are a crucial determinant of spending.

The link exists because people's desire to hold money bears a definite relationship to their income and wealth. When the Fed creates more money, the money balances of individuals rise. They will not simply hold the added money; they will spend more, each thereby adding to the income of another. Since the total money balances are fixed by the Fed and the banking system, people cannot reduce balances simply by spending faster or more. Collectively, people will keep spending until income and spending grow to bear the same relationship to the increased money balances as spending had to the money balances before the new money was created. To put it another way, spending on goods and services will climb until the new GNP has the same relationship to the new money as existed between GNP and money before expansion. The amount of real income and wealth people want to hold in real money balances changes only slowly. Although monetarists agree in theory that other factors can and do influence the demands for goods, and that the money needed for financial transactions will vary, they hold that such shifts are comparatively unimportant. A simple and almost constant relationship exists between changes in the supply of money and changes in nominal incomes.

However, while monetarists all agree about the importance of monetary influences on spending, they disagree with respect to how and when money's impact will be felt and, consequently, on what should be done about it. A most common view is that changes in the growth rate of money lead, after short lags of a year or less, to predictable changes in the level of spending. Demand for money and the velocity of money are quite stable (except in the very short run).

In recent years, the most popular representation of this view has emerged from a model developed by the St. Louis Federal Reserve Bank. In this version, spending begins to change almost as soon as the growth rate of the money supply alters; virtually the entire impact of money on spending occurs within a year. The influence of an additional dollar on spending is spread fairly evenly through these twelve months. Others put more emphasis on the relationship between changes in the quantity of money and prices. In some popular versions, injections of money do their work within a few months to a year, and prices in this time can be expected to rise by the amount money grows. In other theories, the relationship is held to be long-run. Only after a decade, or decades, can we expect the full impact of money on prices to be effective. In the interim, money will affect real output and liquidity as well as prices. Still another approach stresses the importance of money, but holds that one should not expect to find any simple relationship between changes in money and spending or prices. How money affects the economy will differ depending on changes in the demand for money, how it is created, and the supply and demand for goods and services.

Finally, during the 1970s, some monetarists stressed still another approach, but one which would not be acceptable to most. In this version, money may have an even faster impact on interest rates, spending, and prices. As soon as changes in the growth rate of money are reported, people project these rates into the future. They form expectations of price and interest rates from these extrapolations. Thus if money is growing faster than normal, observers sense inflationary dangers; they immediately demand higher interest rates and alter their spending. Adherents to this concept are again uncertain as to when money will affect spending. Nor is the direction of its effect sure. Some people spend less if they fear inflation, aware that they may need all future earnings and savings for necessities. Others may rush to buy more goods, trying to beat price rises.

Probably more important than the differences between the theories of monetarists is that they end up with two very different prescriptions for proper Fed action. All agree that the money supply is the critical target. Most specify the monetary target as the narrow definition of money: currency and demand deposits adjusted (M_1). After that, they split. Some agree with the majority of economists that the amount of money supplied must be varied with the state of the economy. If fiscal policy or other spending threatens inflation, money should grow more slowly. If unemployment and recession are the danger, money growth should speed up. Others, including many academic economists, believe that the Federal Reserve should follow the target with a fixed rule. Money should be supplied automatically at a constant rate of increase. This argument is not related to the debate over what is the best target. It is based on the idea that because of deficient knowledge and political weakness, an automatic rule is better than a discretionary monetary policy. (Others have advocated similar automatic rules based on different targets, such as the gold standard.)

To the Fed, the main thrust of the monetarists' theory seems to be the injunction "Increase currency and demand deposits at a constant rate of 4 percent a year and most of the economic problems of the country will disappear."

Some Problems with Monetarist Theory

Even though the monetarists' position has been brilliantly expounded and won major support in the Nixon Administration, in some academic circles, in parts of the Federal Reserve System, in some banks, and in parts of the financial press, it has not been accepted by the Fed as a whole and probably not by a majority of any of the other above groups except, perhaps, the Administration. Why not? There are as many degrees of sophistication in the arguments to reject the monetarists' views as there are in those to accept them.

The primary reason for their rejection, I believe, is that the Fed, for example, saw the monetarists' prescription as far too simplistic. It did not accord with experience or with the theory still propounded by a majority of academic economists. Most unconvinced analysts doubted whether so simple a prescription would improve monetary policy as much as promised.

A wide gap divides the careful academic theorizing of monetarists from their empirical forecasts and statements. The empirical results emerge from what is technically known as a reduced form equation or set of equations, more popularly known as a "black box." Money goes in one end, spending comes out the other. No one knows what goes on within the box or why. No one knows what will happen if other factors in addition to money change. Yet other forces are in a constant flux. The absence of theory in the models is dismissed as irrelevant since the models work. How-

ever, upon careful examination, they do not seem to work that
well. The relationship between money and income turns out to be
rather imprecise. The margins of error are too wide for money to be
a useful target or indicator by itself.

Furthermore, to follow a rule of holding the growth in money
constant, the Fed would have to neglect the factors that influence
the demand for money. While many monetarists simply assume
these forces to be stable or unimportant, this point is debatable.
Closely related is the question of how much attention to pay to
events in financial markets. Should the Fed disregard changes in
the values of securities?

According to the prescription, the money supply is crucial; yet
there is no agreement as to what is meant by the money supply.
The velocity of money is held to be predictable and not to vary
much; but it is hard to find a period when this has been true. A variety of lags are acknowledged, possibly long ones. In fact, some
monetarists claim lags are the primary reason for following the
fixed rule. The data on the money supply are subject to large estimating errors and revisions. Published figures do not accord with
most theoretical concepts of money. Many feel that, whatever the
merits of the theory, following the fixed rule would be contrary to
the monetarists' theory, since, while the Fed was controlling the estimated money supply carefully, money balances would not increase at a regular rate because of errors in the data. As a result,
the Fed, while consciously attempting to follow the rule as a policy, would unconsciously be adopting a policy in conflict with the
rule.

It is recognized that unwanted demand may arise from other
forces, such as fiscal policy or a speculative housing or investment
boom. On the other hand, unemployment may be high. Monetarists
are split among themselves as to whether monetary conditions
should be altered to aid in bringing about the desired level of
spending.

But probably a more important element than any of these reasons in many economists' rejection of the monetarist doctrine is the
belief that, because our economic system is complex, it cannot be
realistically analyzed without complex theories. We must take into
account changes in demand, whether due to government spending,

psychological factors, endogenous cycles, shifts in liquidity, the money supply, or innumerable other forces. We do better in explaining and predicting the course of the economy by considering as many as possible of the large number of variables which alter income, employment, and prices. A flexible monetary and fiscal policy can be more efficient than a single-variable policy in reducing the amount of instability and increasing the growth rate of the economy.

An oft-cited simile to the problem of steering the economy to its goals is that of a bus driver trying to get to the top of a mountain. If the road were completely straight with a constant slope, it might make sense for him to lock his steering wheel in place and hold his accelerator at a fixed level. If, however, the road curves and the mountain changes its slope rather frequently, nothing could be more disastrous than such a course. He could reach his goal only by using his steering wheel, his brakes, and his accelerator to help adjust to the variations in his road.

The Role of Demand for Money

In policy statements, monetarists assume a stable link between money and income, but in their theories, they point out reasons why such stability may not exist. It is the assumption that other forces can be neglected that allows the relationship between money and income to be stood on its head. Money is thought of as the tail which wags the dog. The Federal Reserve determines the amount of money. To make the public willing to hold the money stock, income must adjust to the level of money. It follows that the amount of income can be determined by picking the right amount of money.

Yet when we look around, we see many forces that we know change the demand for money relative to income. Both monetarists and their critics agree that if these factors raise the demand for money and if its supply is not increased, the result will be less spending, less income, and less employment. Among the major forces which frequently shift the demand for money are,

—The need for money to pay for financial transactions and other nonincome payments

—The demand for greater liquidity or hoarding
—Expectations of future prices and profits
—Interest rates

It is interesting that these demands play a significant role in most monetarists' theories. If the demand for money fluctuates, following a fixed rule will cause demands for spending to fluctuate. The rule will be destabilizing for the economy. Those who advocate the rule either neglect the other changes in demand or believe they are unlikely to be significant; their impact is small or adjustments occur which reduce the pressure on spending fairly rapidly.

In addition to payments for current spending on goods and services, a great deal of money is held to cover financial transactions. For example, the demand for money shifts with international capital movements, stock market volume, and balances which banks require customers to hold to back loans or commitments. There are large variations in such nonincome demands for money in both the short and the long run. Furthermore, many of these shifts are directly related to monetary policy actions. When money grows tighter, people search harder for money substitutes. When we examine the money held by separate groups in the economy, we find that the growth of each varies widely from that of the total. (Even experts are surprised to find that consumers who purchase most of the GNP own less than one-third of demand deposits.) It would be surprising if differential money growth rates among groups did not change the relationship of the total to spending. None of these shifts is haphazard. But if they are treated as such and neglected, they will cause undesired movements in income that are haphazard.

In examining past financial crises, we note rapid increases in the amount of money held. Households and firms want greater liquidity. They raise their precautionary balances. The scramble for liquidity is the key to financial crunches. Although crises are fortunately not a common occurrence, other shifts in liquidity demand lasting from a week to several years are not at all unusual. Increasing the money supply to meet these demands is proper under normal conditions and necessary at times of crisis.

The monetarists have also stressed expectations, which can lead to sharp changes in the demand for money. Recent periods have seen wild gyrations in the spread between short- and long-term interest rates. Opinions as to the future of profits and of common stock prices shift rapidly. Expectational changes such as these may cause the public to rush in and out of money in an attempt to adjust its spending and investing to the new expectations.

Finally, all theories agree that the demand for money depends upon interest rates, among other factors. If interest rates rise, less money is demanded. A constant growth in money under such circumstances will lead to too much spending, as households attempt to reduce their holdings of money in relationship to income and interest rates. Disagreement exists as to how important the changes in interest are and how long they will last. Both how sensitive interest rates are to more money and how sensitive spending is to changes in interest are at the heart of the debate between the monetarists and post-Keynesians as to whether a change in money will have a one-to-one or even a significant effect on spending. If people are willing to hold large additional amounts of money with small changes in interest (if the demand for money is highly interest elastic), then the added money will not lead to much change in spending. Similarly if spending does not respond readily to lower interest rates or more money, the added money will not bring an equivalent increase in spending. Instead the velocity of money will simply fall. There will be more money, but the added spending will be less than expected by one who assumes no changes will occur in velocities.

Nonmonetary Causes of Spending Shifts

A basic difference between those who advocate the fixed monetary rule and the rest of the economists, both monetarists and others, centers on the monetary targets to be selected when nonmonetary forces are causing shifts in spending. Wars, population movements, technological changes, government spending and deficits, expectations of profits from investments, changes in consumer attitudes, securities speculation, all can cause spending to shift. Their impact on income may become cumulative.

Believers in the fixed rule hold that most of these problems would disappear, or at least be diminished, if money growth were constant. In their view almost all critical income fluctuations result from changes in money. Even if these nonmonetary forces do create instability, higher interest rates and lowered availability can force enough of the excess demand for goods out of the market to return the economy to its optimum course. Conversely, in a weak economy, they expect the lower interest rates associated with sustained monetary growth and the relative increase in money balances to bring forth additional spending.

Most other analysts believe, however, that purely monetary reactions arising from a stable money supply will be too slow, and perhaps too weak, to offset the instability arising from nonmonetary causes. Velocities will shift, interest rates vary, desires for liquidity will change. Because of lags, immediate market reactions can increase rather than offset instability. The differing views as to what would happen remain a matter of opinion, however, since the fixed rule has never been tried in practice and no one can really know.

War finance, for instance, is an area where the fixed rule would be severely strained. Most students of war finance believe that a steady growth in money of 4 percent is insufficient to make the tremendous adjustments in the government's demand effective. Wars are not run well without major changes in money, taxes, and spending. Some monetarists would agree, holding that no rules apply in wartime.

A mixed strategy can create a more efficient system of transferring resources. The pattern of government demand differs greatly from that of households. If monetary measures alone are relied upon, higher government borrowing will raise interest rates, causing major alterations in the flow of funds. Some users of credit lose out; they cannot purchase as much as before. Demand depends on the very arbitrary factor of how funds have been raised in the past. Those with large cash flows are not required to sacrifice resources to the war. Those who operate on credit are. There is no necessary relationship between availability of funds and contribution to the war effort or to national welfare.

A tax program and a flexible money supply are far more efficient than a fixed rate of monetary growth in freeing the type of resources required for war, while at the same time insuring that no large quantities of resources láck demand. Furthermore, using policies other than monetary to bring about the changes in demand makes a real difference in who really pays for the war and how income is distributed. While war is an extreme case, similar problems arise with regard to transfer of resources and sacrifices whenever a constant money supply is used as the primary policy tool to adjust shifts in nonmonetary demands.

An Increased Stress on Monetarism

The Administration's 1969 game plan relied on the power of monetary policy and gradualism. Trust in their efficacy reached its zenith in the 1970 Economic Report of the President. In the 1971 Economic Report, the gradualism had been replaced by activism; but faith in monetary policy was still strong. In the 1972 Report, monetarism had taken a back seat and other policies, notably wage and price controls, had superseded monetary policy as the primary weapons in the anti-inflation battle. The 1973 Report saw a renewed emphasis on control over demand, but principally through fiscal changes.

As we saw in Chapter 10, there was nearly unanimous agreement on the need for a restrictive monetary and fiscal policy in 1969. Growth in the current dollar GNP was to be held to 7 percent, accompanied by a growth in net output of 3 percent and in prices of 4 percent. The Administration believed that with money (M_1) expanding at 4 to 5 percent and unemployment rising to 4 percent, the rate of increase in prices by year's end would fall close to an initial goal of 3 percent. The higher unemployment and lessened expectations of further price rises would then lead to still smaller price increases. When the year ended, spending was not too far from the initial forecasts. The GNP was about .5 percent higher than had been projected. The overrun was entirely in prices, which had risen at about a 5 percent rate in the last half of the year. Real output grew in accordance with the forecast and plan, but unemployment was a good deal less than expected.

However, the slight excess spending had been accompanied by far tighter monetary and fiscal policy than projected in the policy assumptions embodied in the forecasts. With the tax surcharge extended in midyear, the government's surplus on national income accounts was close to $10 billion, or more than three times what had been assumed. The money supply also grew at a slower rate. It had increased 2.5 percent (later revised upward to 3.2 percent). Reserves had declined. Interest rates kept climbing to record levels, instead of reaching a peak and declining as expected. Even working much harder, the government policies had not quite slowed the economy as projected.

While there was some concern over the fact that money was growing too slowly, the 1970 Economic Report showed general satisfaction with the economic results. It called for somewhat easier monetary policy (4 to 5 percent growth rate), but otherwise more of the same. "The best hope of curbing inflation and restricting the rise in unemployment to a relatively small and temporary increase rests with a policy of firm and persistent restraint on the expansion in the demand for goods, services, and labor" (p. 22).

When the results of 1970 were in, however, a major revision of the game plan seemed called for. The first substitution had already been made. In July, President Nixon announced that, in the future, the "essential" balance in the federal budget would be measured on a full-employment basis rather than on the traditional surplus or deficit obtained when the government totaled its receipts and expenditures. The full-employment deficit would be calculated, as many economists had been urging, by adding to actual revenues an estimate of how much the government would have collected in revenues if the GNP had been high enough to lower unemployment to 4 percent. This shift in definition was prompted by the knowledge that the traditional deficit for calendar year 1970 would be over $10 billion and that for fiscal 1971 would be over $20 billion.

In 1970 monetary policy also turned out to be somewhat more liberal than had been anticipated. Partly, we have seen, this was due to the Penn Central debacle and the great demand for liquidity. Partly the increase was larger than intended because of errors made in adjusting the estimate of demand deposits. Near the end of the year, a revision in the data showed the growth in the money supply to have been 45 percent more than had been contemplated or shown by measurements within the period. As a result of the revisions, the money supply was seen to have grown at a rate of 5.4 percent in the year—a good deal more than policy had contemplated. There was no quarter in which the rate fell as low as 4 percent.

Even with these more stimulative conditions, the economy looked bad and was worsening. Unemployment rose to 6 percent from only 3.5 percent a year earlier. For the first time since 1958, there was a fall in real output, to a level below that when the Administration had taken office two years previously. Price rises were accelerating. Consumer prices rose over 6 percent in the year, by far the sharpest increase in any year since 1951.

Those facts meant that by the start of 1971, both economic and political problems had become serious. The consensus of most economists was that the GNP would grow by $70 billion (the actual increase was $73 billion), or slightly over 7 percent in 1971. Prices would slow slightly; output would grow considerably less than potential supply, and, as a result, unemployment by the end of the year would be over 6 percent. This was a completely unacceptable scenario to the White House. The results of the 1970 congressional elections had been disappointing from the Administration's point of view. If the forecast was correct, the 1972 elections would take place with unemployment close to 6 percent. The answer was clear. The President's economic staff was informed that the forecast for the economy for 1972 had to be higher. Overnight the estimate for GNP growth was raised from just over $70 billion to $88 billion, or by almost 25 percent, to reach a level of $1,065 billion.

The higher projection was accompanied by only a slight shift in the fiscal posture. Some additional expenditures, as well as added depreciation allowances for industry, were included in the 1972 fiscal budget. The net effect, however, did not add much to demand. The unified budget called for a full-employment balance, while there was to be a considerable surplus in the national income accounts on a full-employment basis.

It was clear that the last-minute fiscal changes would not bring about the projected additional $18 billion in spending. It was also clear to the White House where new expansionary pressures ought to be generated. The finger pointed right at the Federal Reserve. Because of the independent position of the Fed, no direct orders could be issued, but the White House made its views plain.

The rule of gradualism no longer satisfied George Shultz, director of the Office of Management and Budget and the strongest economic voice in the Administration. He now espoused an activist monetary policy. Money would determine spending. If an election were to be won, the Federal Reserve would have to increase the money supply at far more than the 4.2 percent average of 1969–70. In his words, the "real juice" for the expanding economy had to come from monetary policy. To make the message clear, the statement in OMB's official briefing chart book that called attention to the need for an adequate money supply growth was printed in bright red. The estimates of how fast money was to grow were not as precise, but in various speeches and off-the-record briefings, the range of 6 to 9 percent became clear.

That the message of the White House briefings penetrated to newsmen is clear in the headlines in the press. The Washington *Post* wrote, "A Basic Challenge to the Fed: An $88 Billion Growth Requires Easier Money Policy"; the New York *Times* said, "Nixon's Budget Mystery: Electronic Bullishness"; The *Wall Street Journal* headed its story, "Nixon's Flight from Friedmanism." The stories made clear that the reason other forecasts for the year were so much lower than the official one was that they failed to take into account the power of the Federal Reserve to expand the economy. They failed to recognize how promptly added money would show up in spending. OMB sent a monetarist model to Congress and other agencies to show how clear the correlation was between added money and added spending. As long as the Fed cooperated, the traditional forecasters would be proven wrong.

The Challenge to the Monetarists

For several months prior to the budget bombshell, Herbert Stein, then a member, later chairman of the Council of Economic Advisers, and I had been scheduled to address, on February 23, the 1971 National Agricultural Outlook Conference. Our topic was to forecast and explain our views on the economic outlook for the coming year. The conference included the national press, the agricultural press, and farm extension specialists.

I decided to accept the White House challenge and ask them to answer two critical questions which we had been discussing informally with the CEA for the past two years:

—If they were depending on the money supply to raise spending by $10 to 20 billion, what definition of the money supply should the Federal Reserve be using?

—How much added money would be necessary to get the expanded spending? Monetary velocity varies greatly, depending on which past period is chosen. On which velocity should we base our 1971 money supply changes?

The point on which I wanted to focus attention was that those who stressed the rigid rule or who concentrated on small movements in money in a period even as long as a year were, in my view, neglecting a great deal of what we as economists know about money. At the same time, they were urging that policy be guided solely by movements which could well have no economic meaning and certainly were not valid statistical statements. I wanted to emphasize again my belief that the monetary aggregates were a better measure of what was happening to money, but more particularly the fact that judgment is vital in interpreting any reported movements. Money is a sensible measure or target, but only when used properly. The use now being urged by the monetarists, and in this case the Administration, was not a logical one.

What is Money?

Money has meant many different things throughout history. Table 6 shows the amount of money outstanding in the United States in 1973 using four different definitions. The amount varies from the approximately $100 billion of high-powered money, or the monetary base, to $840 billion if we include as money currency plus deposits at all financial institutions.

We frequently hear money defined as whatever is generally ac-

TABLE 2. *Common Definitions of the Money Supply: Growth Rates and Relative Growth Rates*

DEFINITION	BILLIONS OF $ OUTSTANDING MAY 1973	ANNUAL RATES OF CHANGE		4 MONTHS ENDING:		RATES OF CHANGE RELATIVE TO M_1 †		4 MONTHS ENDING:	
		1969 °	1970 °	JAN. 1970	JAN. 1971	1969	1970	JAN. 1970	JAN. 1971
1. Currency and demand deposits adjusted (M_1)	$260	3.8%	5.0%	3.9%	3.6%	1.00	1.00	1.00	1.00
2. Currency and demand and time deposits adjusted (M_2)	$540	3.2%	7.5%	2.2%	10.7%	.75	1.25	.38	2.01
3. Currency and deposits at all financial institutions adjusted (M_3)	$840	3.5%	7.1%	1.7%	11.5%	.80	1.20	.30	2.20
4. The monetary base: currency and reserves adjusted (M_0)	$100	5.2%	6.5%	4.9%	5.9%	1.03	.97	.71	.93

° 4th quarter to 4th quarter.
† All rates of change have been standardized with average growth in 1969 and 1970 equal to 1.00.

cepted as a means of payment or a medium of exchange. Such a definition leads straight to the first line in Table 2, the money supply (M_1) measured by currency and adjusted demand deposits in the hands of the public. In some ways this is the simplest definition; but questions of how to define the public, how to adjust deposits, what to include (as, for example, travelers' checks and credit cards) raise some ticklish issues.

Many analysts stress the use of money as a store of value or wealth, or they have a portfolio explanation of how the quantity of money influences spending and saving. They add what some call "near money" to the narrow definition. Line 2 shows the movements in one of these broader versions, which includes currency and demand deposits plus time deposits at commercial banks (other than large certificates of deposit), called M_2. Line 3 shows M_3, which is defined to include M_2 plus deposits at nonbank thrift institutions. All three definitions are published weekly and monthly by the Federal Reserve under the title of "Measures of the Money Stock."

Another approach to policy is to measure high-powered money, which consists of currency and member bank deposits at the Federal Reserve, or the monetary base shown in line 4. It is the money created by the government and the central bank. High-powered money can be more accurately measured and targeted. It has important theoretical advantages, since it reflects what the Fed does in contrast to what banks and others do.

The right-hand side of the table shows how the definition alters our estimate of how money is growing. If, prior to the Outlook Conference, each concept of money had grown at equivalent rates, all of the numbers in this section would have been 1. They are standardized in terms of M_1 to correct for the fact that historically the different concepts of money have expanded at quite different rates.

Now we see one facet of the dilemma the Administration had handed to the Fed when it asked the Fed to furnish the reserves necessary to cause spending to expand at 9 percent. If the Fed followed those (such as Friedman) who believed that M_2 was really money, it would supply, on the basis of what had been happening for the past four months, just half as many reserves to get the identical increase in spending as would be necessary if it listened to those who defined the money supply as M_1.

As I sat in Open Market Committee meetings and saw projections of different versions of money, varying as they do in the table, I often wished that someone who was a true believer in the money supply theory could make the proper choice of definition for me. Frequently, when I raised the question of the discrepancies between the different versions of money with monetarists, they simply brushed the problem aside. In some cases they were surprised at the variations, because they tended to look at the levels of money (the money stock), which clearly do not change as much. Usually they answered that the variations arise primarily because the Federal Reserve retains Regulation Q, which sets interest rate ceilings and thus distorts deposit flows. If the Fed did away with Regulation Q, no problem would exist. Obviously, this answer was no help for a policy decision in 1971, since removing Regulation Q would create even more difficult movements to interpret. In any case, I do not believe that repealing Regulation Q would serve a useful purpose, since it would do away with an instrument that can and has been helpful. But certainly the mere fact that its elimination would make the problem of monetary theorists and analysts somewhat easier is not a sufficient reason for abolishing it, as some argue. I would prefer to see analysts work a little harder rather than to discard a useful instrument. Furthermore, in my opinion this contention misses a significant point. Even if Regulation Q did not exist, different measures of money should be expected to diverge significantly for periods of at least several years, a long time by any policy or target standard.

Since each type of money serves a somewhat different purpose, each should react in its own way to what is going on in the economy. Interest rate changes, liquidity shifts, financial transactions, technological improvements in the payments mechanism, competitive shifts among financial institutions, all differ greatly from period to period, but all influence each definition of money in a unique way. Moreover, how they shift varies directly with the degree of restrictiveness in monetary policy. Failing to recognize that what serves as money alters with policy is like insisting that we retain ten feet of water in a reservoir but measure it with an elastic yardstick that shrinks in dry periods and expands in wet ones.

Differences in Velocity

Added to the problem of defining money for use as a target is that of determining the amount of money that ought to be furnished to cause a desired growth in spending. This is the problem of the velocity of money. Dividing spending—GNP—by money gives the rate at which money turns over, or its income velocity. However, this velocity is not constant. It has varied greatly in the course of time. Marginal velocities, the ratio of changes in spending to changes in money, which are critical for monetary purposes, move over a wide range. For example, at the Outlook Conference I submitted a series of tables showing how much money would be required in 1971 to meet the goals of the Administration. The table showed desirable rates of growth in money ranging from 4.9 to 14.1 percent to achieve the 9 percent growth in GNP needed to attain the $1,065 billion level. There is no simple relationship between money growth and GNP for a period such as a year or two. The amounts vary depending on which definition of money and what period are used to estimate the expected changes in velocity.

There are many well-recognized causes for the differences in velocity over the course of time: lags or incomplete adjustments in spending to changes in money, shifts in the nonincome demand for money, lags in the effect of interest movements, and shifts in the payments mechanism in its broadest sense. The effect of each of these is to cause the relationship of income and money or income velocity to vary widely over short, intermediate, and long periods. More significantly, we have noted that many economists believe that adding money changes its velocity rather than leading to increases in spending.

Errors in Forecasts

At times, overexuberant believers in the money supply theory seem to say that it is a waste of time to quibble over the theory because the facts have been proved statistically. There is an empirical, if not necessarily a theoretically valid, law justifying the policy of a constant growth for the money supply. They have asked that their black box be accepted on the strength of its successful performance. After examining the pertinent facts, I see no evidence that would support these claims.

In examining the statistical studies, we face, of course, the usual problem of drawing conclusions about an extremely complex system from partial statistics. Looking at post-Korean data, we can explain about half of the quarterly changes in the GNP in terms of changes in the money supply and money stock. The models giving the best correlations of this type contain lag distributions of three to five quarters. The St. Louis type equation is typical. But explaining 50 percent of quarterly changes is not very good in the forecasting field; and it is poor in the sphere of correlations, given the ability of computers to test all types of different lags in split seconds. Even if shifts in money caused movements in the GNP similar to the past, the errors in the projections would still be large. In fact, they would be larger on the average than the errors found in most eclectic forecasts which were actually made prior to the period and made without any prior knowledge of how much the money supply would grow. Moreover, the difficulty is not simply that the correlations leave us looking at a bottle that is half empty and also half full; it is a good deal more complex. In each case we can, by theoretical reasoning, improve or dissipate the initial statistical results. Most models used in these tests tend to be too simple.

It is well recognized that past correlations are no indication of causality. This was obvious to me as a Federal Reserve policy maker. For the entire period on which the correlations were based, the Fed had allowed changes in spending to be a critical influence on the growth in money. As a result, a definite correlation does exist. As GNP grew, so did money. This correlation, however, tells us nothing about what would happen if the past relationship were stood on its head and the Federal Reserve decided to control the growth of money irrespective of other forces which cause movements in spending.

Monetarists' forecasts have had a fair record. The fact that they did well in 1968 when most others did poorly was a major cause of their initial popularity. Since then their record has not been as good. I have tried to keep track of predictions made by various techniques. At times, monetarists have done better than their models. But I, at least, do not believe their record has been good enough to prove their simplified theory. Many other factors in addition to the money supply alter spending.

A rather simple-minded way of showing this variability of money and spending appears in Table 3. Here we have asked how close would each definition of money have been in forecasting the growth in the GNP if we had known two facts: (1) the rate at which money had been spent in the previous quarter (its income velocity), and (2) the amount of money which would be supplied in the new quarter. In other words, this table shows the degree to which the assumption that income velocity remains constant is true, which is simply another version of the assumption of a constant or regular change in velocity.

It seems obvious from an examination of the table that the simple assumption misses rather badly. Furthermore, results over the period are not random or self-correcting. In most examples, the errors accumulate. Misses go in the same direction. Line 5 of the table compares these simple monetary-based forecasts to an actual set of forecasts derived from a judgmental-type model of the sort discussed in Chapter 8. While these figures come from actual forecasts, their errors were smaller than those based on the growth rate for the money supply. On any type of comparison, the actual forecasts had considerably smaller errors.

A simple relationship between money and income does not exist in the real world. We recognize that lags occur in the adjustment process which are only dimly understood. Money acts as a buffer stock. Changes in income and transactions are reflected initially in changes in money balances. Only gradually does the public adjust its new balance to the desired relationship. In the interim, velocities are not at their final equilibrium. They fluctuate. The time it takes to return to a more normal relationship appears to vary greatly, depending upon existing economic and financial conditions.

The St. Louis type of equation includes time lags in an attempt to handle part of this problem. Still, its record for this period does not differ greatly from the assumptions of a constant velocity and no lag. The fourth row of Table 3 contains quarterly estimates from the St. Louis equation, not based on a forecast but using the actual movements in the money supply. Thus, even if we know what the changes in the amount of money and past relationships to spending were, we do not do too well in explaining movements in the GNP.

If we examine the relationship of money to prices, we find still more erratic movements. Whether we look at the United States or at other similar economies, we find only a small year-to-year or even five- or ten-year relationship between movements in money and prices. The main exceptions are countries with extremely rapid or hyperinflations, where prices and movements in money are far more closely related. For example, we can examine the changes in money (M_1) and consumer prices for seventeen major developed countries for the five- and ten-year periods ending in 1971. For the five-year period there is absolutely no correlation between the way money and prices changed in these countries. For the ten-year period, correlation explains about 20 percent of the comparative movements; but, with this small sample, such a number is not statistically significantly different from zero. The apparent randomness leading to these results becomes evident when we examine individual countries. Canada, for example, was second highest in its money growth rate and second lowest in price increases in this decade. Sweden found itself in almost the reverse situation.

The Dog Days of 1971

While the economic and budget messages of 1971 were the high point of acceptance of the monetarist doctrine, its low point came on August 15, 1971, the day on which President Nixon introduced a price-wage freeze and his new economic policy. This marked his and the Administration's admission that changes in money were not sufficient to solve the economy's problems.

Partly because of unusual events and partly because of poor operating procedures, monetary policy in the first seven months of 1971 provided all of the "juice" the White House had requested. In

TABLE 3. *Differences between Actual Growth in GNP and Predictions Based on Changes in Money with Constant Velocity (in billions of $ at annual rates)*

| | 1969 | | | | | 1970 | | | | | 1971 | | | | |
| | BY QUARTERS | | | | | BY QUARTERS | | | | | BY QUARTERS | | | | |
	1	2	3	4	YEAR	1	2	3	4	YEAR	1	2	3	4	YEAR
M_1	−0.3	−5.7	−12.9	−4.1	−23.2	1.8	2.8	−2.5	5.3	7.4	−14.8	8.5	6.1	−18.6	−18.8
M_2	1.9	−5.7	−19.1	−6.3	−29.2	−2.4	5.4	8.0	17.7	28.7	4.3	18.8	5.9	−3.7	25.3
M_3	0.6	−5.7	−16.8	−5.1	−27.0	−3.6	3.7	7.3	18.5	25.9	6.6	22.8	12.7	2.5	44.6
S.L. °	1.5	1.1	−2.5	6.0	6.1	5.0	6.0	2.0	10.1	23.1	−16.6	5.1	17.7	4.4	10.6
Judgmental	2.7	−0.2	3.4	−4.1	1.8	1.1	0.9	1.3	−9.3	−6.0	3.4	2.3	−5.6	−6.0	−5.9

° St. Louis Equation which also includes a fiscal variable.

the six months after the budget message, the money supply (M_1) had grown at more than an 11 percent annual rate. The increase in M_2 was at a rate above 14 percent. Growth in spending had also shot up, partly because it was being compared to the period just prior to the economic message, which had included a major auto strike. However, most of the increased spending was ending up as increases in prices rather than in output and employment. Just prior to the President's move, prices appeared still to be rising at record rates. Industrial production was growing, as was other output, but not fast enough to reduce unemployment. Those out of work remained at just about the 6 percent level, the rate that had been reached at year end.

Monetary policy was pushing hard to help the recovery. Sufficient reserves were added to bring down market interest rates. As market rates fell, the discount rate followed fairly closely. It was lowered from 5.75 to 4.75 percent in four moves of a quarter point each between November 30, 1970, and February 12, 1971. Even prior to the Economic Message on February 1, members of the White House staff had indicated that the slow growth in output and increasing unemployment were unsatisfactory. They felt that more money was required to speed up growth and output. From the President down, the Administration looked at each squiggle in the growth rate of M_1 as a significant and momentous event.

No official communication traveled from the Administration to the Federal Reserve Board concerning the amount of money that would be desirable. However, there were many informal contacts socially, in meetings on related economic problems, and in official sessions with the Council of Economic Advisers and the Treasury. In their speeches and meetings with the press, many of the Administration's top officials, including the President, stressed the importance they attached to the money supply. It was clear that the Administration had forgotten its previous criticism of too rapid an expansion of money. An election was approaching; from their point of view, the faster money grew, the better was monetary policy.

This White House view seemed to affect some members of the FOMC who otherwise might have preferred a slower growth in money and higher interest rates in order to hold back price increases, even if it meant higher unemployment. With less emphasis on money in the Administration, I believe the swing votes in the center would probably have opted for tighter money. I supported the Administration's policy. I believed, as I had during the December 1965 dispute, that the President and Congress were responsible for determining the proper goals for the economy. I would have quarreled with them only if I felt the goals were illogical and selected for political gain, regardless of the public interest. Moreover, it seemed to me that in this instance a policy to get us out of the recession rapidly and with the least possible additional unemployment was sound. I assume that most FOMC members who voted for an expansionary monetary policy followed a similar line of reasoning.

Money market conditions and market interest rates reached their lowest levels at the end of the first quarter of 1971. From then on, it became a constant battle to regain control over the expanding monetary aggregates. Everyone agreed that no matter which definition of money was used, the rate of monetary growth was unsafe. Even if the $1,065 billion goal were reached, the great amount of liquidity in the economy could create excess demand in succeeding years. I believed that the runaway monetary growth resulted from poor operating guides used by the Fed, although statistical revisions and other factors also played a part.

During this period, the monetarists outside the Administration had numerous complaints, but they focused on two issues: They disagreed with the Administration's goal. On the whole they were deflationists who desired a more rapid increase in unemployment in order to halt too great a rise in price expectations. They felt that the money supply was expanding much too fast, especially the broader versions of M_2 and M_3. They were also greatly concerned because the weekly and monthly reports on the money supply showed extremely sharp variations in the annual rate of growth. In view of the large month-to-month swings in these growth rates, they found it hard to believe that the Fed was paying much attention to the money supply.

The explanations offered by the Fed were not accepted. Perhaps random events, preliminary estimates, and difficulties in controlling the monetary aggregates would lead to some month-to-month variations. It was true that multiplying these variations by twelve to put them on an annual basis might tend to overemphasize the movements. Nevertheless, the fact that annual growth rates varied from plus to minus 10 percent meant that something was wrong. They believed the Fed was allowing these large month-to-month changes in order to hold down rapid swings in interest rates. The result would be much too rapid a rise in spending. The Fed was using an improper objective.

The Federal Reserve, on the other hand, maintained that these sharp month-to-month movements were due in large part to statistical flukes, or noise. They would average out (as they did) and have minimal impacts on spending. On the other hand, if reserves were changed in an attempt to iron out these random movements, there would be a depressing effect on the economy and on financial markets.

In any case, President Nixon ended the debate by deciding that traditional monetary and fiscal policies had to be supplemented with another form of policy—price-wage controls.

Incomes Policy

In the 1965 March–April *Harvard Business Review*, Professor Arthur F. Burns wrote a strong attack on the Kennedy-Johnson wage-price guideposts. The article pointed out that the problem with guideposts was that they would throttle competition, become a drag on economic growth and, most dangerous of all, might lead to actual control over wages and prices by the government. His movement away from this position was gradual. In May 1970 he told a group of bankers that, because of the failure of prices to moderate "there may be a useful—albeit a very modest—role for incomes policy."

People were confused by the term *incomes policy*. It means the use of government action to stabilize the share of national income going to business and labor. In an inflationary situation, labor may try to gain at the expense of the rest of the population by boosting its wages faster than productivity rises. Business may raise prices in an attempt to increase profits per unit of output. An incomes policy consists of programs aimed at holding the income of each group relatively stable in comparison to others.

In December 1970, in a speech at Pepperdine College, Chairman of the Federal Reserve, Arthur F. Burns went still farther by suggesting a voluntary wage-price board. As the year progressed and crises multiplied, Burns actively supported the concept of actual controls.

In late 1972, when the question of completely removing controls was raised in a public meeting, he spoke up again strongly for the need to continue them in some form. When asked how he could harmonize his later views with the *Harvard Business Review* article, his answer was simply, "I was wrong in 1965."

I believe this action is very revealing of Arthur Burns's approach to economic policy. In 1965, as an academic economist, he was willing to base his arguments primarily on pure theory. When he became responsible for policy making, he became more pragmatic, examining the situation as it actually existed, using his vast economic knowledge and analytical ability to arrive at a practical solution which differed greatly from that of pure theory.

This approach contrasts sharply with the more traditional approach of the monetarists, as evidenced by Chancellor W. Allen Wallis of the University of Rochester, another Nixon adviser whose background was primarily the University of Chicago. In an article in the December 22, 1971 *Wall Street Journal*, he stated,

> The prospects that wage and price controls will succeed in checking inflation are nil. Wage and price controls will affect many things but inflation is not among them. . . . Inflation can be generated only by the government. Business firms, labor unions or consumers with excessive market power can do many objectionable things that are contrary to the public interest; but one objectionable thing that they cannot do is to cause inflation—or, for that matter, prevent it. Within our government the only important power to cause or prevent inflation lies with the Federal Reserve Board. . . . There is one, and only one, way to achieve the price stability at which the wage and price controls aim, and that is to control the rate of growth in the stock of money and credit.

Why Prices Rise

The debate over price-wage guideposts and controls is a debate over why prices increase. What are the factors that cause inflation? Why do prices rise when labor and capital are unemployed? What is the proper policy when rising prices are coupled with a level of unemployment unsatisfactory both to economists and, even more, to politicians? The Wallis quotation reflects the traditional monetarist viewpoint that such a situation can result only from too much money. The majority of economists and most businessmen, however, disagree with this simplistic explanation.

The wage-price problem arises because we live in an imperfect economy. The problem was recognized when, between 1955 and 1959, prices rose over 11 percent, even though unemployment remained around 5 percent. In the year prior to August 1971, the record was far worse. In that single year, prices rose more than 5 percent while unemployment was over 5.5 percent.

Two explanations are possible for such situations. The simplest is that of a lag. Even though unemployment is high, prices continue to rise because wages are being pushed up in the wake of previous price and wage increases. However, if only past pressures were at work, increases would gradually taper off. Supporters of an incomes policy do not believe they will do so. They see another situation developing, with new pressures which can push prices and wages ever higher in a never-ending wage-price spiral.

Most modern mixed capitalistic economies have a record of unacceptably fast increases in wages and prices, i.e., inflation, even when no general excess demand exists. Stable prices result primarily from either severe depressions or price-wage controls. This causes a dilemma for governments that want to avoid inflation: Since they and the voters also place a high value on employment and output, they do not want to halt expansion while resources are still available for growth.

Looking at the record, three prime possibilities exist for avoiding controls. The first is simply to accept inflation. The second is to restrict demand sufficiently through monetary and fiscal policies to keep prices reasonably stable. The third is to improve information and cause markets to move closer to the model of pure, perfect competition so that whenever there are excess resources, prices will not rise.

Everyone prefers the third possibility, but unfortunately neither theory nor practice indicates that it can be accomplished. While many problems could be eliminated by better information and by removing artificial restraints in the market, these appear to be longer-run solutions, impossible as an immediate alternative and unlikely even in the long run. Competition is extremely important in restraining many price rises, but the competitive market has many forces within it that allow general price-wage increases to continue even without an excess of aggregate demand.

Thus, the real choice is between accepting inflation or depression and imposing some restraint on wages and prices. Those who think that inflation or serious deflation is not too costly urge their acceptance. Others are adamant that neither good economics nor practical politics will allow such a choice, which they feel is defeatist. A majority seems to believe that occasional controls, even though in theory they may be a second-best policy, turn out to be the best practical solution.

The belief in the necessity, or at least desirability, of an incomes policy is based on certain theories of inflation. Some economists distinguish between demand-pull, or excess demand inflation, and cost-push inflation, but most agree that many situations are a mixture. Demand-pull refers to orthodox inflation. If aggregate demand exceeds the capacity to produce goods and services, purchasers will raise their bids for goods in short supply. Prices will rise to eliminate some potential buyers.

At the same time, the higher prices add to the income of the suppliers. They can now buy more. Their bids cause prices to spiral upward still faster. Purchases become income, which, in turn, becomes purchases. The fundamental feature of a demand-pull inflation is the bidding up of the prices of resources in short supply. The increased transactions are possible either because of more money, or because existing money is used more rapidly; i.e., the velocity or turnover rate of money increases.

It is agreed that in periods of too great aggregate demand, excess incomes should be cut back by either monetary or fiscal action. However, in recent years, studies of the price-making mechanism have brought recognition that excess demand is not an all-or-nothing concept. Shortages in particular industries may accompany aggregate excess unemployment and a great deal of unused capacity. Lumber can be in high demand even as textiles are in balance and shoes depressed. For resources move only slowly from one industry to another, and usually will do so only if attracted by increased wages or prices in the areas of short supply. Because they are not offset by falling prices elsewhere, rising prices and wages in particular industries may bring about inflationary rises in the general price level, despite overall excess unemployment.

The problem is often even more complex. Other forces may also act to raise prices. In a period of general stability, a strong union or a monopolistic or oligopolistic group of companies may try to increase their income. If they have enough power, they can do so, even though excess unemployment exists elsewhere. It is theoretically possible that other prices would fall as they raise their prices, but this is unlikely in most modern economies, where wages and prices are too rigid to react to minor increases in unemployment. In fact the opposite occurs. Workers in industries with somewhat lower demand will strive for higher wages also. Thus we see the possibility of cost-push. Actual real income can rise only through greater productivity or increased employment. Higher wages without increased productivity must be passed on in higher prices or lower profits; and, since profits are generally not that large, over time any increase in wages must show up in higher prices. Thus cost-push inflation arises from temporary market power due either to a high industry demand or to a strong position of labor or corporations. In fact, most price movements show a mixture of the two.

The reply of the traditionalists to this generally accepted analysis is that, if power strong enough to raise wages or prices existed, it would be used anyway. Wouldn't firms maximize their profits and labor unions increase wages as rapidly as possible? The answer is that they do not. That is simply not the way the economy works. Few if any price or wage bargains reflect the total amount of power possessed by the participants. Most are made in line with surrounding bargains and prices.

Another rejoinder is, Why not force other prices and wages down by not supplying the money? Even if demand increases in a particular sector, inflation could be avoided by refusing to supply the necessary cash to allow prices to be maintained elsewhere. One answer is that transactions are handled not just by the amount of money alone, but by the amount of money times its turnover. Thus even if money is held constant, increased velocity will allow prices to rise. More important, however, is the unwillingness, for valid economic and political reasons, to allow the economy to suffer the necessary recession or depression which would accompany a policy of not expanding money because incomes are being pushed up from the cost side.

Another way of summarizing the discussion is to point out that experience in our markets, and in those of most developed nations, shows that without some type of government intervention in the price-wage bargains struck by labor and industry, the trade-off between inflation and unemployment is unsatisfactory. The level of unemployment required to stabilize prices without any outside pressure on incomes and prices is higher than that which the economy finds acceptable.

The idea of an incomes policy is that outside pressures, greater information, and focusing attention on the basic, underlying problems, will lead to bargains based on the recognition that higher incomes can result only from increased productivity or more hours of work. The race for higher income primarily through price increases can thus be avoided. In the battle of increasing prices, no group as a whole can win, although obviously some individuals, groups, and firms can and do improve their own relative shares. Since it is in the national interest to avoid both inflation and deflation, the hope is that these outside pressures from incomes policies will be accepted, thus diminishing the inflationary pressures.

Wage-Price Controls

The decision by Chairman Burns that in the current situation the traditionalists' view of the price problem was wrong and the new economists were right in this intance on the need for wage-price action nearly led to an all-out fight with the White House. It certainly was important to the eventual shift of President Nixon from his former position.

The background of Burns's shift was the unsatisfactory wage-price situation at the end of 1970, already described. Unemployment was approaching 6 percent and threatening to rise still higher. But neither the recent sharp increases in unemployment nor the relatively low usage of business plant and equipment was bringing sufficient pressure to bear on wages and prices to end the inflation. Price increases were expected to continue between 4 and 5 percent. Contrary to all statements of the two previous years, current policies were not likely to end inflation without increasing unemployment.

It was this analysis of the current needs that led Burns to give his Pepperdine speech. Since it was the first major speech in which anyone closely connected with the Nixon Administration called for a price-wage policy, it resounded through the media. It struck an extremely responsive chord in the hearts of most businessmen and financiers who had been calling with an ever-increasing clamor for such action for several years.

The need for a new policy was spelled out more clearly in the Federal Reserve Board's official statement to the Joint Economic Committee of Congress on the condition of the economy, presented shortly thereafter in February 1971. This statement pointed out that the current expansionary pressures from fiscal and monetary policy were necessary but dangerous. Money was growing at a rate previously seen only in years of sharp inflation. Adverse effects on the balance of payments and prices were developing. Future dangers were still greater. Yet with all this, the rate of expansion in real output would not be adequate for the needs of the economy or the full employment of the labor force. Speaking for the Board, Chairman Burns concluded,

> We recognize also, as do an increasing number of students around the world, that the problems of economic stabilization policy currently plaguing us cannot be solved by monetary policy alone, nor by a combination of monetary and fiscal policies. Monetary and fiscal tools can cope readily with inflation arising from excess aggregate de-

mand. But they are ill-suited to dealing with the rising price level that stems from rising costs at a time of rising unemployment and excess capacity. . . . The stimulative thrust of present monetary and fiscal policies is needed to assure the resumption of economic growth and a reduction of unemployment. But unless we find ways to curb the advances of costs and prices, policies that stimulate aggregate demand run the grave risk of releasing fresh forces of inflation.

In view of this new problem, it is the considered judgment of the Federal Reserve Board that, under present conditions, monetary and fiscal policies need to be supplemented with an incomes policy—that is to say, with measures that aim to improve the workings of our labor and product markets so that upward pressures on costs and prices will be reduced. . . . If I read the national mood correctly, widespread public support now exists for vigorous efforts to bring wage settlements and prices in our major industries within more reasonable bounds.

The call for such a policy was an anathema to those on the White House staff who believed in the traditional remedies of demand management to create a labor surplus in the market. Governmental pressure to speed up the process would only upset the classical mechanism. The President had been elected as a spokesman for a Republican doctrine which emphasized minimal restrictive relations between the government and business. In public meetings, senior advisers stated that anybody who suggested that the President might adopt any type of incomes policy was being disloyal. In fact, however, the Administration was split on the matter. Some saw the problem in the same way as the Federal Reserve.

While the Fed and its Chairman believed that a change in policy was necessary and stuck to their guns, all were well aware of the problem facing the System. In the summer of 1971 it became clear that the White House staff was preparing a major campaign against the Federal Reserve. The foundation for it was laid in July, with an extremely personal, blistering attack on Chairman Burns emanating from the White House. According to the *Wall Street Journal* of July 29, 1971, observers felt that, among other aims, the attack hoped to "embarrass Mr. Burns either to diminish his impact on public opinion or to force him to resign and make room for a more docile central bank head" and "to set the stage for making the Reserve a scapegoat in case inflation and unemployment are political handicaps in 1972."

Two factors caused further attack to be postponed. The first was a strong adverse reaction in the stock market and in the business world to the first attack. Whereas they were attacking the Federal Reserve primarily for political reasons to explain the continued recession, their words and actions appeared to be having policy repercussions and to be making the recession worse. The second factor was the threat of serious international consequences. The dollar was under major pressure abroad. The attack by the White House on the central bank was not helping its already poor international image. In the end, the President issued a public statement reaffirming his friendship and support of Chairman Burns. While the statement partially offset the effects of the attack, this episode was one of the forces that accelerated the economic crisis and led to the development of a changed economy policy.

At the start of August, the internal fight within the White House approached a climax. It was clear that the activist monetarist game plan was in trouble. Prices seemed to be rising at record rates. Unemployment was not falling. The economic projections for the year continued to forecast the most sluggish recovery from recession of the entire postwar period. Added to domestic problems, the international monetary situation was steadily worsening.

Former CEA chairman Arthur Okun has suggested that there is a very simple index of discomfort in the economy. It is derived by combining the unemployment rate and the annual rate of change in consumer prices. This discomfort index had risen 40 percent during President Nixon's first two years. By August 1971 it was still rising and threatened to approach the previous postwar record, set in 1951. It was clear that this degree of discomfort would be a major political liability in the 1972 campaign.

Herbert Stein, who did yeoman service at the Council of Economic Advisers in devising the new economic policy, cited four elements which finally caused President Nixon to decide in favor of wage-price controls. The first was the failure of inflation to subside at the expected rate. Second was the growing clamor in the press, in the business community, and among politicians for an incomes policy. The do-nothing approach to prices and wages was amazingly unpopular, particularly among major business groups. Third was the fear that the economy could not be pumped up enough to start unemployment down without some inflation control. A rise in demand sufficient to start unemployment decreasing would have required a far more aggressive fiscal policy and an even more aggressive monetary policy than was contemplated, and would have caused continuing inflationary difficulties far into the future. Finally, there was the international situation; it was the critical factor that determined the timing of the change. Dollars were pouring out of the United States. Foreign governments, which previously had been willing to accept dollars, demanded either that they be converted into gold or that the United States guarantee them against losses if devaluation occurred.

As a result of all of these pressures, President Nixon determined to make a bold attack upon the entire problem. He could have attempted to patch up the critical leaks in the existing programs. But it was clear that a patched up vessel would remain weak and subject to constant pressures and further leaks. Consequently he took what I felt to be the proper action. Seizing the initiative with a striking display of leadership, he made a comprehensive attack on the fundamental problems that had developed under the previous game plan.

The crucial elements of the new economic policy were the devaluation of the dollar, a price-wage freeze to be followed by price and wage controls, a more activist fiscal policy, and a more active foreign trade promotion or balance of payments policy. Together they added up to a major initiative. The economy would be pushed from its stalled position in order to achieve a more rapid recovery with diminished inflationary pressures.

This new economic policy was clearly the antithesis of all of the programs that had previously been publicized. The idea that stability in the economy could be guaranteed purely through monetary action by controlling the money supply went out the window with other parts of the doctrine of the two previous years. It was recognized that the new policy would also contain problems. Monetarists and those who opposed the change in policy would have many opportunities for future criticism. Action was taken because inaction in the price-wage sphere had become increasingly difficult and unpopular. Even though advisers in the Administration did not revise their economic dogma, the President acted when it seemed clear that voters, and especially business leaders, had become convinced that only an activist policy could defeat inflation. While gradualism and minimal action retained a high priority in the White House, many opinion leaders interpreted delay and hesitation in the price-wage sphere as indications that the Administration was willing to accept too high a rate of inflation. The conflict between the White House views and theoretical and business opinion was not resolved. It was, however, temporarily papered over.

The decision to act did not, however, end the search for a solution. Debates within the White House and among advisors to the President as to a viable incomes and price-wage policy continued. The vacillating price-wage "phases" of 1973 reflected the acceptance and then rejection of opposing views as each proposed solution encountered difficulties. Monetarists continued to argue that the best solution would be to furnish the "proper" amount of money. Their views were significant in the semidismantling of controls in early 1973. But again, because a majority deemed results unsatisfactory, new actions were taken.

Unfortunately the choices remained difficult. Either accept inflation or deflation or find new procedures for our market system to determine prices, wages, and income distribution at a constant price level. The underlying forces did not alter either. Our economy is complex. Wage-price decisions result from millions of independent choices. Except under the pressure of recession or depression, some wages, costs, and prices rise. As long as some prices rise and institutional rigidities stop others from falling, a failure to increase money leads either to rising velocity or to some sectors with a lack of demand and unemployment. However, if spending expands to cover both higher prices in those sectors with cost-push and greater demand as well as full employment elsewhere, then inflation remains a continuing problem. The need for incomes policies to alter the price-wage mechanism will remain a source of constant debate.

CHAPTER TWELVE

Operating Guides and Instructions: The Golden Mean

MY SERVICE on the Federal Reserve Board ended while the FOMC was engaging again in one of its periodic debates over ways to improve procedures. I am certain that this subject will continue to plague future FOMCs at the same frequent intervals as in the past. An exploration of why this is such a knotty problem serves also as a way to summarize the problems of managing the dollar.

As did so many of the others, the 1971–72 debate over operating guides and instructions grew in part from analysis done inside the Committee, in part from developments in the monetary and economic sphere, and in part from outside pressures. At the time wage-price controls were imposed, a report of the directive committee was before the FOMC, reminding it that in 1970 only a portion of our suggestions had been adopted. We now recommended that the FOMC go beyond the initial action and revise both its instructions to the account manager and his operations.

In the fall of 1971, the monetary measures were mixed. A rapid expansion in monetary aggregates had occurred between February and August. Interest rates, at a low in March, had climbed steadily until August, retracing about a third of the sharp decline which had begun in mid-1970. The imposition of controls had reversed both of these trends. The growth in the aggregates slowed to a trickle. Interest rates fell somewhat. Views as to the state of the economy were divided. Economists, including those at the Federal Reserve, were unanimously optimistic. The year 1972, they believed, would see record growth in spending, with less than 3.5 percent of it in prices. Businessmen, on the other hand, were extremely pessimistic. The directors of the Federal Reserve Banks carried the same message to the Board that others were carrying to the White House. They saw little or no prospect for an end to the recession.

Pressure increased on the Fed to expand money more rapidly. While the White House staff were no longer primarily monetarist, they became apprehensive during the fall as the slow growth rate for money (M_1) continued. With the presidential election less than a year away, why take a chance? They wanted the Federal Reserve to increase money faster.

As in similar situations, a split within the Open Market Committee slowed its action. It was agreed that money should expand at a moderate pace, but the operating instructions to the manager were not bringing this about. Furthermore, it seemed to me that the manager believed that a majority of the FOMC supported this slower expansion rate, and he therefore failed to move, even though the new theory of the directive should have brought more rapid reactions.

Because open market operations were not expanding money, the Board took control of the situation, with the cooperation of a few presidents and District Bank directors. For two months in a row, the Board lowered the discount rate just prior to FOMC meetings. In each case, some presidents were upset because they disliked foregoing prior consultation over such actions at FOMC meetings. But there was no question of the Board's right to make policy in this manner; it felt that the debates within the FOMC would be improved if at the start of a meeting a clear understanding existed of the Board's views and willingness to act. However, because the Federal funds rate declined slowly even with a falling discount rate, the aggregates continued to expand only gradually. Especially for believers in the narrowly defined money supply (M_1), monetary policy by mid-December was far tighter than desirable, given the goal of a large expansion for the economy.

The Failure To Change Operating Procedures

When in 1970 the FOMC agreed to shift its target from money market conditions to monetary aggregates, it still failed to face up to the requirements of a sound decision-making process. It adopted a new target and extended its policy horizon by one or two months, but it failed to change its operating procedures. Money market conditions were still used to instruct the manager and for his operating guides. The staff projected the way they expected the monetary aggregates to move in response to money market conditions, with a separate estimated growth for each alternative set of conditions. The FOMC then selected the growth rate for the aggregates best suited to its goals, together with the related money market conditions expected to move the aggregates properly. These conditions then became the manager's operating guide. If money failed to track the Committee's desired path, he was instructed to alter the money market conditions to bring the aggregates closer to the Committee's target.

A hypothetical situation shows how this procedure was expected to work. Let us say that, after a major debate over the objectives for the economy, the FOMC agreed that its goals for 1971 would be an 8 percent increase in total spending (the growth in current dollar GNP). Along with this GNP forecast, assume that a monetary model showed that the money target most likely to help achieve the desired growth in the GNP would consist of a 7 percent growth for total reserves, 6 percent for M_1, and 11 percent for M_2. If both the monetary aggregates and income and spending grew at these targeted rates, interest rates would be at 5 percent for the three-month Treasury bill and 7.25 percent for Aaa corporate new issues.

The money market conditions to bring about this growth in money might be estimated as (assuming the discount rate was at 4.75 percent) Federal funds at 5 percent and net borrowed reserves at $350 million. The manager would be instructed to create the reserves to maintain Federal funds within a small range around the 5 percent rate, together with a $350 million net borrowed reserve position. However, if the monetary aggregates grew too slowly, to speed their growth he would have to furnish more reserves to decrease the net borrowed position of the banks and the Federal funds rate. More importantly, the next time the FOMC met it would have to decide whether or not to set a new lower range for the Fed funds rate to insure that the monetary aggregates moved at the desired pace along their targeted path.

I felt that this technique was awkward and unsatisfactory. In the first place, we did not know enough about the relationships between money market conditions and changes in the monetary aggregates to operate the system. We know far too little about the supply and demand for money to pick the Fed funds rate needed to elicit the proper growth in money. I felt the FOMC could come closer to its monetary target if we furnished a certain quantity of reserves and then allowed the market to establish the Federal funds rate that would equate demand to the supply we had furnished. We would not get the exact growth we wanted because the market could maintain excess reserves, but over six months or a year we could come close.

The problem of good operations is almost identical to that of choosing a good target. Which operating guide is best depends on how much you know about short-term relationships among reserves, interest rates, the demand for money, and the growth of the monetary aggregates. While we lacked major pieces of information, I was convinced that we could do better now and improve more rapidly if in our week-to-week operations we fixed supply (reserves) rather than the rate on Fed funds (prices). (It should be noted, however, that for technical reasons the Fed funds rate has day-to-day advantages.)

Another problem that concerned me was that we still had too short a horizon. A reserve target path extending several months into the future was necessary, in my opinion. Furthermore, picking such a target would force the FOMC to look farther ahead and put less emphasis on day-to-day vacillations in the funds rate. Our current problems were aggravated by the fact that the target debated was the monetary aggregates, while operating guides were still money market rates. If the Committee decided to lower the growth for the aggregates from 7 percent to 5 percent, for instance, no one at the meeting would know how much the Fed funds rate would have to move to make this choice effective. Although the staff would estimate the needed change later, those concerned with the rate would be lacking a vital piece of information when they were asked to vote. In contrast, since a desired shift in the aggregates would require a nearly similar move in reserves, the necessary change in operations using reserves as a guide would be known in the debate.

Beyond this, I felt that continued use of money market conditions led to counterproductive market expectations. Since the Fed's mechanism for controlling the aggregates was publicly known, everyone paid too much attention to the Federal funds rate. As a result, the FOMC tended to move rates too slowly for fear of upsetting the interest rate apple cart. This technique of changing the level of Fed funds rates gradually from one meeting to the next was the type of poor control mechanism that my Directive Committee had warned against. Like an inferior thermostat, it alternately caused over- and undershooting of the desired levels of the monetary variables. It allowed the aggregates to build up momentum. When a reversal became necessary to get back to the target path, the required movement in the Fed funds rate had to be large. To change the metaphor, it was like cracking a whip, putting all the speed at the end of the line. A number of participants risked ending up with a whiplash.

Developing a Good Operating Procedure

The deeper the Directive Committee delved into the problems of working with the monetary aggregates, the more complex we found them to be. Achieving a specific growth rate for the aggregates was more difficult than was generally acknowledged. We at the Federal Reserve had failed to understand several aspects of the problem. As had outside observers, we had assumed away several tricky operating questions.

The problem is similar to that for the target. The Federal Reserve controls reserves, but the banks determine how fast a given reserve creation becomes money and what type of money it becomes. While, over an extended period—say, six months to a year —growth in money will come relatively close to the changes in reserves created and available for new deposits, this is not true in the short run. Banks have alternative uses for reserves. They can be held in excess. If a bank is in debt, it can repay borrowings. By buying assets, banks can create either time or demand deposits. Only this last alternative causes the money supply (M_1) to rise.

Banks' excess reserves serve as a buffer against unexpected movements in deposits and loan demand, thus giving banks greater flexibility. As with most buffers, large and erratic weekly changes occur. Over a longer period, excess reserves are also influenced by changes in interest rates. The progression from the Fed's creation of reserves, through the increase and then decrease in excess reserves, to the actual changes in money is spread out and does not occur at the same rate from one year to the next. There are long lags in the adjustment process. Studies of the time at which changes in reserves have their impact on increases in the money supply indicate that the effects are spread out over a full year; on the average, an increase in reserves may not be effective for six months.

The speed at which banks create money depends upon the demand for credit, the rate at which reserves are supplied, and interest rates. When demand increases, if the banks have additional reserves, they can create more money at stable interest rates. Without new, nonborrowed reserves, they can create more money temporarily, but at rising interest rates. Eventually, too, they use up the reserve flexibility granted them by increasing their borrowing of reserves from the discount window.

Some people ask why the Fed does not avoid having to estimate what banks will do by merely adding a fixed amount of reserves week in and week out. The answer becomes apparent when we compare the high proportion of reserves required to meet seasonal and erratic demands with those serving as a base for the creation of additional money. In many weeks, the account manager must add or subtract $1 billion in reserves to take care of seasonal movements, shifts in balances at tax and Treasury funding dates, changes in holdings of foreign central banks, weather interference with check collections, and similar events. In contrast, the amount of reserves added for growth has been closer to $30 million a week. In any week the total added reserves may be thirty times as large as those required for growth. Yet if these temporary reserves are not added and removed as conditions warrant, extreme and costly fluctuations in short-term lending and interest rates will result. The Fed wants to avoid these costs for the economy if at all possible.

Most observers agree that furnishing seasonal and special reserves makes sense, although a few of the most prominent monetarists do not. Those promoting a steady growth in money say that, even though it may be worthwhile to supply some reserves for non-growth purposes, the Federal Reserve should still be able to control money closely over a longer, more critical period such as six months or a year.

The answer depends on what is meant by closely and also the length of the period. Assume, for example, that you believe that a difference of 2 percent in the growth of money in a year marks the breaking point between a good and a poor monetary policy. This is a sensible conclusion if you believe that the GNP rises percent for percent with money growth over a year, for in most recent years a 2 percent change in the growth rate of the GNP would make the difference between good and unsatisfactory economic policies. Most nonmonetarists, however, would be less likely to agree that such a change of 2 percent, or an even larger one, in money would be that important, since it could be absorbed in holdings of money balances and a change in velocity, rather than exerting much pressure on spending. They would want to analyze what was happening to other monetary and nonmonetary variables before they would agree that a 2 percent annual change in money is important.

The statistics on reserves for 1971 put the 2 percent figure in perspective. Suppose the Fed had wanted to use a rule of steady growth in reserves for the year, while continuing to furnish temporarily those needed for seasonal purposes. In that year, the securities purchased for the Open Market Account increased by $7.5 billion. Member bank reserves increased by $2.2 billion, the difference being absorbed by movements in securities to back currency, other assets, and liabilities other than member bank reserves. The money supply grew by 6.7 percent with monthly changes at annual rates ranging from −2.1 percent to +14.1 percent. Imagine that the target had been to hold the M_1 growth to 4.7 percent. To reduce the growth rate for the year by 2 percent would have required furnishing about $35 million fewer reserves per month, or about $400 million less for the year. Contrasted with this, reserves required to handle expanded activity for the December holidays were between $1.5 and $2 billion. If even a modest error in seasonal reserves were made in the last weeks of the year or if banks used these reserves for growth rather than for seasonal purposes, the steady growth policy would have been scuttled. Even while the Fed thought it was creating reserves for growth at a steady 4.7 percent, the year could easily end up with the reported growth rate of 6.7 percent because of the flexibility given to the banks by the necessary increase in seasonal reserves. As an example, not quite so extreme, in December 1972, the growth rate in money (M_1) for the whole year did jump by 1.1 percent, as a result of an unusually large surge in new money in that month. It was followed, as is usual, by a somewhat slower growth rate in January, but reported 1972 growth remains high.

There is another problem which, when fully recognized, should lessen the attention paid to month-to-month or even quarter-to-quarter movements in a single monetary aggregate such as currency and adjusted demand deposits (M_1). The month-to-month reported movements in money (M_1) are extremely erratic. It is unlikely, however, that the true money supply which affects economic decisions bounces around nearly as much as the reported figures. An indication of the extent of this bouncing is the standard deviation (a measure of the movements about the average) of the reported monthly changes at annual rates in M_1, calculated for 1968–71. It was 4.65 percent, just about equal to the average increase. Any change in a monthly rate from zero to 10 percent had little or no statistical significance. It could indicate simply that growth was proceeding at the normal or average rate. Of course, the longer the period of observation, the less important is any error in the terminal observations. Even so, a 2 percent change in growth rates over six months is as likely as not to reflect a purely random movement or measurement error without economic significance. (Data have also been revised frequently by the Fed staff. The estimated growth in money was raised 0.6 percent for 1968, 0.6 percent for 1969, 1.7 percent for 1970, and 3.5 percent in 1972. Growth in each year was far larger than it seemed at the time policy decisions had to be made. These revisions are due partly to the fact that the reported money supply is an artificial construct. The money for income purposes was probably the same before and after the revisions, but good monetarists sharply revised their views of what was happening.)

These facts do not, of course, reduce the significance of actual changes in that money which is having a basic influence on the economy. They constitute a warning, however, against overemphasizing quarter-to-quarter or even year-to-year changes in the reported level of money without a careful analysis of how much of the reported movements are economically significant. From the point of view of the Fed, decisions must be made to change the amount of money. These decisions may produce an immediate reaction on interest rates, bank loans, and security markets. Before taking the decision to alter the reserve flow, the Fed should be certain that it does not attach too much weight to a reported movement that reflects nothing more than a measurement or data error. If the change threatens a measurable cost elsewhere, the Fed must make certain it is not seeing merely a statistical figment.

Final Report of the Committee on the Directive

As 1971 drew to a close, several significant trends converged: Businesses continued to worry over weak economic activity; the Federal Reserve had again lost control of the monetary variables, which failed to track the desired path; and the White House was pushing for a faster growth rate in money for the coming presidential year. My term as a governor of the Fed was due to end on January 31, 1972, although I would continue to serve until my successor took office. I decided that, just as a somewhat similar series of events had led to the earlier adoption of the monetary aggregates as a target, this might be an opportune time to get the FOMC to revise the manager's operating instructions and guides.

I drafted a report for the Committee on the Directive, suggesting a change in procedures. It acknowledged the lack of certainty and the probable measurement errors in a reserve guide, but pointed out the reasons to expect that reserves would work better than money market conditions in controlling the rate at which the monetary aggregates expanded:

—The necessary additions to reserves compatible with any desired growth rate of the aggregates could be planned for a longer period—three to six months.
—The proper interest rate to equate supply and demand would be set by the market.
—Movements in the Fed funds rate would be less likely to set off expectational surges, since the market could form its own estimates of what proper rates would be.
—The market could step up short-term arbitrage to iron out interest rate movements it felt were wrong.
—We could probably develop a better estimating equation for the relationship between reserves and the aggregates to replace the poor one that connected the Fed funds rate and the aggregates.
—Since the Fed's main instrument is reserves rather than interest rates, it would be easier to explain and justify operations conducted in terms of reserves.
—The use of a reserve guide for operations would permit the target for monetary variables to be more readily reached, since the monetary aggregates would react more rapidly and surely to the Committee's desires.

The operating procedures suggested were simple. The staff would continue to estimate two or three paths for the monetary variables, each expected to help achieve a separate set of objectives. Each target path would list the amount of reserves that ought to be furnished on a week-to-week and month-to-month basis to meet both the desired growth in the aggregates and the expected seasonal movements. (For technical reasons, I recommended that reserves required to back government and interbank deposits be furnished automatically because they are immediately observable, fluctuate widely, and changes in them average out at close to zero over a few months. I wanted the guide to be in terms of nonborrowed reserves, but others felt that total reserves, with the exceptions agreed upon, would be easier to operate. Thus the guide became "Reserves Available to Support Private Nonbank Deposits," known as RPDs).

When the FOMC picked a monetary target, the operating guide would be selected automatically and simultaneously. The manager should be instructed to furnish the selected amount of reserves, with a proviso that he should alter the amount if the Federal funds rate moved by more than an indicated percent on either side of its expected level. I chose a 1 percent range to allow the market to do the adjustment. The limits were based on simulations indicating that more severe Federal funds rate movements could mean something was wrong with the underlying assumed relationships. If the Fed funds rate moved by 1 percent more or less than expected, the staff should reexamine the assumptions in the light of what was happening. The FOMC would then debate the issue and determine what new instructions to give the Desk.

As before, discussion of the advisability of this action was heated. It encompassed not only the question of a better operating guide but implicitly, in my mind, that of whether the Fed was really interested in achieving the target it had proclaimed—that of a moderate growth rate for the monetary aggregates. In the end, the FOMC revised the directive. It put the priority on furnishing bank reserves (RPDs) to achieve the desired target path. However, because some members were not convinced, the FOMC maintained money market conditions at a coordinate point in the directive. The result, in effect, was to limit the swings in the Federal funds rate below the level I believed compatible with most efficient operations.

What Have We Learned?

When I look back at my Washington service, I see the principal accomplishments of the Federal Reserve Board during those seven years as falling into two main categories. The first was composed of the day-to-day decisions on monetary policy made in response to movements in the economy, to other government programs, and to events in the financial world. The second was the slow and halting development of an improved understanding of what monetary policy does, what it can do, and how it should be operated. While many of the day-to-day decisions were extremely difficult and important, they are also transitory. Although I feel that the Board's record for this period was good, I know that some critics feel otherwise. The article by Paul Samuelson from which I quote in the first chapter points up this dichotomy. To my mind, the developments which took place in theory and operations are more important. They continue to evolve.

The basic problem for the Federal Reserve is how best to operate "knowing that it knows not." There is always uncertainty about the economy and financial markets and their future trends. Our information is inexact about the effects of monetary variables on spending, and of spending on prices and output. Movements in money and interest rates result from the interaction of the monetary instruments with other forces in the economy. Improvement in its operating procedures gives the Fed better control of this process, but it is still far from perfect.

Recognizing the extent to which current decisions are still based on judgment, inadequate data, and unknown relationships, we may well ask how much has really been gained over the typical directive of the early 1960s, when the goal was clear—"to foster sustainable economic growth and expanding employment opportunities" —and the single target, measure, and policy instrument for achieving it was also evident—by "restraining inflationary credit expansion."

I think we have gained a great deal. Judgment still is and always will be essential, but it can be enhanced by a specific framework and a better understanding of the task. Even though exact relationships are lacking, both intuition and judgment improve when they are combined with concrete quantities and measurable operations. A good decision framework incorporating what we do know frees us to concentrate on what we do not know and on what is subject to change. When we think quantitatively we can better judge whether our goals, targets, and guides are compatible.

We see that economic policy reactions are felt well into the future and that a trade-off exists among both policies and objectives. Good decisions require options to be specifically set forth with estimates of the magnitudes involved. Judgment must go beyond generalities such as tighter or easier and come to grips with the specifics of how much and when.

We do profit from experience. Important progress has been made in both forecasting and operating knowledge. We have done well in projecting next year's economy and how spending will divide between output and prices. Knowing where we would like the economy to go and what forces outside the monetary sphere seem to be driving it, we can set objectives for monetary policy with far greater assurance.

The fact that we have a better picture of the limits of our accuracy means that anlysis can be concentrated where the need is greatest. We need estimates of whether the system is out of the equilibrium assumed in most economic equations. We need to, and can, refine the techniques by which policy decisions can account for potential costs of uncertain outcomes (loss functions). Work on these questions is still embryonic, but such problems are amenable to gradual improvement as more effort is devoted to necessary research.

Goals and Objectives

The gradual recognition that, as a nation, we have a multiplicity of goals has had profound implications for monetary policy. No longer could decisions be taken solely in the light of possible price increases or balance of payments deficits. The fact that monetary policy has indirect impacts on jobs, output, and prices through its effects on the level of spending means that all of these semicompetitive goals, and not any single one, must be taken into account. At the same time, consequences spread beyond the primary spending sphere. By altering flows in money, credit, and interest rates, policies affect sectors of the economy in unique ways. We have seen the divergent influences in 1966 on housing, small business, state and local financing, the spending of large corporations, and the international sphere. The extent of a sector's reaction to monetary policy and the speed with which it is felt depend partly on economic relationships such as methods of financing and partly on existing institutions.

Policy makers must appraise the divergent costs and sacrifices that result from the use of their instruments. In my opinion, the Federal Reserve has sometimes erred in refusing to take into account costs in some sectors of the economy while giving undue weight to others, notably the international sphere. The Fed at times has justified its neglect of certain sectoral problems, claiming that if the government felt they were sufficiently serious it would deal with them through legislation; but actually, many Fed actions have been taken on the assumption that monetary policy must be adjusted to the absence of legislation. However, increasingly, experience and the course of events have led to giving more consideration to all impacts of policy.

We have also learned that it is important to articulate the costs or benefits growing out of major financial movements. The Fed has always factored them into its objectives, but has done so hesitantly and apologetically and not always on the most logical grounds. When it spoke of its goal as the removal of all restraints in financial markets, it failed to recognize the importance of underlying economic and institutional constraints. This policy was almost disastrously expensive in 1966 and 1970. Experience shows that a central bank must be cognizant of the effect of its action on wealth in securities, real property, and the relationships among holders of various claims. It must also concern itself with liquidity and the general safety of financial institutions. Changes in interest rates, just as in prices, can cause arbitrary swings and redistributions in income, wealth, and productivity. It is not sensible to stress one cause—inflation—for such undesirable movements while simultaneously neglecting changes in credit and interest rates which also cause large and costly swings and redistributions.

A Framework for Analysis

I have said that the adoption of a quantitative expenditure-financial framework for analysis marked a tremendous step forward for monetary policy. It has greatly expanded knowledge and understanding. I am not without sympathy, however, for those who wish they could continue to make policy on the basis of the "tone and feel of the market" and in terms of "more" or "less." Their preference reflects in part their, and everyone else's, frustration with the lack of hard knowledge in some areas as well as their experience that, because human reactions are at least partially unpredictable, things do not always work out as the numbers suggest. I do not believe, however, that we can return to a system that did not work. We must continue to develop better procedures.

At the Fed, I advocated at least four changes in the framework which were not adopted, but which I believe would speed progress. The first is that there should be more explicit discussion of the goals of policy decisions in terms of trade-offs among objectives and of sectoral gains and losses. If no attempt to weigh these is made, decisions are hard to make with respect to output versus prices versus financial stability, or the distress of specific sectors. It is especially necessary to show alternative costs because potential losses rise as pressure on a specific point builds up. The costs of monetary policy do not move along a straight line, but accelerate as money grows tighter. We need estimates of the disruptive effects and losses from higher interest rates and altered credit flows. These must then be balanced against hoped-for gains, the costs of other types of policies, of institutional changes, and of maintaining the *status quo*.

As an example, I point again to the international sphere. Here the costs of maintaining a particular exchange rate or of allowing it to rise or fall can be counted. If the alternative costs are dispassionately weighed and the relative importance of various objectives is logically determined, I doubt that we will again see Federal Reserve Banks advocating policies which risk recessions for the purpose of maintaining a fixed exchange rate, or sacrificing large amounts of output to hold a floating rate within too narrow limits.

Second, although the best interval for changing monetary targets has not been worked out, I believe it should be less frequent than in the past. By reconsidering policy every month, the FOMC pays too much attention to transient and statistically meaningless data. While provision should exist for monitoring the situation and making changes in unusual circumstances or when developments clearly are not tracking expectations, on the whole, policy decisions should not be made more often than once a quarter. Such self-restraint on the part of the FOMC would also free financial markets from their excessive preoccupation with Fed policy. It would allow traders and investors to spend more time on a more fundamental analysis of the conditions underlying the markets.

The third change I would like to see adopted concerns the amount of information the Federal Reserve makes public about both its objectives and its operating procedures. Part of the reason the Fed has not specified its goals more clearly is fear of political attack and public criticism and the belief that political pressures would lead to more inflation. I have always believed, however, that publishing more information would improve monetary policy.

Although the published reports of the actions of the FOMC and the Board are more complete and are issued with less delay than formerly, they continue to use deliberately fuzzy language to describe goals and operations. Since the Fed's decisions depend as much on value judgments as on analysis, and since they are made by a not too representative, though dedicated, group of men, the implicit biases and trade-offs contained in them should be reported clearly for public inspection and discussion. In addition, the policy records should convey specific indications of the targets and operating instructions, and they should be issued at the end of each meeting of the FOMC, just as they are now issued immediately when the Board changes its policy instruments. Monetary policy is too important to too many people to allow its record to remain so ambiguous. In the past, the more information the Federal Reserve has made public, the better its operations have become. I think further progress would result from even more openness. The effect on the financial markets would be beneficial, rather than harmful, if they were told outright and immediately what the Fed was trying to achieve.

Research and criticism from outside the System could contribute to the development of better procedures. While I understand why the Fed wants to protect itself from being graded on its performance, from my own experience as a student, a parent, a school board member, and a professor, I have always believed in report cards. Nothing in my experience as a governor of the Federal Reserve has led me to change my mind. In the case of the Fed, however, judgment should be made not on the basis of how successful the result, but rather on how well it performed within the limitations of its knowledge and tools. In any case, providing enough information to make the public aware of what monetary policy can and cannot do would be helpful.

Finally, I believe that because the Fed's procedures still contain so much that is vague and indefinite, too little effort has been given to improving them. Too much time is still spent fighting fires rather than in developing a long-range decision framework. A great deal more work needs to be done on measurement of monetary aggregates, on obtaining better estimates of uncertainty, on estimating potential gains or losses from reaching or failing to reach particular objectives, and on determining what institutional changes are needed to make policy more effective. Too much of the vast amount of data available is wasted or useless because it has not been organized to be used efficiently in a logical system of managing the dollar.

A Further Look at Targets and Procedures

Operations should continue to use reserves as an operating guide and the monetary aggregates as a target. As always, actions must take into account uncertainty, lack of data, and lack of knowledge. It is not uncommon for the predicted movements in the monetary variables to fail to work out as expected and to conflict with the underlying assumed relationships. The FOMC must then decide whether, in seeking to reach its goals, it should put all its faith in money or in interest rates or some in both. It may be useful to examine a typical situation in which such problems arise.

On the basis of a forecast, the FOMC has picked $125 billion as a desirable growth for the GNP for the year. The compatible monetary targets are a 6 percent increase in money accompanied by a 5 percent level for Treasury bills and a 7.25 percent interest rate on new issues of corporate bonds. The operating guides require the manager to furnish reserves at a 7 percent rate. Federal funds are expected to trade at 5.25 percent.

During the first two months of the year, the manager has supplied reserves at the desired rate. Money has also grown as expected, and the economy appears to be conforming to its forecast. However, Treasury bills and corporate new issues have both risen by .5 percent above their targeted level.

What should determine whether or not the FOMC ought to step up the rate at which reserves are created? At least three factors should enter into the decision: the accuracy we attach to the observations and the estimated relationships; the harm which may result from the movements in money, credit, and interest rates; and our analysis of the situation based upon as much qualitative and quantitative information, no matter how fragmentary, as we can obtain to supplement the monetary readings.

The Committee could decide that rising interest rates are just what the doctor ordered. That would be true if an unwanted, potentially inflationary, increase in income was causing the higher rates. Even though the GNP showed no evidence of overexuberance, the higher interest rates could reflect a potential surge of spending. Higher interest rates would be desirable to counteract such forces and to hold spending closer to its noninflationary full-employment path. The Committee might also want to allow interest rates to rise if the movements reflected anticipated inflation. The higher market, or nominal, rates would not signify a rise in real interest rates. The financial impact might be undesirable, but with real interest rates unchanged, the nominal rates would not be working against the desired growth in spending.

On the other hand, there might be good reasons to interpret the higher rates as a warning and to supply more reserves and money in an attempt to bring them down. An increase in the nonincome demand for money might be causing the higher rates. In this case, a failure to furnish more money would drive spending below the goal of a $125 billion gain. In 1971, for example, the rate of increase in money and interest rates both shot up together. Although explanations offered were dissimilar and at times seemed conflicting, there was considerable evidence that the increased demand was for precautionary and speculative balances. Some households wanted to hold more money because they feared the possible loss of jobs in a growing recession. Others were holding more because they feared a fall in the prices of stock and securities. Money in the bank could be used to buy cheaper securities later. A surge in international speculation was occurring. Businesses were forced to be more liquid. Banks would lend them money to buy foreign exchange, but they demanded larger compensating balances to be held in demand deposits here.

Another reason for furnishing more reserves could be that the higher interest rates occurred because data errors and measurement problems caused the change in money to be overestimated; it was in fact increasing at less than 6 percent. Monthly and quarterly estimates of changes in money are erratic; the higher interest rates might reflect a real shortfall of cash. This could also be true even if the data were correct. The targeted growth rate for money could be too low to achieve the goal of a $125 billion spending increase. Better information might show that the demand for money had not been in equilibrium when we made our choice. Or we might have picked an incorrect relationship. The equations used to estimate expected velocity movements could be too high and the required growth of money too low.

All of these would be good reasons for increasing the growth of reserves above 7 percent and money above 6 percent. If the $125 billion GNP was not sufficient to bring about full-employment, this might be another reason to give more weight to the interest rate rise than to an increase in money. In 1971, with unemployment at 6 percent, most observers welcomed a greater than normal increase in money.

The several possible interpretations of the data show why decisions should not be based solely on an arbitrary rule or even on the best modern economic equations. We know that a probability of error exists. We must reexamine circumstances at each new decision point. The choice should be based on all the available knowledge of both the monetary variables and the costs of alternative paths. The losses both from failing to achieve specific objectives and from the likelihood of failure are significant. When diverging variables force a decision, it may be wise to refrain from driving any variable too far without very strong reasons.

As I noted earlier, both analysis and some model simulations indicate that, when the movement in a measure is larger and faster than expected, it should flash a warning. A strategy which shifts or switches between interest rates and money (and takes into account what is happening to the various concepts of money) is preferable to one which neglects surrounding movements because of undue concentration on a single variable. Such a switching rule is especially useful if costs accelerate the more a specific variable moves from its usual path.

A decision to change should be specific and carefully documented. Too many decisions are not. At present no one, including the Fed, really knows why many changes in monetary operations are being made or what each is supposed to accomplish. The absence of documentation handicaps the decision makers in making subsequent choices as well as current ones.

The Golden Mean

Today's monetary policy evolved under the pressure of events and criticism from both within and outside of the Federal Reserve. There has been not a lack, but a surfeit of both theories and ideas. The Fed's problem has been to pick and choose and not be overwhelmed by the smorgasbord spread before it. In my view, it has avoided a serious case of indigestion by rejecting the beautifully packaged appeals based on a single solution and easy answers to economic and monetary problems.

It would be nice if we could all become better off by simply creating enough money to keep interest rates low. It would be fine if inflation could be stopped merely by failing to create much money. It would be even nicer if we could have the best of both worlds, low interest rates and no price rises, by generating exactly the right amount of money. But all such simple ideas are unrealistic because they overemphasize some highly theoretical possibilities for monetary policy, while underemphasizing the difficulties of making the real world fit the abstract world and the economic costs of following any simple idea to its logical conclusion.

At the beginning of the 1960s the Federal Reserve had a split personality. It correctly pointed out the great uncertainty in the monetary sphere. No one knows exactly what will happen when new reserves are created or destroyed, and what will happen varies greatly from period to period. On the other hand, the Fed initially appeared to believe and to promise that it could accomplish a great deal of what its critics in the anti-inflationary field expected, namely, stable prices and a fixed exchange rate, through its influence over credit creation.

The Fed failed to recognize two vital flaws in its theory. Its doctrine was based on a period of mild, not wild, gyrations in demand. It underestimated the large potential costs of an overuse of monetary policy in idle men and idle plants and to financial markets and institutions. Secondly, simply to recognize the need for a decision to tighten or loosen money was an inadequate technique for making monetary policy. To use or to avoid abusing the money generating machine, those at the throttle must be concerned with more than just acceleration and deceleration; they have also to decide how much fuel the economy needs and when. Money market conditions as a measure of policy were simply unequal to their tasks.

The Fed has moved forward, but hesitatingly, often with two steps forward and one back. I believe that the words of Guttentag, quoted in Chapter 8 (page 170), continue to explain a great deal of the failure to advance more rapidly. The Fed has a psychological barrier to developing fully its strategy. It is understandably reluctant to expose its procedures and objectives explicitly to public scrutiny, or even to itself. In its attempt to protect itself from both outside critics and internal disappointment, it weakens its ability to improve its performance.

Good monetary policy depends upon admitting how much we do not know, but at the same time recognizing that the dollar must inevitably be managed. Furthermore, by using the knowledge and judgment we have, we can do better than by following a rigid rule. It follows that we must expend more effort on improving knowledge so as to raise the level of our accomplishments.

My analysis of the current state of monetary operations and theory leads directly to the conclusion that, for monetary policy, as for many other activities, we should be governed by the rule of the Golden Mean: At no point in the decision process should we put our faith in a single element. We will do better and will sharply decrease the danger of extreme and costly reactions if we recognize the value of employing several instruments, multiple variables, and even a variety of theories. My reasoning stems directly from the lessons of the past and my awareness of how much we still do not know. Lack of knowledge impairs even the best intuition, judgment, and theories. Still, although we cannot prove what the result of any decision will be, we cannot avoid taking action. This means that, whether formally or informally, we need to consider the likelihood of error, the possibilities that other theories are right, the variety of responses which might occur in the economy. Rather than attempting to find the point that would be best if everything worked out exactly right, we should select a path that points to the lowest probable cost, given our lack of knowledge, the factors of uncertainty, and the losses from different possible outcomes. Such an approach will achieve far better results than trying to pursue a single track to a particular goal.

What is true of monetary policy is also true of economic policy in general. Reliance on a single type of policy can rapidly raise the costs to the economy and to specific sectors. These costs rise in an exponential manner; the greater the pressure being exerted by any single policy, the faster costs climb. The use of a package of policies—monetary, fiscal, incomes, and institutional change—reduces the likelihood that any one of them need be pushed so far as to cause accelerating inefficiency in the economy's operations.

The effectiveness of any policy tends to diminish the more often and more intensively it is used. If money is tight, people create substitutes. When credit rationing threatens, businesses make certain that they are not caught with their liquidity down the second time around. If interest rate policy is used, the patterns of borrowing and lending change. Firms plan now for future wage-price controls. As a result, similar movements at different times do not have the same effect. It took much higher interest rates in 1969 than in 1966 before spending was cut back. Now still higher rates, with a greater disruption of financial markets, may be needed if monetary policy is depended upon as the primary tool to curtail prices. With time and the ability of the economy to plan, there is less bang for the buck of monetary restraint. Policies must be flexible and change with the times. Surprise may greatly increase the effectiveness of a policy, while familiarity breeds contempt.

The same factors which I have discussed in relation to operating guides apply to the choice of overall economic aims. Again, it must be recognized that no single goal can be attained without attendant costs. Economists preach that there is no such thing as a free lunch; gains in one sphere exact sacrifices elsewhere. The more aware we become of the many pressing national goals, the more we realize that all are not simultaneously attainable. We have to settle for the best package possible.

There has been considerable disappointment over the inflationary price increases of the past decade and the costs involved in reducing them. But what must be weighed are the alternatives that were available. Is the existing trade-off the best possible? The country has had relatively full employment; output expanded constantly for a record number of years; we went to the moon; we fought a war; we avoided a financial crunch. But we have also suffered inflationary price increases.

We certainly have not tracked the optimum theoretical path. The question really is whether we have done as well as we should have with what we know or what we could have learned. We do know the mistakes of economic policy are not random; they tend to be on the inflationary rather than the deflationary side. This is particularly true the closer we come to full employment. When excess capacity exists in the economy, an error that increases demand will merely close the gap to full employment and maximum output more rapidly. But when full employment has been attained, such an error leads to higher prices. Many economists believe, correctly, that political considerations enter into the more frequent occurrence of errors on the up side. People do not give equal weight to unemployment and price movements. A job lost or goods not produced cannot be recouped. Resources have been wasted. In the case of price pressures, the dangers are not as clear and immediate.

Another element in our general dissatisfaction with economic policy is greater expectations. A superficial acquaintance with economic issues has become more common, leading to higher aspirations than our policy skills can satisfy. Successful policies have brought about excellent rates of growth in jobs and output, stability has been improved, and nationally we are better off. But we may be psychologically poorer in the greater awareness of the inequities that still remain and the great gap between the actual and the desired.

The 1973 difficulties in finding a satisfactory anti-inflationary policy are not unique, nor were they unexpected. Choices are hard. People dislike inflation, controls, taxes, high interest rates, and less available credit. No single policy or even diversified package can guarantee a desirable outcome. Debates over policy remain heated because they require not only a choice of workable targets and operating procedures, but also a decision as to who shall pay for policy moves. While proponents of a particular policy frequently neglect or gloss over costs, those who must sacrifice income, standard of living, or jobs do not and should not. While wise policy choices can reduce costs both to some individuals and to the economy, they cannot make the costs disappear, and may raise them for others. Any promise to the contrary should be automatically suspect.

I expect to see continued dissatisfaction with economic policy. We want, and should want, more than can be delivered. All goals are not equally attractive to all segments of our nation. What is good policy for one group may appear disastrous for another. When the necessary trade-offs are chosen, some will be disappointed.

We should expect periods of relative calm and noninflationary prosperity, but such periods will be unstable and will generate their own demise. Although our knowledge of how to choose and operate economic policy is expanding rapidly, the problems may be growing even faster. The international monetary sphere is an excellent example. We were forced to abandon the old system. We recognized what was wrong; yet the solutions that seemed adequate even a year or two ago are not capable of coping with current conditions.

Although we will not find the perfect solution to our problems, we should not be discouraged. We know a great deal and are steadily learning. Our economy is now operating far better than it did when we had less understanding, and far better than it would in the strait jacket of a single goal or automatic rule.

Still, it is probable that we shall continue to demand better economic performance for the nation than we now experience. It is hard to accept the fact that, despite continuing improvement in economic understanding, our techniques cannot completely solve the problems of fluctuations in overall demand and supply. We tend to blame human error for the fact that inflation and recession are still with us. However, most of our basic economic problems are not due to the mistakes made by economists in policy positions, but, rather, are inherent in some of the desirable attributes in our system. We need a complex and dynamic economy to insure the progress and growth which make our nation great. Yet it is this very complexity and dynamism that make it hard to perfect our knowledge and to develop workable techniques. Even if economic and monetary planning could be carried on entirely independently of political or social concerns, the intricacies of the task probably place the hoped for stability out of reach. But economics is a developing science that has come a long way. As our knowledge continues to expand, we should expect improved performance both from those who manage the national economy and, particularly, from those who manage the dollar.

Index

317